Inspired
Innovations

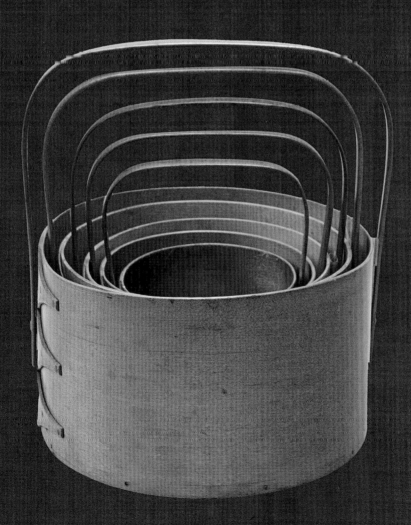

Inspired Innovations

A Celebration of
Shaker Ingenuity

M. Stephen Miller

University Press of New England

HANOVER AND LONDON

This book is published in conjunction
with the exhibition
Inspired Innovations: A Celebration of Shaker Ingenuity,
organized by the New Britain Museum of American Art.

January 16 to April 11, 2010

NEW BRITAIN MUSEUM OF AMERICAN ART
56 Lexington Street
New Britain, Connecticut 06052
860.229.0257
www.nbmaa.org

University Press of New England
One Court Street, Lebanon NH 03766
www.upne.com

Designed by James F. Brisson

Library of Congress Control Number: 2009934604

ISBN 978-1-58465-850-4

Printed in China

5 4 3 2 1

THIS BOOK IS DEDICATED
TO THE MANY STUDENTS
OF SHAKER HISTORY
AND CULTURE,
PAST AND PRESENT,
WHO HAVE STRIVEN
TO TELL THE
SHAKERS' STORY
TRUTHFULLY
AND FAIRLY.

YOUR GOOD WORK
WILL ENDURE.

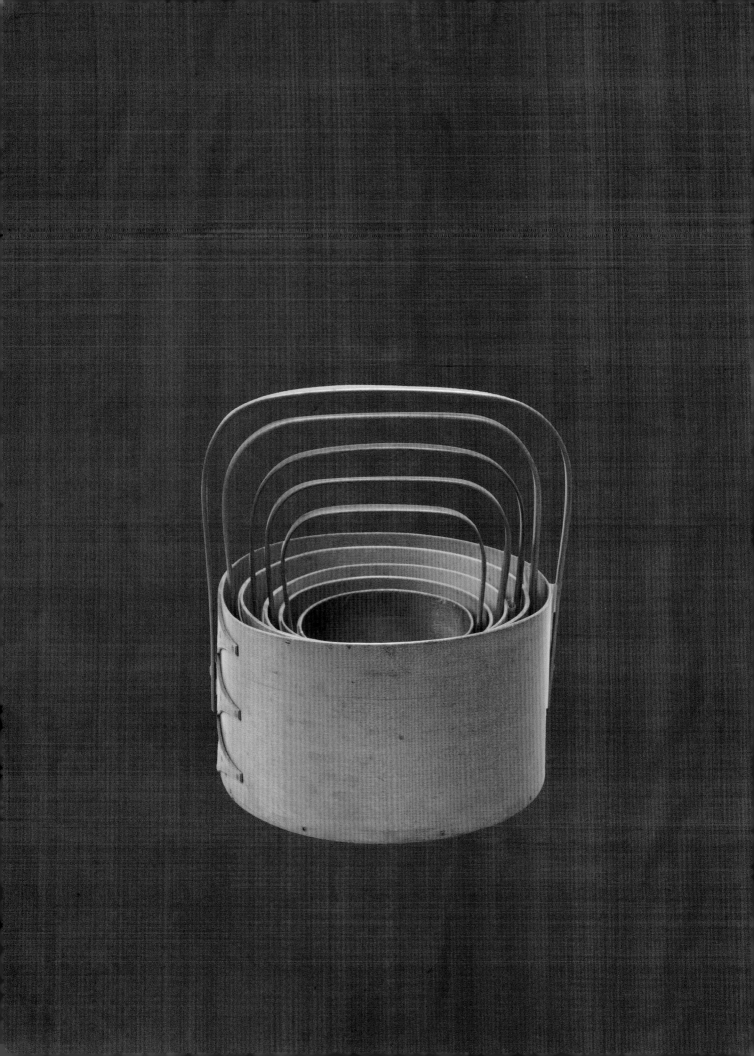

Contents

Acknowledgments

ACKNOWLEDGING THE MANY PEOPLE who have made this book possible is a task both daunting and pleasurable, and one that I undertake with deepest appreciation to each of them. The contributing writers are some of the brightest and the best in the field of Shaker studies. Nearly all are published authors in their own right and all have given generously of their knowledge, time, and expertise in order to make this volume a significant addition to the body of information that explores what the Shakers have contributed to the World—*our* world. You, the reader, will soon discover why this is also a most pleasurable task.

Only a few of the members of what became "Team Miller" are engaged in full-time Shaker-related activities, yet each has already made important contributions to our understanding. Their backgrounds are diverse: a former nurse, licensed private detective, newspaper publisher, FBI agent, and international rock musician. There are also: a successful entrepreneur, a crafts instructor, and several teachers and college professors. Some are grandparents and at least one, a recent parent. All are committed to one quality above all else in their work in Shaker studies—seeking out the truth. I have made every effort to allow their individual "voices" to be heard in their essays. One will find their biographical information at the end of this volume. I am extremely grateful to each for the excellence of their work.

This book began life as a catalog, an accompaniment to an exhibit of the same name mounted at the New Britain Museum of American Art in early 2010. Founded in 1903, it was the first museum anywhere devoted solely to American art. Now it is housed in a modern structure barely three years old. When its director, Douglas Hyland, approached me in the spring of 2008 to ask if I would be willing to assemble a large-scale Shaker exhibit there, I was delighted to accept. The opportunity to present a significant slice of an indigenous culture to an audience in an art museum setting—a progressive museum, able to see the Shakers' works as simply another expression of America's cultural values—was compelling.

As work on an exhibition catalog proceeded, it became apparent that in addition to documenting the exhibit, we had an opportunity to add to our knowledge of Shaker culture, for their many innovations have not been explored in depth before. Thus, an embryonic catalog expanded with the contributions of other scholars until it emerged as a full-length book. At that point Michael Fredericks, James F. Brisson, and Robert I. Cottom were engaged: Michael to take virtually all of the photographs that appear in the book, Jim to organize and design it, and Ric to serve as copy editor for all of the text. Each is highly accomplished and broadly acknowledged in his field, and all have been a delight to work with. This book stands as a testimony to their thoroughgoing professionalism and unusual sensitivity to this subject.

I thank Mike Burton, director of University Press of New England, for his eagerness to take on this project and his expressions of confidence in me. UPNE published my previous book, *From Shaker Lands and Shaker Hands,* and I am thrilled to be working with them once again.

The following institutions granted me access to comb through their collections, including materials that were in storage. Some have never been reproduced in print or placed on exhibit before, and for the rights to reproduce them here I am very grateful to: the Art Complex Museum, Duxbury, Massachusetts, Charles A. Weyerhaeuser, director and Maureen Wengler, registrar; Canterbury Shaker Village, Canterbury, New Hampshire, Funi Burdick, executive director and Renee Fox, librarian and archivist; Hamilton College, Clinton, New York, Randy Ericson, Couper Librarian, Burke Library; Hancock Shaker Village, Pittsfield, Massachusetts, Ellen Spear, executive director, Christian Goodwillie, curator of collections, and Lesley Herzberg, collections manager; Shaker Heritage Society, Albany, New York, Starlyn D'Angelo, executive director; the Shaker Museum and Library, Old Chatham, New York, David Stocks, president and Jerry Grant, director of research; and the United Society of Shakers, Sabbathday Lake, Maine, Lenny Brooks, museum director.

I also would like to recognize Christian Goodwillie for the many ways in which he helped me with this book, all in addition to his curatorial role at Hancock Shaker Village and then as curator of special collections and archives at Hamilton College Library. His enthusiasm and energy are a constant source of inspiration to me. I am grateful to Dr. Magda Gabor-Hotchkiss for reading and providing a most useful critique of my Introduction as well as other parts of the book. Magda's keen intelligence and meticulous approach to every aspect of Shaker scholarship made her the ideal indexer for this book. Finally, I want to express my appreciation to my friend Amy Lynn Silverman. Amy proofread the entire text and made many invaluable suggestions and corrections.

The patrons and friends of the above institutions are vital in keeping the Shakers' story alive. All students of the movement, and each of the contributors to this book, are grateful to them. Although it is impossible to acknowledge them individually, for they number in the thousands, their ongoing, enthusiastic support insures that the World will not forget the achievements of the United Society of Believers. It is my sincere hope that this exhibit and book will help to keep the flame of the Shaker legacy burning brightly.

When asked to contribute anywhere from a single piece to thirty objects from their private collections to this project, a number of individuals stepped forward. Though they prefer to remain anonymous, nevertheless I wish to publicly thank them for entrusting highly valued portions of their collections to the exhibit and allowing them to be reproduced in this book. Each object adds to our understanding of Shaker innovations in a significant way.

I am grateful to the members of the board of directors of the New Britain Museum of American Art for granting me their full measure of trust and allowing me to organize the first exhibit there that focuses on the creative output of an entire culture—the United Society of Shakers. My special gratitude goes to Douglas Hyland, director, Maura O'Shea, deputy director, and John Urgo, collections manager, and to the many staff members who contributed to this project in ways large and small.

Finally, I wish to acknowledge—with my greatest affection—my wife Miriam. She has patiently stood by me for than the more thirty years that I have indulged my passion for all things Shaker and shared the many other joys in our lives. For this project, she has provided frequent computer expertise and steady encouragement. In so many ways this book is hers as well.

Preface

DOUGLAS K.S. HYLAND

To visit the Hancock Shaker Village, tour its collection of buildings, and study the contents of each is to immerse oneself in a world without parallel in the history of American architecture and decorative arts. The aesthetic of the Shakers is so remarkable that once one is exposed to their ingenuity, their achievements are readily recognized. It was a pleasure to have Dr. M. Stephen Miller and Christian Goodwillie, former Hancock Shaker Village curator, as our guides because each has a passion for the Shakers and a wealth of knowledge about their history, folkways, and accomplishments. Dr. Miller has collected furniture, decorative arts objects, and ephemera from all the Shaker settlements over the last thirty-two years. Along the way, he has gotten to know the remaining inhabitants of the Sabbathday Lake, Maine settlement who may be the last of a dying breed.

As a result of his appreciation and understanding of the Shakers, he has wisely gathered objects for this exhibition that amply demonstrate the multiple ways in which the Shakers have demonstrated their inventiveness. This exhibition, for the first time, examines the full range of innovations that have helped define them as a cultural force. It is vital, too, that we appreciate how the Shakers have influenced *our* lives because these innovations continue to have an impact on American design and commerce.

I am most grateful to Dr. Miller for not only lending objects from his personal collection and for writing his illuminating essays but also for curating this watershed exhibition. The Art Complex Museum, Duxbury, MA; Hamilton College, Clinton, NY; Hancock Shaker Village, Pittsfield, MA; Canterbury Shaker Village, Canterbury NH; the Shaker Museum and Library, Old Chatham, NY; the Shaker Heritage Society, Albany, NY; and the United Society of the Shakers, Sabbathday Lake, Maine also have generously loaned key objects and I thank them for their cooperation. Dr. Miller has enlisted the participation of twelve of the country's leading authorities and their contributions to the book guarantee that the publication will be a major addition to the literature and scholarship on the Shakers. I am indebted to his team of experts for their insights.

The New Britain Museum of American Art receives funding from the American Savings Foundation, the Connecticut Commission on Culture and Tourism, the Greater Hartford Arts Council, and the Community Foundation of Greater New Britain. In particular, I wish to express my gratitude once again to the hardworking and resourceful staff of the Museum who have worked so closely with Dr. Miller. For those unable to see the exhibition at the New Britain Museum of American Art, and subsequently at Hancock Shaker Village, this book will serve as a timeless document of many of the Shakers' most *inspired innovations.*

Douglas K.S. Hyland
Director

Using This Book

THE OBJECTS ILLUSTRATED come from numerous public and private collections. Institutional lenders are identified in the accompanying captions. Objects from the collection of M. Stephen and Miriam R. Miller are identified as having come from the "Miller Collection"; all other private lenders have chosen to be identified as "Private Collection." Carol Medlicott supplied the captions for chapter thirteen, "Music and Song." M. Stephen Miller, editor, wrote all the others.

Dimensions are given in inches, height by width, and by depth or diameter where appropriate. Where only height or length is given it is signified by h- or l-. The height of objects with handles is measured with the handles fully extended. Printing technique(s) and materials used are provided when appropriate. Where the cost of an item in the past is given in current dollars, a table of Consumer Price Index Conversion Factors, developed by Professor Robert C. Sahr, Oregon State University, Corvallis, Oregon was used.

Michael Fredericks supplied the great majority of photographs used here, and several other photographers should be credited as well for the excellent work they have contributed. For objects from: The Art Complex Museum, Duxbury, Massachusetts, Lance Keimig/thenightskye.com; Canterbury Shaker Village, Inc., Canterbury New Hampshire, Bill Finney, Douglas Hamel, and Scott T. Swank; The United Society of Shakers, Sabbathday Lake, Maine, Lenny Brooks. Some private collectors furnished images of the objects from their collec-

tions. All other credits for illustrations appear in the captions.

A note about spelling and punctuation of certain terms that are commonly used when discussing the Shakers is also appropriate here, for there are some inconsistencies in usage found in both the primary and secondary literature. Although it is the editor's intent to permit contributors latitude in usage, certain words and terms need clarification. The most reliable current source for matters of style in this regard is the *Historical Dictionary of the Shakers* by Stephen J. Paterwic.

For brother and sister, elder and eldress, and similar positions, the lower case is generally used unless a specific individual is named. Likewise, the term family uses the lower case unless a specific family is identified. The Shakers tended to capitalize Ministry, Office, and Trustee, even when these words were used independent of an individual or community. A Shaker Meeting House generally uses two words, each capitalized; a worldly one is spelled meetinghouse. This writer uses World, others use world, when referring to non-Shakers, the Shakers themselves used both.

The name of the New Lebanon community was changed to Mount Lebanon in 1861, after it was granted a post office separate from that of the town of New Lebanon, New York. In 1930 the Church Family at Mount Lebanon closed, and the community's postal address reverted back to New Lebanon. Most authors use the two communal names interchangeably. The Harvard, Massachusetts, community became known variously as South Groton from 1849 to 1862, Groton Junction from 1862 to 1871, and finally Ayer, from 1871 until it closed in 1918.

A "Notes" section, containing the notes for the individual chapters, is located at the back of the book. A short biography of each contributor follows the notes.

For further information concerning any of the above the editor may be reached at: shakermiller@gmail.com. 🌾

Introduction

I N 1928, *The Magazine Antiques* published an article titled "Craftsmanship of an American Sect." Written by Edward D. and Faith Andrews, this was the earliest exploration of Shaker material culture, and it set the table for a veritable banquet of books, magazines, pamphlets, and monographs about the sect that followed. Two years later, Shaker culture was put on display for the first time. The New York State Museum in Albany mounted a summer exhibition of materials collected from the Mount Lebanon and Watervliet New York communities, ". . . household occupations of spinning and weaving, and the medicinal herb industry."[1] This led to an almost gluttonous public appetite for exhibitions about the Shakers, and hundreds more followed over the ensuing eighty years. Their themes varied widely and focused on almost every conceivable aspect of this unique American monoculture. Curiously, though many of these publications and exhibitions spoke about the important role of innovation in Shaker communal life, none before now has concentrated on that particular aspect of their culture. It brings to mind a remark attributed to Mark Twain: "Everybody talks about the weather, but nobody does anything about it."[2] This book, as well as the exhibition of the same title, aim to "do something" about the subject of Shaker innovation.

In terms of their religious beliefs and practices, social structure, communal organization, economic activities, material culture, and more—all of which have been part of the fabric of American life for more than 225 years—there has never been a group quite like the United Society, commonly called Shakers. Yet, even after more than two centuries, we are privileged to speak of them using the present tense; although they are now reduced to just a few members, this small band continues to live much as their forebears did. In fact, it is an article of their faith that if the first founders of the sect were to reappear at their sole remaining community at Sabbathday Lake, Maine, they would fully recognize and be "in union" with the Believers there.

It is the major goal of "Inspired Innovations: A Celebration of Shaker Ingenuity," to amply demonstrate that innovation is and has always been central to their way of life. The Shakers are consummate problem solvers. This legacy of finding or creating ingenious solutions to everyday challenges has, to a large extent, defined them as a successful social and economic experiment. However, a vital subtext of any conversation about Shakerism is the understanding that they are, above all else, *believers*—that every aspect of their lives is guided by religious principles. Ingenuity aside, the essence of Shakerism is a profound and all-encompassing spirituality.

From the time the Shakers first gathered into communities separated from the World,[3] they have had to develop strategies for survival that often were unique for their time and place. With little precedent for a tightly knit group of relatively self-sufficient co-religionists to make its way within the larger American society, the Shakers very early on developed creative responses to the needs of communal living. Simply stated, necessity was the parent of innovation. Shaker innovations to be considered here include inventions, adaptations, improvements, and refinements, as well as the development of new approaches for growing or crafting, packaging, and marketing the products of their lands and their hands. Challenge and response, all of it mediated by innovation, is an enduring legacy of Shakerism.

It should also be understood at the outset that Believers have never attached any spiritual significance to objects—any objects—including those they made themselves. Again, the "inspired" in the title of this book refers rather to the realm in which Shakers conduct every aspect of their lives. They strive to live the Christlife at all times, inspired by their understanding of the life of Jesus and Mother Ann, and to simply do their very best in everything they undertake. In this context, work and worship are inseparable—one's labors are in the service of God at all times. Worship, then, is not reserved for a time and place, such as Sunday Meeting, but rather exists at *all* times and in *all* places.

Non-Shakers, by contrast, sometimes want to imbue Shaker-made objects with an aura of spirituality, using such terms for their crafts as "religion in wood." This concept, which is completely alien to Shaker doctrine, past and present, and is actually a form of idolatry, took hold in the World only after their crafts became "collectable" in the early twentieth century. Present-day Believers separate themselves entirely from any such notion. Everything they grew or made was intended first to feed, clothe, and house themselves and, second, to raise money so they might live according to their non-traditional ways. Put even more bluntly, Shakers do not live in order to "make things." Although their work is guided by their beliefs, work must not, of itself, be the object of worship.

It will be necessary to briefly review the history of the movement before we can begin to dissect what it is that leads them to be considered unique.[4] In eighteenth-century Britain, the Anglican Church was the established church, the ultimate spiritual authority. Nonetheless, a general tolerance prevailed towards the small numbers of English Quakers until mid-century, when a small group of dissident Quakers in the industrial city of Manchester broke away and were later joined by Ann Lee, a lowborn, illiterate woman from that city. The group became notorious for its ecstatic form of worship—jumping, dancing, whirling movements, and speaking in tongues—and was derisively called "Shaking Quakers." By 1769 their name had been conflated to simply Shakers. They called themselves the United Society of Believers.[5]

Relatively little is known of Ann Lee's early years in Manchester. Born in 1736 and married at the age of twenty, she gave birth to four children—none of whom survived early childhood. Ann constantly ran afoul of British authorities for her advocacy of physically demonstrative worship, and on several occasions she was imprisoned. Impressed by her visions while in jail and her charismatic personality, the group elevated her to a position of leadership. She was now called Mother Ann (and later, simply, Mother). During the last of these incarcerations, in 1773, she had another vision in which she saw that the full flowering of her faith could only occur in the English colonies across the sea—the soon-to-be United States of America.

Upon her release from jail, Ann and seven followers sailed for New York, arriving there in August 1774. This was a time of gathering political restiveness in the colonies and only one month before the First Continental Congress was to meet in Philadelphia. All British "imports" were viewed with suspicion. Only a few generations earlier, for example, it had been illegal to be a Quaker in New England, and for years to come Ann Lee, in particular, would be further vilified for preaching her views of the Gospels, marriage (i.e., celibacy), and pacifism.[6] She was again jailed for a short time in New York State under the pretext of being an English spy. Following her release, she was often subjected to severe verbal and physical abuses as she traveled around rural New York State and New England, proselytizing.

Political unrest in the colonies was accompanied by a more urgent search for spiritual meaning, which became evident in various forms of revivalism. As Mother Ann preached, hundreds of mostly country folk—farmers and tradesmen, with their families—answered her call to live out her vision of the Christlife. The final form of Shakerism as a *communal* experience was still several years away.

What exactly was Mother Ann's vision? Brother Ted Johnson, a latter-day Shaker at Sabbathday Lake, Maine, once wrote, "We do not worship Mother Ann Lee. Mother was not Christ, nor did she claim to be. To Mother was given the inner realization that Christ's Second Coming was a quiet, almost unheralded one within individuals open to the anointing."[7] Another contemporary Shaker, Eldress Marguerite Frost of Canterbury, New Hampshire, explained the revelation received by Ann Lee this way: "Although God is one Being, Eternal Unity, God is also both male and female. In the depths of the human spirit, man's and woman's put there by God, resides the latent Living Christ, the Christ of all Ages."[8] Perhaps the simplest way to think of Shakerism was enunciated by present-day Shaker Brother Arnold Hadd, who once said, "Mother taught a way of life," a statement as all encompassing as it is succinct.[9]

This "way" is often summarized as the "three C's": community, celibacy, and confession of sin. It will be worthwhile to look at them individually, as each has been the source of controversy and even conflict for much of Shaker history.

Community, for Believers, is a way of life idealized by Jesus. It includes not only the places where members live, work, and, pray but, most importantly, common ownership of all goods. It also extends to the common dedication of labor to one's community and, taken all together, leads to the most idealized form of communism possible—giving according to one's abilities and taking according to one's needs. Nowhere else has communism flourished in such a pure form for so long. In many ways, individualism is discouraged in Shaker life with personal needs subordinated to the greater good of the group. Thus, communalism is fostered.

Celibacy is, without doubt, the most controversial aspect of Shaker life and has been from the beginning. When people today learn that the Shakers' numbers have decreased from almost five thousand in the mid-eighteenth century to just a few at present they will often respond with: "How can a group survive if they do not reproduce?" They seem to conveniently overlook the fact that there have been Shakers for more than twelve generations. They have survived, and for many decades thrived, by taking in converts and children. More to the point—what is the idea behind their tenet of celibacy?

The answers are somewhat complex, for no single response can fully address them. The founding Shakers believed that the millennium had already come, and that *they* were the embodiment of the Second Coming. Succeeding generations of Shakers have come to believe that their time for procreation has passed and the time for regeneration, building their "Heaven on Earth," is at hand.[10] There is also the general pattern of the life of Jesus that Believers choose to emulate, one aspect of which is celibacy. Additionally, to quote historian Stephen Paterwic: "Through prayer and desire, every person could achieve that indwelling union with God. As a consequence, no other relationship should stand between God and humanity."[11] Finally, Mother Ann was convinced that sexual relations were literally "original sin." Needless to say, this last message was not received well by the World. Although Shaker life today is often seen as "quaint," perhaps as a comforting reflection of halcyon times, in the 1780s it was far more often seen as a threat to the "natural" order of family life among the World's people. The idea of enforced separation—wives from husbands and both from their natural children—was a continuing flash point.

Confession of sin has always been a part of Shaker life. It is for Believers an acknowledgement of their human frailties, an expression of humility, and an affirmation of their desire to rise above their faults. It is how they strive to be accepted into the "community in Christ." Indeed, confession is an important part of a Shaker's spiritual travel. The lifelong journey of sisters and brothers is a constant striving to be more perfect human beings within themselves rather than to judge those around them as less perfect. Occasionally, they were harsh in their judgment of apostates, especially in the early years when some members who had "fallen away" were vicious in their attacks on the Shakers. (Apostate writings actually became a small cottage industry in the nineteenth century.)[12]

It should be understood, though, that the "three C's" is simply a shorthand encapsulation for the group's philosophy. Of equal importance is that Believers view Shakerism as a *living* movement, an ongoing experiment in a new social order of thinking, worshipping, and honoring work and each other.

Shakers are committed to pacifism, equality of the genders, and complete tolerance of other races, ethnicities, and religious persuasions. Finally, they are passionate in their belief that humans are blessed by their creator with special gifts and talents: their mission here on earth is to use these for the benefit of one another and for the World around them.[13]

Given the scope of Shaker beliefs it may seem inevitable that they follow a single source of spiritual knowledge, a religious "code." That is not so. Their earliest printed statement of theology was a brief publication, *A Concise Statement of the Principles of the Only Church . . .*, written in 1790 by their first American-born leader, Joseph Meacham, and a mere twenty-four pages in length. It was but the first of many volumes devoted to their religious beliefs, the last major one being Calvin Green and Seth Wells's *A Summary View of the Millennial Church . . .* last revised and printed in 1848. There has never been a Shaker equivalent of a single holy text. Today, in Sunday Meeting at Sabbathday Lake, the lectionary used for readings includes texts from the Jewish and Christian Scriptures. At the same time, inspiration from "within" remains the center of Shaker worship. Services consist of various readings and more or less spontaneous spoken thoughts, all of which are interspersed with the singing of Shaker hymns. Of great importance: between each of the foregoing are moments of silence, times for reflection and contemplation.

Mother Ann died in 1784, ten years after arriving in what was, by then, an independent nation. She was only forty-eight years old and her death was likely the cumulative result of abuses suffered during her travels around the Northeast "gathering souls." She had been the first woman to found and lead an enduring religious sect, and this too was a source of her public persecution. Her brother, William, took up her ministry and soon was followed by the last of the English group, Father James Whittaker. After Father James's death in 1787, the first American-born elder and eldress stepped up to Shaker leadership— Father Joseph Meacham and Mother Lucy Wright. This began a pattern of dual, male and female leadership that has lasted to the present—an extraordinary example of innovation that will be examined at length in another chapter. Of equal importance, under these two an organizational scheme for com-

munal living developed that almost certainly was not envisioned by Mother Ann and the English ministry.

Thus in 1787 the stage was set for the founding of the first fully organized community, New (later Mount) Lebanon, located just outside the village of New Lebanon, New York, about thirty miles southeast of Albany.[14] Actually, the only wealthy member of the first group of English converts to arrive with Mother Ann had bought a piece of swampy land north of Albany called Niskeyuna (later known as Watervliet) some years earlier, and the first Shakers settled there well before 1787, but New Lebanon became the social and political model for the seventeen communities that followed. The Central Ministry was located here, and it was the "center of union for all the Shaker societies" until it closed in 1947.[15] New Lebanon's importance in the movement, its large size (up to 615 members in 1842), early settlement, seat of authority, and relatively late date of closure, help explain why so much more Shaker material of all kinds survives from here than from the seventeen other communities combined. In addition, it had opened its doors to collectors by the mid-1920s and was quite generous in its dispersal policies.

By 1793, ten other communities had been formed: in Maine (2), New Hampshire (2), Massachusetts (4), Connecticut (1), and at Watervliet, New York. During the first decades of the nineteenth century, six more long-standing communities were organized in the west, in Ohio (4) and Kentucky (2), plus one more in western New York State. In all, there were eighteen Shaker villages that lasted for at least fifty-five years each and a handful of shorter-lived ones in Indiana, Georgia, and Florida. Today, Sabbathday Lake, northwest of Portland, Maine, is the only one remaining. Others have become correction facilities, a hospital, a retirement community, museum sites, or have largely disappeared, leaving only fragments of their former lives to be found.

A Shaker community—then and now—is essentially a large communal farm with most of its acreage devoted to fields, orchards, and woods. Separated from the World for religious and political reasons, these collective farms had an advantage over their rural neighbors—an economy of scale. At least until the second half of the nineteenth century, there were enough hands with specific knowledge of soil culture and husbandry to successfully compete with farmers in the World. The earliest converts, in addition to being farmers, were "mechanics," usually from nearby towns. The term "mechanic" at that time applied to almost anyone who worked at a trade with his (but not her) hands: blacksmiths and tinsmiths, harness makers, carpenters, tanners, wood workers, stone masons, and the like. In order to be self-sustaining, Shaker villages had need of all of the trades. Capable, healthy adult males were especially prized.

Early on, women's work was mostly confined to what were then traditional roles centered around the home—growing kitchen gardens, preparing and preserving food, making butter and cheese, milking cows, sewing and weaving, cleaning house, and laundering.[16] This was to change radically later in the nineteenth century as the number of able-bodied Shaker men declined disproportionately, and women came to dominate their communities in numbers and in responsibilities. (Hired men also assumed a more prominent—and more problematic—role as the century wore on.) Child-rearing, however, was always the responsibility of both sexes, sisters (for girls) and brothers (for boys). By the early twentieth century women at Mount Lebanon were working at some jobs traditionally held by men, for example making oval boxes with handles (called "carriers") and assembling chairs—all for sale.

Although the various Shaker societies strove for the greatest possible degree of self-sufficiency, they themselves could not produce certain goods that were not part of the farm culture of the Northeast. For example, foodstuffs such as coffee, tea, salt, and sugar had to be bought. So did metals commonly used in building and crafts: brass, copper, tin, and tin-plated iron. Glass and ceramic containers were needed to package medicines, cotton cloth and thread for clothing. The result was that an early economy developed, based on bartering with neighbors for excess farm products. This was succeeded by cottage industries that supplied local farms with pails, tools, implements, harnesses, and the like, all of it crafted for the express purpose of producing income. Finally, highly organized industries emerged, such as the garden seed enterprise, which initially sold its product locally, then regionally, and finally across the country. The challenge was

the constant need for income; the response was the production and sale of commodities, the means for which often hinged on innovation.

By the early nineteenth century, converts came from other countries as well, mainly the British Isles. They too brought skills and talents, and—importantly—children. These latter helped to swell the ranks of the Shakers, and many of the youngsters remained in their communities as faithful and productive members for life. That would decidedly not be the case as the nineteenth century wore on. Eventually, children proved to be one of the most important reasons for the Shakers' decline.[17] Most who came without at least one parent eventually left, usually after a huge investment of time, care, and resources on the part of those Shakers who formed the core of their villages. This, as much as celibacy or shifts in demographics or ineffective leadership, was a prime reason the movement weakened after the 1840s.

The year 1850 is a convenient point at which to interrupt the story of Shakerism for a closer look. Although in many ways this was a time of unprecedented prosperity for most communities, the high point of about sixty years of almost uninterrupted growth, trouble was brewing on many fronts. A period of spiritual revival, called "the era of manifestations" or "Mother's Work," had recently swept through the eastern societies, reinvigorating many members who had not known any of the movements' founders. Yet, shifting demographics in the World were transforming a mostly rural, agrarian society into a more urban, industrial one. It was a trend that forced Believers to alter certain patterns of commercial production.

Communities began to see increasing numbers of youngsters who would not remain in the faith, declining numbers of able-bodied men, a lack of new, committed recruits, a general falling-away again of religious fervor, and the presence of ineffective, inept, and sometimes even corrupt business leaders. To this litany of woes would soon be added the burden of a civil war that nearly undid the two Kentucky communities and severely hampered the economy of some northern ones like Enfield, Connecticut, that depended on selling garden seeds in southern markets. This is not to say that all of the news was bad, for, as we shall see, there were some stunning successes as well. A look at some of those forces that threatened the movement will reveal just how resilient Shakers have been over the past 160 years.

At mid-century the Shakers were, to a large extent, farmers—albeit now concentrating in specific areas such as cultivating medicinal herbs, utilizing orchard products, and raising garden seeds. According to the United States Census of 1840, more than four out of every five workers were involved in agriculture. Ten years later those numbers showed the beginning of a long-term shift: from 89.2 to 84.8 percent rural and from 10.8 to 15.4 percent urban. Looking back on this period, it is clear that the Shakers were moving against the grain. Manufacturing aside, even farm activities in the World were coming to be conducted on a scale at which they could not compete. Nor could they compete with the seed companies and drug houses that sprang up after the Civil War. The last seeds were sold by Mount Lebanon in 1888, and after 1876 most herb sales were made to other, worldly medicine manufacturers such as Ayers in Lowell, Massachusetts, and A. J. White in New York and London.

A small medicine business at Sabbathday Lake, a robust coopering business at Enfield, New Hampshire, and an active business making women's cloaks at Mount Lebanon, all arose in response to the wasteful or criminal acts of men—trustees—who had been entrusted with the financial dealings of their respective societies. At Sabbathday Lake, "The Shaker Tamar Laxative" was made between 1881 and 1890, but its sales were modest at best. At Enfield, a thriving business making tubs, pails, and sap buckets was carried on from about mid-century until about 1890. It was said that the largest number of sap buckets used in the maple sugaring business in northern New England was made there. At Mount Lebanon, the community was forced to develop new sources of income following the wildly speculative excesses of several of their trustees, including the ill-advised purchase of land in Florida. One of the businesses communities settled on to address these debts was the making of women's woolen cloaks. Eldress Dorothy Durgin at Canterbury developed one popular pattern, supposedly by using an old raincoat as inspiration. All of the new ventures—a pill-drying machine invented at Sabbathday Lake,

a series of cutting and polishing jigs for pails developed at Enfield, and new fabric patterns designed at Mount Lebanon and Canterbury—involved a degree of innovation. Challenge, response, innovation. This is the Shaker way.

How do the Shakers use innovation? If a system or process or technique for accomplishing a task was already available, they took that and adapted, improved, and/or refined it. While some people tend to lump them together with entirely distinct Anabaptist groups such as the Old Order Amish, their differences are far greater than their similarities. The Amish are generally reluctant to accept "the new," whereas Shakers are and always have been progressive. For example, when moving water was the main source of power for driving machinery, the Shakers harnessed water in the most efficient ways possible, by building reservoirs, check-dams, and sluiceways that took advantage of the contours of their lands in order to maximize the work that could be gotten from each drop. They went on to develop—and patent—improved water wheels and, later, a water turbine.[18] When steam power, and then electricity, became available they were usually the first people in their area to embrace it. Their willingness to accept new developments held true with the telephone and then the automobile, some villages trading for newer models every few years. At Sabbathday Lake, they have conducted their dried culinary herb and herbal teas business over the Internet since the mid-1990s. Shakers view progress as a "gift" and feel that it is a duty as well as a privilege to use it.

Some incorrectly assume that the altruistic nature of the Shakers forbids them from participating in the patent process. This misunderstanding exposes two problems: what a patent is and who the Shakers are. A patent is "a grant made by a government that confers upon the creator of an invention the sole right to make, use, and sell that invention for a set period of time."[19] While patents protect the patentee, they also make public the details of the invention, allowing others to sufficiently alter and improve upon it so that they may then be granted their own patent. In this way patents can stimulate even more creativity. As for the Shakers' motives: two disparate forces drove them. On the one hand, they found that others were imitating their creations, such as the chairs that they themselves adapted from vernacular forms and made for sale by the tens of thousands. These could not be patented but, as we shall later see, they were trademarked (as the *Genuine* Shaker Chair). On the other was the profit motive. In order to support their unique way of life they had to have an economic base to support their communities. Nothing in their religious philosophy runs counter to this.

Nevertheless, Shakers are and always have been generous to friends and neighbors in need. They have consistently paid property taxes to their local town or county, even though they are exempted from having to do so by law.[20] Because they very much want to be responsible "partners" in the affairs of the towns or counties with which they interact, they contribute what they see as their "fair share." It is not a matter of altruism; this is what they believe it means to be a Christian community and a good neighbor.

Inventions were sometimes intended to solve problems within communities and sometimes made as products to market in the World. An example of the former was the tilter ball made for the bottom of the rear posts of chairs. The problem: rear posts broke when brethren tilted the chairs backwards, often marring the floors. The solution: a ball-and-socket device. To accomplish this, the bottoms of the rear posts were hollowed out, and round wooden pieces with flat bottoms installed. Each rounded piece was retained by a leather thong knotted at the bottom and threaded through an opening higher on the chair leg, where it was held with a tack. Alternatively, a cast-brass sleeve fitted with a ball and a socket was fitted over the bottom of the chair leg. This latter device was granted a U.S. patent but in the end was only used to outfit a handful of chairs, all for use within the New Lebanon community.[21]

An example of an invention intended mainly for sale to the World was the chimney cap, the brainchild of Elder Elijah Myrick at the Harvard, Massachusetts, community.[22] Patented in 1869, it consists of varying lengths of three-sided, cast-iron pieces, each connected to its neighbor with a pin-and-socket fastening system. These were made in several widths and designed to fit over the edges of the brick capping at the top of a chimneystack. A decorative outer flange and plain inner flange give it lateral stability. The device was used to protect the mortar at the top of chimneys from the elements. It is not known how many were actually sold, but apparently Harvard was the only Shaker community to use them on their own buildings. Several are still in place there.

Adaptations and improvements were so common in every Shaker village that it is difficult to extract a sole example. The round stone barn at the Hancock, Massachusetts, community—now a museum setting called Hancock Shaker Village—is a wonderful illustration of innovation writ large. In order to tend their herd of dairy cattle the Shakers there built a barn with a round shape that ultimately had three levels.[23] The main floor accommodated fifty-two head of cattle in stalls around the perimeter, their heads facing inward. In the center is an enormous round open area for hay. An earthen ramp leads to the upper level, which has a circular floor with its center open. A Shaker brother drove a wagon around the perimeter of this level and hay was pitched down into the central space. This brother then walked down to the main floor where he moved the hay a short distance to where cows could reach it from their stanchions. A third circular level beneath the cows caught manure shoveled through trap doors at the back of their stalls. The same brother then drove his wagon down the ramp from the top level to a second earthen ramp leading to the lower level. Here he circled the perimeter, collecting the manure for use in the fields. All of this meant that a single Shaker could efficiently feed a full herd of dairy cows and collect its waste for use as fertilizer. From hay to milk to manure—all through the ingenious use of gravity.

Examples of Shaker refinements abound as well. In fact, virtually every product of their hands is an example of their refinement of an existing form, for they "invented" almost nothing in the way of furniture and little in the way of small crafts. Their genius lay in paring down forms to their very essence, with no "extras" that could catch debris or display vanity. Humility was a guiding principle in the simple, recto-linear lines and flat surfaces of almost all Shaker-made furniture—as it is in their lives.

One example of extreme refinement is the simple and humble candle stand, also known as a light stand or tripod stand. It consists of a top—almost invariably round—a turned shaft with little or nothing in the way of additional turnings and no carvings at all, and three curved legs that generally end in narrow "pad" feet. A round or rectangular cleat is screwed to the top, and the shaft is threaded into it. Six pieces of wood (cherry, maple, and/or butternut); that is all. It is a perfectly functional piece, sturdy enough to hold a lighting device, light enough to be easily moved, unadorned so that it does not trap dust or dirt—yet totally elegant in its simplicity.

Mother Ann once admonished her followers: "Do all your work as though you had a thousand years to live, and as you would if you knew you must die tomorrow."[24] By this she meant: Do the very best you can but don't tarry in doing it. The Shakers always had a reputation for excellence in virtually everything they made. Moreover, though they did not take an excessive amount of time to do it, they nonetheless had the relative luxury of more time than their worldly counterparts. The results were sometimes stunningly innovative. In 1820 a visitor to the New Lebanon community reported: "Instead of wooden posts in front of their gates and doors, they use pillars fashioned of a single stone block."[25] The reason the brethren took the time and applied the expertise to carve posts from slabs of granite rather than simply sawing them from pieces of timber is that wood rots in the presence of water. The bottoms of traditional fence posts need constant replacement; the Shakers expected theirs to literally "last a thousand years." Later, the Canterbury Shakers modified this process by making granite bases with square cutouts on top into which square wooden posts could be fitted. This, too, overcame rotting.

Finally, there was the development of systems for growing or crafting, packaging, and bringing to market the products of Shakers' lands and hands. Here there are several examples to choose from but none better than garden seeds. Before about 1794, the only way to buy seed was in fabric bags in bulk and just about the only people who bought seeds were farmers. If individuals had a small "kitchen garden," their seed came from previous plantings or by exchanges with neighbors. At that time there simply was no such thing as a retail seed industry. The Shakers changed that forever and, in the process, created an industry that more than any other underwrote the first sixty years of their movement at New Lebanon and other communities. Although virtually nothing

remains from this endeavor at other Shaker villages, it is all but certain that every one of them engaged in raising and selling seeds at a retail level. (It also paved the way for a thriving non-Shaker industry in America, from after the Civil War to this day and will be re-visited in detail in Chapter 1.)

As the movement progressed from its formative years in the late eighteenth century through its greatest prosperity in the mid-nineteenth century, its means of supporting itself gradually shifted from the production of goods needed to support agriculture locally to raising and selling products for non-agrarian consumers in more distant markets. Better roads, the opening of the Erie Canal in 1825, and the dominance of railroads all spurred the expansion of markets. Later in the nineteenth and into the twentieth century, groups of Shakers made the rounds of hotels, fairs, and exhibitions, especially at resorts near the seacoast and in the mountains, selling their wares.

Meanwhile, the clouds gathering over the society in the 1850s became storms by the 1870s. Many more were leaving than joining, and the population of the faithful was aging. The first long-standing village to close was Tyringham, Massachusetts, in 1875. This was a small society with never more than a hundred members (1850), and of that number more than half were under sixteen or over sixty years of age. Next to close, in 1889, was North Union, Ohio, the present site of Shaker Heights. By the early 1930s, another ten villages had closed, and only a handful of Shaker men remained at the five surviving communities.[26]

At Mount Lebanon and the other eastern communities at least, the number of girls and women who came and stayed continued to outpace the number of boys and men who did, although in both cases the data show a general decline. After about 1880 the Shakers came to depend less on income from the products of their farms, fields, and orchards—"men's work"—and relied more on a group of handcrafted pieces that are called fancywork or "fancy goods"— "women's work." Fancywork is labor-intensive but not backbreaking the way farm work is. The farming that was still carried out to supply the remaining communities' needs late in the nineteenth and early in the twentieth centuries usually depended upon either young Shaker boys or on hired labor from the World. Among the latter were a few thieves and even an arsonist, further adding to the Shakers' misfortunes.

Fancywork, made by the sisters for sale to non-Shaker women, consisted primarily of items used for sewing and mending. The major item in this category is "poplarware"—a craft wholly developed by Shakers and almost entirely carried out by sisters. This will be extensively covered in Chapter 9. Suffice it to say this craft alone was probably the reason why the Alfred, Maine, Canterbury, and Sabbathday Lake communities lasted into the twentieth century. The other large category of sisters' work made for sale were clothing items—cloaks for children and adult women as well as sweaters for men and women. Canterbury led the way here. Finally, a plethora of small notions, knick-knacks, and foodstuffs were crafted or put up at every Shaker village and sold in gift stores located along well-traveled roads. Items included knitted wares, potholders, gloves, potpourris, and comestibles: candies, flavored waters, and jellies. The gift store at Sabbathday Lake remains active in selling this merchandise.

Brother Theodore "Ted" Johnson's arrival at Sabbathday Lake in 1960 heralded a virtual rebirth of some of the most highly prized traditions that had fallen away there. A new scholarly publication, the *Shaker Quarterly*, was begun in 1961. The historic 1794 Meeting House reopened for Sunday worship in 1963 for the first time in seventy-five years. In the early 1970s the community resumed growing, harvesting, processing, and packaging a wide variety of dried herbs and herbal teas. They soon began selling these to distant markets by mail order, then through the Internet. This enterprise, along with the sale of wool from their herd of sheep, continues to this day.

The Seventh Census of the United States was conducted in 1850. Slightly more than twenty-three million people were counted; 3.2 million of them slave. That was an overall increase of 36 percent from the census of ten years earlier. By way of contrast, in 1850 there were approximately 4,800 Shakers—their highest number ever but only fractionally higher than their total for 1840. Thus, at the time when their movement counted its largest number of Believers, it still only constituted a mere .0002 percent of the U.S. population.

The number of Shakers assumes greater significance when we consider their impact on the country. From the development of far-ranging businesses in garden seeds, medicinal herbs, and woodenwares the Shakers were already well known east of the Mississippi River in 1850. In the next twenty-six years, up until the time of the Centennial Exhibition in Philadelphia, their fame spread even farther, thanks primarily to the quality of their medicinal herbs and herbal products, and a thriving chair business. Both earned medals for their respective communities—Canterbury and Mount Lebanon—at the exposition. In 1900 the population of the United States had risen to just over seventy-six million, while the Shakers in their nine eastern villages numbered 627 and the western villages had only two hundred.[27]

Today, though only one out of every hundred million residents in this country is a Shaker, they are a source of seemingly endless fascination to many. They and their world continue to be written about, exhibited, and collected. Annual seminars, symposia, and forums are organized to discuss every conceivable aspect of their lives. One can only conclude that in spite of the fact that there are just a handful of Believers today, *the Shakers still matter*.

Yet, one nagging question—sometimes whispered, more often stridently posed—remains: Is this the end? Are we about to witness the closing of the Shaker Gospel in America after almost 225 years? Are these the last Shakers? Will the World soon bear witness to the demise of a sect whose influence has always been vastly disproportionate to their small numbers?

The Shakers are not unaware of these questions and of what others view as their precarious future. For their part they believe the future is simply in the hands of Father/Mother God[28] and that their numbers are not a meaningful measure of their worth in God's eyes. They have served the ministry of Father/Mother God here on earth and delivered to the World through everyday living what they believe is God's message. Nobody knows what lies ahead: the future will be what it will be. Meanwhile, day by day, Sabbathday Lake's Believers continue doing what Shakers have always done, putting their hands to work and giving their hearts to God. 🌿

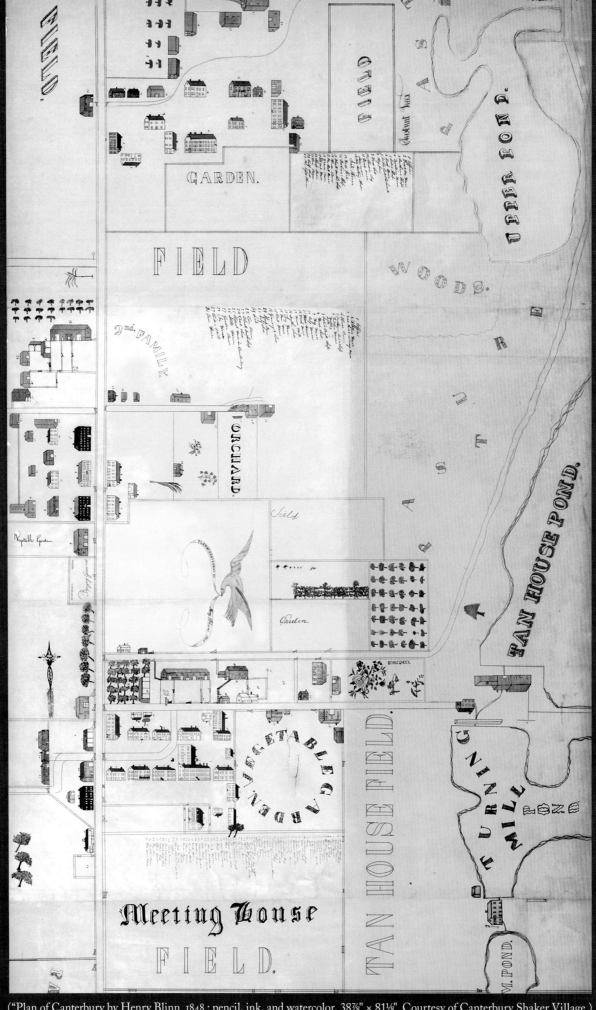

("Plan of Canterbury by Henry Blinn 1848 : pencil, ink, and watercolor, 38⅞″ × 81⅛″. Courtesy of Canterbury Shaker Village.)

Innovations in Shaker Architecture and Planning

Scott T. Swank

I N 1792, the newly formed group of Shaker believers in Canterbury, New Hampshire, faced a dilemma. After meeting for several years in the homes and barns of believers in the Canterbury area, Benjamin Whitcher gave his farm to the Shakers in order to build a community, and the New Lebanon Ministry was calling the community to "order." The first priority was a Meeting House for worship. As the first Shaker building in New Hampshire, the Meeting House would be a symbol for the Shaker faith. Where would it be built? What would it look like? How would it address multiple functional needs? Who would build it?[1]

In the twenty-first century, only one active Shaker community survives, at Sabbathday Lake, Maine, but Shaker innovations are still evident throughout the physical landscapes of former Shaker villages. Some exist only in the historical record or in physical fragments ensconced within modern prisons, educational institutions, or urban sprawl. Several former communities are well-maintained museums and historic sites, such as Hancock Shaker Village, Massachusetts; Pleasant Hill, Kentucky; and Canterbury Shaker Village, New Hampshire. The latter, in fact, is arguably the best vantage point from which to study the original architectural and spatial intentions of the Shakers, and to actually see the innovative Shaker architectural program that can be called the "Pattern from the Mount." This designation derives from the fact that the early Shaker leadership in New Lebanon, New York, where Joseph Meacham defined Shaker gospel order, also first sanctioned the

basic principles of Shaker architecture and spatial planning. New Lebanon was situated on the shoulder of a small mountain in eastern New York, and was known from its founding as the "Mount." In 1861 the Shakers changed the name from New Lebanon to Mount Lebanon.

From the 1780s through the 1830s, the Shakers hitched their innovative religious movement to the revolutionary social fervor of the era in order to create "Heaven on Earth" in their burgeoning communal villages. The Shakers' way of life in their communities radiated from their core belief in "gospel order." This was a fundamental and defining principle of Shaker society that called for life to be lived collectively rather than individually; separate from the outside society; in harmony with God and other Believers, and with disciplines rooted in established patterns of Shaker social organization and village life. Those patterns included the specific buildings needed for worship, living, and work; the division of spaces and functions within those buildings; and "zones" of organization for efficiently implementing their principles.

Canterbury (hereafter used to identify the Shaker village, not the nearby town of the same name) was planned according to general guidelines established at New Lebanon, but the ruling elders and eldresses of the New Hampshire Bishopric shaped the actual village plan locally. This bishopric was responsible for overseeing the needs of Believers at Canterbury and Enfield, New Hampshire (not to be confused with the Shaker community of the same name in

Connecticut). To live in gospel order, a Shaker community needed three core buildings: a Meeting House for worship, a dwelling house for communal, celibate living, and an office to manage their economic enterprises. To achieve their goals, the Shakers could not just borrow ideas from the "corrupt" prevailing society around them. They had to shape existing society to their purposes, and create new systems of belief and practice.

The Shaker Meetinghouse

At the time of their founding in 1792, the Canterbury Shakers needed a Meeting House. (The Shakers traditionally separate these two words.) We know a great deal about the outcome of the Shaker deliberations concerning their first building in New Hampshire because this 1792 Meeting House still stands at Canterbury Shaker Village in its original location, with only a few modifications over time. We also know that the master builder was Brother Moses Johnson, sent from New Lebanon to supervise its construction in order to implement the specific Meeting House "template" established by the Church Family's own Meeting House built in 1784.

In 1792, in most of New England, Congregation-

alism was the established religious faith, and Congregational churches dominated the architectural landscape. If a congregation or town wanted to build a new meetinghouse, a local building committee would be delegated to visit recently erected structures in other towns, and return to make a proposal. Town fathers wanted their meetinghouse to conform to the style of a "proper" New England meetinghouse. The actual building process was a community event since meetinghouses in the eighteenth century served as both a church and a meeting place for town residents. The Shakers, on the other hand, did not want their Meeting House to look like a Congregational church, or a town meetinghouse. They wanted to make a fresh statement.

The New Lebanon template for a Meeting House probably developed from the earliest buildings used for Shaker worship in Ashfield, Massachusetts, and Watervliet, New York, during Mother Ann Lee's ministry, but we know very little about these early structures. With the fully developed template first given form in 1784, and with the imprimatur of New Lebanon's leaders, Johnson supervised the construction of eleven more Meeting Houses in as many Shaker communities in the eastern United States. Although he did not build any in the Shaker West, those Meeting Houses also followed the same basic pattern. The Shakers had invented an architectural form that met their specific spiritual requirements. Design and function were determined by the following:

1. The Shakers embraced dance as their principal form of worship. Dancing required a large open room with no liturgical center such as an altar or pulpit, without supporting posts, but with a reinforced floor. The entire building had to be engineered to provide a square dance floor at least thirty-two feet square with seating benches built around the outside wall.

   Dancing was associated with taverns and Native American paganism. Few large eighteenth-century taverns had second- or third-floor ballrooms, and no one in New Hampshire had ever designed or constructed a *church* for dancing. Moses Johnson, who had already built several in the New York and Massachusetts communities, imported to Canterbury in 1792 a Hudson River Dutch framing tradition (anchor beam construction), married it to basic timber frame practice of the time, and subordinated the entire construction process to Shaker principles of "use." No other religious movement in the new United States used dance as a principal expression of worship, so the concept of a meetinghouse as dance hall was shockingly new, and scandalous to non-Shaker Christians.

2. The Shaker Meeting House had to serve as a residence for four lay Shaker elders and eldresses. The Canterbury Ministry was expected to be in residence at each community for six months of the year. At each they would live on the second and third floors, apart from other brothers and sisters of the community. This meant that Enfield and Canterbury needed identical Meeting Houses. New England Protestant churches had no precedent for unmarried men and women living together. The Shakers created two apartments on each upper level of their Meeting Houses to accommodate one elder and eldress on each floor. Separate staircases for men and women reinforced the concept of separation of the celibates, yet each floor had a wide central hall for passage, work, and most likely dining, and there were no physical barriers to prohibit the mingling of the ministers.

3. These two major building requirements—to accommodate dancing and to accommodate ministerial living—shaped the interior of the three-story Meeting Houses, but they did not determine the exterior appearance. Their overall architectural form was much more conservative than the unusual interior arrangement and socially controversial uses. Shakers were mostly drawn from the yeoman farmer and artisan classes of society. They were not versed in European town planning and architecture, so they were limited to the styles, materials, and techniques at hand, and they insisted that their place of worship not look like the established churches of their time. Among religious traditions, that left only the Dissenting English tradition (which included the Quakers, Presbyterians, and Methodists) to provide precedent. Shaker buildings and Dissenter meeting-houses do share some architectural characteristics, especially double entries for men and women and the interior division of space into male and female spheres, but the Shakers chose to adopt a common domestic form for their Meeting Houses. Shaker Meeting Houses are a clever adaptation of the classic eighteenth-century gambrel roof houses found in the port and river valley towns of New York and New England. In short, the Shakers chose a domestic building type that was passing rapidly out of style in the 1780s, and elevated it as their preferred architectural style. They replaced the central door on the façade with separate entries for men and women, and revolutionized the interiors.

The Shaker Village

When the Shakers located their first building on the southern ridge of land on Benjamin Whitcher's farm, the Canterbury Shakers had killed the proverbial two birds with one stone. They had chosen the gambrel roof, timber-frame structure as the architectural model for other buildings in the village, and they had re-affirmed New Lebanon's principle of arranging villages relative to the Meeting House. This spatial organization of the entire village is another inspired innovation and one as remarkable as the invention of the Shaker Meeting House.

The Dutch in New York and the English in New England had been establishing towns and villages since the early seventeenth century, and in the late eighteenth century mill villages added a new model for settlement. In the mid-Atlantic region, the Moravians had established standard communal settlements. The Shakers did not directly borrow any one established settlement pattern, nor did they insist that only one was acceptable. Instead, they developed a core pattern in New Lebanon that dictated the relationship of the Meeting House to the dwelling house and let each village work out the details of its own development. The Shakers intended that their faith in general, and their villages as the "patent models" of that faith, would be a living, growing organism, with buildings and spaces emanating the spirit of Shaker life in community. As Stephen Paterwic so aptly observes in his essay on innovations in Shaker social organization, "Shakerism is a way of life that is progressive and responsive to change." That is as true of architecture and building use as it is of the organization of the Shaker ministry.

The community plan in Canterbury is not exactly like the one in New Lebanon that was centered on a crossroads and generally laid out along the principal road in and out of the village. Canterbury Shakers set their Meeting House back from the road on a hilltop and developed their community with a series of streets running perpendicular to the main road. The only other Shaker community built exactly like Canterbury was Enfield, New Hampshire. That is not surprising since the two were under the same ministry. Many other communities in the East and West followed the New Lebanon crossroads model. A third pattern emerged at Watervliet, New York, which adopted an open courtyard plan.

There are almost no meaningful similarities between known American settlement models and Shaker communities. The most congruent are the Moravian communities in eighteenth-century Pennsylvania, but no one has yet documented a direct connection between German Moravians and English Shakers. There are some striking parallels of spatial zoning and social organization between Catholic monastic communities and the Shakers, but the similarities can be explained by shared religious principles and do not assume direct knowledge of monastic practice. The dominant New England settlement pattern in the eighteenth century was what Joseph Wood in *The New England Village* calls the "dispersed village."[2] Americans did not want cramped, nucleated "Old World" settlements. They valued their land and did not want to live in town and till outlying land parcels. They wanted the largest contiguous landholding they could afford, and they wanted to live independently on that land. Their village center might hold structures that were used by all, such as the meetinghouse, town hall, store, or blacksmith shop, but otherwise the farmers' homes were dispersed throughout the geographical entity known as the town.

The Shakers' rural, nucleated settlement was an innovation in the 1780s and 1790s. Shak-

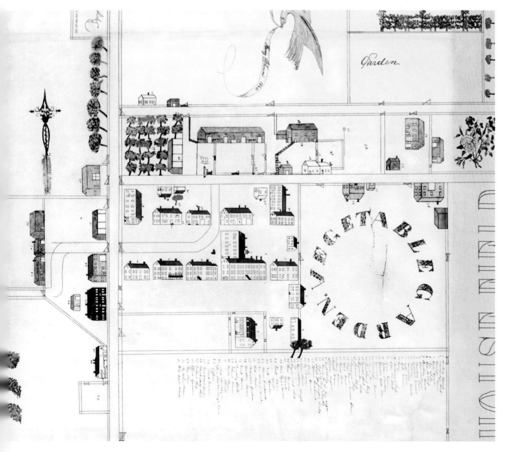

ers needed to live together and apart from the World for religious reasons. They had to encourage one another in the face of social persecution and reinforce their beliefs and practices by living in gospel order. The Shakers anticipated another powerful reason for nuclear settlements, namely, the economic efficiency that spurred manufacture and commerce. Given their concentration in communal villages, and their progressive views of society and life, the Shakers were primed for the economic changes sweeping the new American Republic. They took to the industrial revolution like the proverbial ducks to water. Their philosophy primed them to accept new ideas and social change as evidence of God's progressive revelation. Their social organization encouraged cooperation rather than competition, and their type of entrepreneurial communism supported making money and using profits for the benefit of the larger community. Consequently, Shaker villages were not at all like mill villages, where the workers lived next to their factory in meager housing while the owners lived up the hill in mansions. Shaker villages made no distinction between owner and worker in status or housing (even though the ministry did live apart), and all forms of competition were discouraged.

The Shaker Dwelling House

Based on the "Pattern from the Mount," three specific building types formed the core of each Shaker village, regardless of which settlement type the leaders chose to follow. The first building in any new community was the Meeting House. The expectation and practice was that every Shaker community would have one. The family living around that Meeting House was known as the First or Church Family. As the community grew, there could be additional branches of the Church Family, or other families, but only one Meeting House. When it came to the dwelling house, it was assumed that as the movement grew, there could be an unlimited number of villages and multiple dwelling houses in each. The Shakers developed a concept of home unlike any other social or religious group in the eighteenth century. Although they lived in dwelling houses—organized as families, calling their first founders "father" and "mother," and calling each other "brother" and "sister," these were communal rather than kinship designations. In that sense, the true Shaker physical home was the village, which the average Believer rarely if ever left.

The dwelling house was in many ways the center of Shaker life. It was the "bell house," the source of daily ritual and communication and the daily gathering place for meals, meetings, and rest. It was the largest building in the village, other than barns, because it was designed at first to house up to sixty members and, in later generations, up to one hundred. In the eighteenth century, the Shakers built at least two dwelling houses for every Meeting House. The New Lebanon Pattern from the Mount required that the dwelling house or houses be built directly across from or in close proximity to the Meeting House. In many villages, this meant that the dwelling was across the main road from the Meeting House. At Canterbury and Enfield, New Hampshire, the first dwelling houses faced the Meeting House across a dooryard. If more than one dwelling was required, others were placed in a row next to one another but still facing the Meeting House. The Canterbury Church Family erected two dwelling houses side by side in 1793 and 1794. The Harvard, Massachusetts, Church Family erected three dwelling houses in a row across the road from their Meeting House. In the eighteenth century, the Shakers built at least twenty dwelling houses and at least eleven Meeting Houses. Three original Meeting Houses survive intact (Canterbury, Sabbathday Lake, and Shirley, now relocated to Hancock), with several more surviving in altered states. The only eighteenth-century dwelling house in a Shaker museum setting is the 1793 dwelling house at Canterbury, but it is encased in a much larger structure which has been expanded five times since it was first built. The 1793 timber frame and several third-floor rooms survive within the existing structure.

To support gospel order, the dwelling house had to provide gender separation and promote community harmony among scores of residents. Each dwelling needed kitchens, cellars, and pantries, a large communal dining room, common space for meetings, sleeping chambers, and storage areas for clothing and bedding. In order to accommodate gender separation, the dwellings had separate entrances for men and women, separate staircases, and separate sleeping and storage areas. In effect, the large building was split down the middle, but true separation was maintained through social discipline, not by means of a solid partition. These dwelling houses relate to the large academic buildings that constituted the first American colleges, but colleges were never coeducational in the eighteenth century. In short, the Shakers once again adapted an existing building type—eighteenth-century residences for groups of the same gender—and created an entirely new building type. Remarkably, the earliest Shaker dwelling houses were also gambrel roofed structures that looked very similar on the exterior to the first generation Meeting Houses. The Shakers took a common structural form, used standard eighteenth-century construction methods and materials, and created two innovative interior arrangements to address two essential but different functional needs: worship and daily living.

The Office and Other Community Buildings

Even more astonishing is the fact that, especially at Canterbury and Enfield, although less so at other communities, the Shakers took this same gambrel roof model and adapted it to build their first office and their first gender-specific work building—the 1795 Sisters' Shop at Canterbury. Leaders here believed they had an inspired design into which they could shoehorn every major function just by changing the physical dimensions. This ambitious effort broke down very early at New Lebanon and most other communities, and even Canterbury and Enfield abandoned the gambrel roof by 1797 or 1798.

The Shaker Office served the temporal and business needs of the community. In the earliest years, it was a small structure that served as the work place for four office deacons and deaconesses who supervised the economic enterprises of the community. It was also the community's public face to the outside world. The latter function required that the office be located along the main road through the village where it would be easily visible and accessible to non-Shaker business travelers. In the 1830s the first office at Canterbury was replaced with a commodious Trustees' Office. Over time, the deacons and deaconesses were called trustees, and the office served as a Shaker hostel as well as a business center. Many other building types were developed as the Shakers grew in numbers and enterprises, all of which were laid out in the community plan in their respective zones, which included a ministry zone (Meeting House and ministry shop), residential zone (dwelling houses with service buildings such as privies, cheese houses, and woodsheds), brothers' and sisters' work zones, an agricultural zone, and a mills zone.

Regardless of the building type or purpose, the Shakers continued to expand their villages according to concepts of order first developed in the New Lebanon's Church Family. Once the Meeting House and one or more dwelling houses had been erected, Believers quickly turned to the construction of farm and industry buildings/workshops that would enable them to generate income to support their community and fuel its growth. In order to accommodate this rapid expansion, every village needed a plan. These extensive and dramatic plans can be seen most clearly on the many Shaker maps published in the seminal study *Shaker Village Views* by Robert Emlen.[3]

From the vantage point of the twenty-first century, it is sometimes hard to grasp the scale of the Shaker communities. They were dense clusters of buildings surrounded by thousands of acres of land, some of which the Shakers engineered into mill-ponds, mills, roads, gardens, and orchards, and most of which were open pasture, cultivated fields, and woodlands. At its peak, New Lebanon had some six hundred Believers living on and working six thousand acres of land. Canterbury and Enfield, New Hampshire, reached peaks of about three hundred Believers living on between three and four thousand acres of land. The Shakers quickly advanced to the forefront of American agriculture by taking a position at odds with most farmers in the Northeast. The average American farmer in the early nineteenth century had no conception of sustainable farming. The prevailing ethic was one of intensely using the land since land was cheap and plentiful. Many farmers assumed they would move on when their lands became unproductive. The freedom to waste was, for them, a hallmark of democracy.

The Shakers, on the other hand, were highly invested in their communal homes. They formed new communities and expanded old ones, but they had no intention of abandoning highly developed sites. Rather than exploiting their land, they borrowed from early agricultural reformers and experimented

with ways to improve their soils, expand crop yields, and achieve balance among woodland, pasturage, and plow land. Their progressive views provided fertile ground for new ideas and new practices, and they achieved a remarkable synchronicity between their religious beliefs and their economic practices.

Shaker Interiors

Shaker innovations in architecture are not confined to the exteriors of buildings, or to village plans but appear inside buildings as well. They developed plans for the highly efficient use of interior space, organized that space into distinctive patterns, and differentiated it according to gender and function. The result was a system of interior designs marked by features such as dual entries and staircases, a profusion of storage units, repetition of peg rail, and the use of "borrowed" light. In New England, prevailing fashion directed that patrons spend their money on those exterior and interior features that conveyed status. A house's façade required more attention than the back; the front hall and front parlors sported finer paneling and fireplace treatments than the upper or back rooms. A hierarchy of ornamentation conveyed social messages to occupants and visitors. None of this mattered to the Shakers. They did not live by ordinary social norms or according to current fashion. Their mission on earth was to please God and facilitate harmonious, collective living and working.

For example, peg rail for hanging clothing was a feature of most New England residences, often in the form of short strips near a back entry or in closets and chambers. The Shakers took this ordinary, unfashionable device  and elevated it to an art form and a distinctive mark of their design. Instead of confining peg rail to a small functional strip in an out-of-the-way location, they expanded its use and put it on all the walls of rooms and hallways, sometimes in double and triple rows. Peg rail served not only as a place to hang the many Shaker garments, tools, and light furnishings, it became a marker of Shaker space.

Another example of this same principle is found in the multiplicity of Shaker storage units. Wealthy and fashionable Americans of the time put their money and attention into architectural features and fine furniture that would speak to the rest of their social world. They certainly would not have directed their builders to spend as much time and money on finishing the attic as they did on the front parlor. By contrast, the Shakers devoted inordinate amounts of time and material to building the most spectacular attics in American architecture. The glories of many Shaker dwelling houses lie in functional staircases, built-in storage units, and storage attics such as the ones at Canterbury, Hancock, Enfield, New Hampshire, and Pleasant Hill. Once again, the Shakers took a common necessity and elevated it to an art form. Since Shaker joiners, all of them men, were committed to building heaven on earth, their work on the multiple built-in storage units in sisters' attics is as superb as their work on the living and dining spaces two stories below. It is remarkable to think that once their work in the sisters' attic at Canterbury was completed, the brothers who built it would never see the attic again. Only the sisters would see their stunning workmanship until the attic was opened to the public in the twentieth century.

A final example of Shaker innovation lies in the manipulation of natural light in Shaker buildings. The Shakers did not invent either skylights or borrowed light (the technique of creating interior windows that would convey natural light from outside through a series of windows into the darkest interiors of a building). However, they took a concept known mostly in European academic architecture, one that harkened back to classical Greek and Roman architecture, and adapted the concept to their own buildings. Nearly every Shaker building uses borrowed light to illuminate staircases, rooms, and storage areas, and there are occasional instances where as many as three openings are used to move light from the exterior windows to the deepest recesses of interior closets. Although intended as practical devices to facilitate daily life and work in a time when artificial lighting was expensive and dangerous, these interior windows today add great beauty to the aesthetics of Shaker buildings.

One of the myths of Shaker design is the common belief that the essence of Shaker aesthetics is simplicity. Shaker design is, in fact, the result of numerous complex options and choices. In making their choices, the Shakers first of all were rejecting the prevailing religious views and popular fashions of their day, then selectively choosing options that they could incorporate into their distinctive designs. In the process, whether it was a building style or function, social organization, community planning, spatial arrangement, or gender separation, the Shakers applied innovations that fulfilled their ideal for a harmonious community. Their ultimate goals were to achieve gospel order and create a heaven on earth, and each of these innovations contributed toward those ends. 🌱

All images courtesy of Canterbury Shaker Village, Inc

Equality of the Sexes as Shakers' Inspired Innovation

GLENDYNE R. WERGLAND

To fully appreciate the Shakers' accomplishments in achieving equality of the sexes, it helps to know what preceded their inspired innovation in women's rights. In 1780, unmarried women had most of the rights that single men had, with the significant exception of the right to vote. As long as women remained single, they could own property, pay taxes, run their own businesses, and manage their own affairs without a man's interference—but they could not vote or hold public office. Most women married, but some avoided wedlock because singleness ameliorated the unequal power relations between women and men.[1] Marriage changed a woman's status.

American culture inherited its concept of the hierarchy of marriage from England. According to this tradition, by marrying, a man and woman became one. A wife experienced "civil death" when her legal identity merged with her husband's at marriage. In effect, she became the property of her husband. A married woman (a *feme covert*) could not make contracts, buy or sell property, sue or be sued, or draft a will without her husband's permission. Her husband owned any wages she earned, and unless she protected her assets with a prenuptial agreement, he controlled her dowry as well as any other property she brought to the marriage. If a couple divorced, courts typically awarded custody of children to the father, and they might never see their mother again. A husband could have his wife committed to an asylum against her will. Women could not vote. In the United States before 1920, men made all the laws governing women and their rights—usually privileging men over women, but by the nineteenth century, women had begun to protest their disadvantaged status.[2]

The Shakers were more than a century ahead of the rest of American society with their radical notions about equality of the sexes. Ann Lee, the founder of Shakerism in America, was one of only ten women preachers identified before 1800.[3] By preaching to the public, Mother Ann violated gender norms. By leading a group of men and women, she violated norms of male dominance. Her inspired leadership outraged some observers and mystified others. A thread of gendered incredulity ran through one visitor account. "It hath appeared to many persons a riddle altogether inscrutable," this skeptical clergyman wondered, "how it was possible for an indigent stranger to effect what this woman effected, when labouring under all the disadvantages with which she was burdened."[4] Because Ann Lee was a woman, an immigrant, illiterate, and poor, she was "in the eyes of the world" unqualified for church leadership. Yet she actively proselytized, and her congregation grew.

The radical nature of Shakerism began with celibacy, which established women's equality by eliminating the hierarchy of marriage. Celibacy was not, of course, unknown. Roman Catholic priests and nuns had vowed celibacy for centuries, although that church did not insist that married couples of the rank and file set aside their marriage agreement and live as celibates. The radical nature of Shaker celibacy, then, lies not only in living without sexual relations, but in the sundering of marital ties. By eliminating marriage, Ann Lee may have intended to co-opt the husband's authority over wife and children and transfer that authority to the Shaker church, but the practical effect, as things turned out, was to make men and women equal in the eyes of the church. By eliminating marriage, Shakers removed men's traditional source of patriarchal authority over women. One has to wonder how that first generation of converts adjusted to their new roles.

After Ann Lee died in 1784, the Shakers had no official female leader for several years. Mother Ann was succeeded by a series of men, including Joseph Meacham. Meacham instituted the next inspired innovation in Shakerism: he elevated Lucy Wright to be his partner in leadership. He might have chosen a man or men, vested all authority in males, and caused Shakerism to veer off the path toward equality. Instead, he chose a woman who was already a leader among her peers, a woman who made her own decisions. Together, Meacham and Wright restructured Shaker social relations to provide women with opportunities that, if not exactly equal, were similar to those of men.

After Meacham died in 1796, Lucy Wright remained the acknowledged lead of the Shaker ministry until her death in 1821. Thus, Shaker sisters continued to have a strong female leader as a role model for the rising generation. Men unwilling to live under "petticoat government" left the society.[5] Over the next few decades, the population of sisters grew until they outnumbered brethren. Because more women than men joined the society, and remained Believers, we can infer that Shakerism had more to offer women than it offered men, who were accustomed to the perquisites of patriarchy. By banding together, Shaker sisters had more power in their society than most other women enjoyed. As an equal, according to church law, a Shaker woman was not under any man's thumb. For women fleeing domestic violence, a peaceful Shaker village provided sanctuary.

Shaker men and women maintained a traditional, gendered division of labor, so their roles were not exactly equal in all ways. In fact, Believers did not expect them to be. Sisters cooked, sewed, knitted, did housework and laundry, and were responsible for a multitude of chores that might be collectively termed "women's work." Though the sisters did sometimes feel oppressed by their work, they seem not to have felt they were subjugated to the men whom they outnumbered. Sisters and brothers generally seem to have viewed themselves as partners in the shared enterprise of Shakerism, each sex helping the other.

In addition to running the farm and several home industries, brethren also sewed, knitted, and supported women's efforts. The kitchen was a case in point. Brethren eased the cooks' workload by installing conveniences such as indoor plumbing, boilers, stoves, and drying racks. In 1818 the New Lebanon kitchen had two large marble sinks, ovens, and boilers, which most farm kitchens lacked. In 1835 an Englishman noted of the kitchen, "None in London could exceed theirs in neatness of equipment."[6] Another visitor concluded in 1888, "The Brethren have devised unheard-of comforts for the indoor workers, and the visitor leaves with the feeling of pity for the housewife who does her cooking in the ordinary way. Here every step tells, every movement counts."[7] The laundry was also arranged to promote efficiency and ease. Brethren built or bought labor-saving innovations such as water-powered washing machines, a wringer for squeezing water out of the wash (or the more expensive "centrifugal dryer"), and hoists to lift heavy wet laundry into the attic for drying.[8] Brothers installed special stoves for heating irons, as well. All those conveniences expressed equality in Shaker material culture. Among the world's people in the nineteenth century, indoor plumbing and mechanical assistance for farmwomen were unusual. Many had to carry water in buckets from a well or stream. Worldly farmers privileged men over women, and often improved men's equipment, but rarely did anything to ease women's work.[9] Shakers' modern kitchens and laundries were enticements for overworked farmwomen to join the society.

After Lucy Wright died in 1821, the rank-and-file sisters at New Lebanon and Watervliet maintained their authority. They continued to do "woman's work," but they also expected equal consideration and received it in ways that reached beyond the kitchen and laundry. For instance, when the brethren wanted to use the sisters' shop for hat making, the sisters demanded another shop. They negotiated as a group, and Eldress Betsy Bates recorded their agreement. The brothers acquiesced and built a new shop as agreed the following year.[10] If brethren had dominated sisters, the men would have simply issued an edict, and the women would have had to accept whatever they got. Among the Shakers equality gave the sisters bargaining power.

Unfortunately, equality was not practiced evenly throughout Shaker society. By one account, even Hancock, Massachusetts, which adjoined the New Lebanon Shaker village, had given up that standard by 1816.[11] At Canaan, New York, the brethren were remiss in providing conveniences for the sisters. They had no washhouse for years; the sisters did laundry in the kitchen at night after supper and lacked indoor drying space until 1838. One unidentified scribe (probably female) wrote, "Sometimes a whole week would elapse before the weather would be suitable to put the clothes out and often would they have to wade through deep snow to put up their lines." The Canaan sisters' frustration with the brethren reached a crescendo with William Evans, an obnoxious newcomer who tried to tell the sisters how to do their work. After two years of his meddling, the sisters finally reached the end of their patience. "As the brethren had not the power or lacked the disposition to get rid of him the sisters undertook the job and succeeded admirably," explained the scribe. Hannah Bryant and Harriet Sellick "took him by the collar and put him into the street and threw his clothes after him." Evans went to the Hancock Shaker village, expecting to be taken in there, but Elder Daniel Goodrich sent him away, saying, "A man that the sisters have turned out doors is not fit to be on consecrated ground."[12] The sisters had the authority to expel a troublemaker—a power virtually unknown among the world's people in the nineteenth century—and the elders respected their right to do so.

Sisters asserted themselves in other ways as they challenged traditional gender relations. In addition to negotiating for a new shop and throwing a troublesome brother into the street, they ran their own businesses, expelled their peers by "spirit edict," refused to milk the cows at two communities, and changed their own dress code. The brethren were unable, or unwilling, to keep determined sisters from getting what they wanted.[13]

By the late 1830s (a decade before the historic first women's rights convention in Seneca Falls, New York), pressure was building for women's rights among the world's people. Traveling lecturers such as Frances Wright, Sarah and Angelina Grimké, and others promoted women's rights in pamphlets, newspaper columns, and public talks throughout the northeast.[14] Shakers kept up with what was going on in the outside world, and promoted women's rights. As early as 1869, a Shaker Elder said, "When women vote wars shall cease."[15] Charles Nordhoff wrote of the Shakers, "They hold strongly to the equality of women with men, and look forward to the day when women shall, in the outer world as in their own societies, hold office as well as men." New Lebanon's Elder Frederick Evans said, "Here we find the women just as able as men in all business affairs, and far more spiritual."[16]

By 1878 even male visitors recognized that Shaker society had become a "woman-ocracy ("gynécratie"), or a government by women."[17] One anonymous visitor, a woman with a keen interest in the Shakers' practical application of the principles of women's rights, recognized that women were the "real strength" of Shakerism while men assumed "no air of superiority" in either religious or temporal matters.[18] In 1888 a visiting Mormon missionary noted that eldresses were "equal in authority" with elders.[19] Because the sisters' equality was evident, even to outsiders who spent only a day or two with the New Lebanon Shakers, there can be little quibbling as to the women's status there, at the sect's "center of union."[20] Shaker women were an increasing majority in a society that made decisions by consensus, so they could—and did—bring pressure to bear on the male minority in ways that most non-Shaker women could not. According to visitor Lida Kimball, the Shakers had "perfect equality of the sexes."[21]

In a sense, that equality was a gift bestowed by Joseph Meacham and Lucy Wright before 1790. It was also one their late nineteenth-century spiritual descendants advanced even further by advocating for women's rights around the world. Over three centuries (from the eighteenth into the twenty-first), Shaker sisters' roles have included leading thousands of male and female Believers, an innovation that was natural and evolutionary within Shakerism, but radical and revolutionary to the rest of the world.

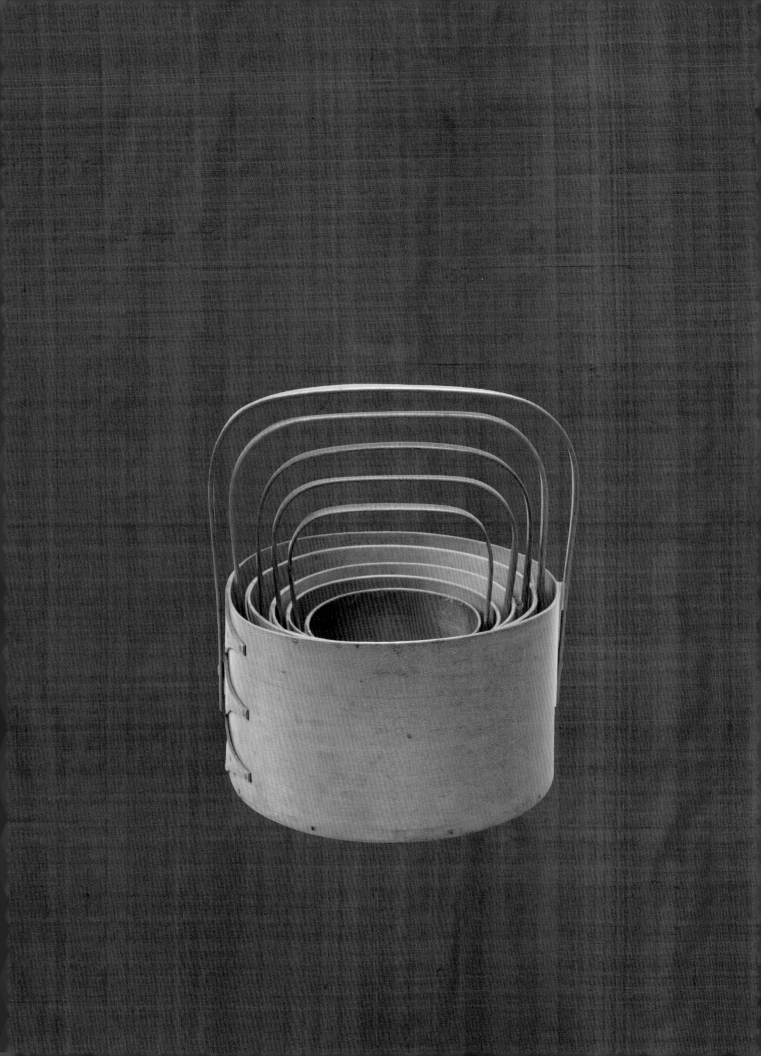

Shaker Innovation: Lifestyle and Governance

STEPHEN J. PATERWIC

IN 1779, a New Light "stir" inflamed the border towns of Massachusetts and New York State. Hundreds of seekers came from all over New England and New York to attend, and for a brief time they were filled with millennial hopes; this was quite a contrast to their struggling lives. As the revival closed and great disillusionment set in, a number of men and women visited Mother Ann and her companions at Niskayuna (Watervliet), New York. They eagerly followed her counsels and joined her society. When it was time for these Believers to go back to their homes, they carried the Shaker message deep into New England and upstate New York.

The Shaker Testimony officially opened to the World in May 1780. After this, Mother Ann, Father William Lee, Father James Whittaker, and other Shaker leaders intensified their efforts to extend their message and solidify the faith of the recent converts. As a result, in 1781 they began a long missionary tour throughout New York, Massachusetts, Rhode Island, and Connecticut. In spite of severe persecution, the faith of Believers remained strong. New Lights and others from northern New England learned of the Shaker Gospel and visited Mother Ann and her followers. The result was hundreds of more converts in New Hampshire, Vermont, and what later became the State of Maine.

When Mother Ann returned to her home at Niskayuna, near Albany, she was exhausted and in broken health from the numerous physical assaults she had endured. Hostile mobs seemed to greet her everywhere she went. On September 8, 1784, merely

forty-eight years old, she died—probably as a result of the ill treatment she had received. Her successor, Father James Whittaker, a young man she had raised in England, was Mother's strongest supporter after her brother, Father William Lee. He continued her pattern of visiting scattered Believers, even going as far north as the town of Alfred in the district of Maine. His time in office was short, though, and he died in July 1787. Leadership of the Shakers then passed into the hands of Father Joseph Meacham, and at once a radical change occurred in Shaker policy regarding the way Believers lived.

Born in Enfield, Connecticut, Father Joseph was the son of a Baptist minister. As a young man he, too, became a Baptist minister and served in a church in New Lebanon, New York. Along with Presbyterian minister Samuel Johnson, he led the large religious revival of 1779 that so electrified the surrounding countryside. Though not the first American convert, he is regarded by Shakers as "Mother's First Born Son in America." Under Ann Lee's guidance he led missionaries and labored long and hard to gain converts. His most important legacy was his implementation of an organizational plan for gathering and maintaining Shaker communities called Gospel Order.

Father Joseph was convinced that if Believers were to live truly peaceful, holy, and dedicated lives, they must separate from the World and live in communities. Since Shakerism required celibacy and confession of sins, it was not practical for hundreds of individuals to live on widely scattered farms. In addition, the newly converted Shakers were sometimes persecuted by members of their own families as well as by local townspeople who had heretofore been their friends. By separating themselves from the World, society leaders would not have to visit remote places to reach scattered Believers; all Shakers could go to a nearby center where a number of others already lived. Adjacent farms could be merged to form a critical mass that would allow for self-sufficiency, with new buildings added as needed to accommodate the growing numbers. People coming into the new communities were expected to bring all they possessed and contribute it to the common purse.

The first community to gather according to Gospel Order was New Lebanon, New York, in the fall of 1787. Father Joseph had only been the Shakers' leader for a couple of months, but his plans for Gospel Order had been made years earlier. For example, as soon as the Meeting House had been build at New Lebanon, young men and women of promise were chosen to live with him in the apartments over the worship hall. Here he prepared them for future leadership in the communities he envisioned. Indeed from 1785 until 1800, no further missionary work was done. The chosen leaders were sent out to gather in the newly formed communities, and all available energy was spent organizing eleven Shaker societies in New York, Massachusetts, Connecticut, New Hampshire, and the future Maine.

The parent society at New Lebanon served as the organizational model for all subsequent Shaker villages. Those who could give their all and live a complete communal life were organized into what was called the Church Family. There were so many new converts at this stage of development that three Orders of the Church were formed at New Lebanon. These were called the First, the Second and the Third Families of the Church. Organized roughly by age, these Church Orders were the first attempt to sort Shakers by spiritual fervor and temporal talents. All other Shakers lived in smaller groups on farms owned by local Shakers. Called the Order of Families, they were the outermost groups of Shakers. They also had spiritual and temporal leaders but were not fully organized into Gospel Order. Outside of New Lebanon, the largest communities organized

themselves into two orders of the Church; one or two other groups formed the Order of Families.

Gospel Order was organized on a "four square" model of leadership. At the apex were the Ministry, two men and two women. In those times no churches allowed women to be ministers and to have equality with men so the Shakers were true pioneers in these matters. Societies were yoked together into bishoprics, each headed by a Ministry. New Lebanon and Watervliet (Niskayuna), New York, for example, formed a bishopric, led by a Ministry that resided primarily at New Lebanon. This Ministry, called the Ministry of New Lebanon or simply the Lebanon Ministry, had general supervision of all other Ministries. Thus New Lebanon came to be called the "center of union" for all Shakers. The other Shaker bishoprics were Hancock, Massachusetts (including the communities at Tyringham, Massachusetts, and Enfield, Connecticut); Harvard, Massachusetts (including Shirley, Massachusetts); New Hampshire (including the primary society at Canterbury and another community at Enfield); and Maine (including the primary society at Alfred and another community at New Gloucester, later called Sabbathday Lake). After 1805, when the Shakers expanded into Ohio and Kentucky, four more bishoprics were formed. In 1826, the last Shaker bishopric was created at Sodus (later Groveland), in far western New York.

Following the pattern at New Lebanon, large communal families replaced individual natural ones. Biological parents and children were blended together in Shaker families that ranged from thirty to more than one hundred members. Each family had two elders and two eldresses, whose duty was to act as spiritual parents to the family. They led prayers and supervised day-to-day religious matters at home. Since spiritual matters were so important under the system of Gospel Order, temporal matters were separated from the duties of the family elders. A foursquare set of deacons and deaconesses was appointed by the bishopric Ministry to oversee everyday matters. The deacons and deaconesses lived in a separate building called the Office. Here they greeted visitors and transacted business with the World.

Outsiders were not permitted to roam the property. Fences and signs deterred curiosity seekers. The deacons acted as trustees and held the deeds and titles for the property. When written covenants were devised after 1800, it was the trustees who witnessed these important legal documents that provided protection for all Shakers and at the same time enumerated the required duties and expectations. (One key provision of these documents, often challenged in court but never overruled, held that members who left were not entitled to back wages for work performed while they were with the Shakers.) It was customary for men and women aged twenty-one and over to sign the covenant of their Shaker family. The covenant was kept at the Office since it had a legal and not a religious significance. Trustees also were permitted to leave the community in order to conduct business in the World.

Shaker families lived in very large dwelling houses. One characteristic making the Shakers unique is that males and females, though not married, lived in the same buildings. Although there had been dual monasteries in the early years of western Christian monasticism, monks and nuns did not live in as close proximity as did the Shakers. Not only did Shaker men and women live under the same roof, they slept in retiring rooms on the same floors, separated, in most cases, only by a wide hallway. In addition, they all ate in a communal dining hall and worshipped together in family meeting rooms. To keep unnecessary contact to a minimum, separate doors and stairways were used.

Since the trustees lived in the Office, each family had family deacons and deaconesses, chosen as needed, to have charge of temporal affairs within the community. Family deaconesses, for example, were responsible for provisioning the sisters so that they had proper clothing, bedding, and the equipment necessary to do their jobs. Other sisters also served as kitchen or laundry deaconesses. The brethren had deacons for the farm, shops, and orchards.

Although many positions of responsibility existed in a Shaker society, most Shakers were without rank and worked in the shops, on the farm, or in the dwellings. Living in spiritual families, they used the title of Sister or Brother before their given names. The titles elder and eldress applied to members of the Ministry as well as the spiritual leaders of a Shaker family.

One of the most positive features of the Shakers is that they did not operate as a monolithic organization where changes were difficult or came about slowly. In spite of the veneration that early Shakers had for Father Joseph, for example, they made significant changes to his plan for Gospel Order within five years of his death. By 1799, it was clear that the society had to undertake new missionary efforts. Some Shakers had left, and the children of the first Shakers were mostly grown up. In addition, scores of people had inquired about membership. As a result, the Ministry of New Lebanon created a Gathering or Novitiate Order.

Once again, a four-square set of elders presided over a Shaker family that was set up specifically to receive new members. When the first Gathering Order was inaugurated late in 1799 at New Lebanon, it was thought that a number of the nearby Shaker communities would send any potential converts there to be molded into Shakers, before they were sent out to other societies where needed. So many people were seeking admission, especially large families, that this scheme did not work. The leaders responded by being flexible and modifying this plan. During the first decade of the nineteenth century, in every community, one of the groups that had been in the Order of Families was turned into a Gathering Order. Almost immediately these orders branched into other Gathering Order families as more people poured into Shaker villages.

In 1811 a further modification of the original Gospel Order took place at New Lebanon, when all of the groups of Shakers still living in the Order of Families were consolidated into a new arrangement called the Second Family of the Church. Subsections of this Second Family lived in various locations called the East House, West House, and South House. Some of these later grew to become separate Shaker families with their own trustees and covenants. Meanwhile, the three Orders of the Church at New Lebanon were consolidated into two.

Similar changes were also made along these lines at the other Shaker villages. The society at Enfield, Connecticut, is typical. At its organization in 1792, Enfield had a large Church Family formed on the Meacham farm. The home farms of two other prominent converts and their families, Lot Pease and the Allen clan, contributed land that became respectively the North or Second Family of the Church, and the

Gathering Order (later, the South Family). This latter also had a small branch called the East Family. In time, another Gathering Order was started, and it became the West Family. Thus Enfield at its largest, between 1818 and 1854, had the First Family of the Church (Church Family), the Second Family of the Church (North and East Families) and two Gathering Orders (South and West Families). When the Shaker communities in Ohio, Indiana, and Kentucky were organized, they used this same pattern of Gospel Order, although in the West the Church Family was commonly called the Center Family.

Another important modification can be noted in the titles the Shakers used for those holding important offices. The first Ministries chosen when the communities were organized used the parental titles of Father and Mother, but these were not continued after those leaders died. That is why so many of the early leaders have the title Mother or Father in front of their names but no subsequent Shaker leaders do. In addition, the men who were office deacons came to be called trustees. By the 1890s, the scarcity of men caused a complete reorganization of the trustees' ranks in some societies. Women as well as men from various families in a particular society formed a board of society trustees, and together they had charge of temporal matters. Adaptation as necessity demanded remained a hallmark of the Shakers.

As the communities continued to shrink and merge, the bishopric ministries were dissolved, and the Ministry at New Lebanon took over their duties. In 1918, when the Canterbury and Harvard Ministries were closed, all of the surviving societies, with the exception of those in Maine, came under the direct care of New Lebanon. Consequently, the Lebanon Ministry, which by that time was called the Central Ministry, also became known as the Parent Ministry. When Elder Irving Greenwood died in 1939, no men were available to serve in the Parent Ministry. The surviving sisters re-organized the old four-square system to one that included women only. In this final version, no fewer than two, and no more than three women could be in the Ministry. It is clear that although they were so diminished in numbers, the Shakers did not remain attached to older forms of governance even though they still revered those who had created them.

When seen in perspective, the Shakers' organizational history can be viewed as a series of innovations designed to meet the demands of a particular time. In the earliest years, Shakers had to gather together for spiritual reasons and for physical safety. They organized themselves into a radically new social system called Gospel Order that sustained them and functioned well for many decades. The admission of large numbers of converts caused the original plan of Gospel Order to be modified to accommodate these new members. Soon afterward, all Shaker families were stabilized into tighter units as the old Order of Families was replaced, echoing more closely the Church Family. Furthermore, when large industries demanded more expertise in finance and marketing, the Office deacons became trustees. One unforeseen and unfortunate consequence of this shift in responsibilities was that it opened the door to occasional, but often devastating, fiscal misconduct. In the late nineteenth century, bad debts were a significant cause of the movement's decline.

As the number of men dwindled, women became trustees. (In contrast to some male trustees, there was never an instance of fiscal malfeasance by any sister.) Finally, after the bishopric Ministries were abolished, a single Parent Ministry functioned for as long as it could before the lack of men caused it, too, to become made up entirely of women. None of these innovations should be surprising since the Shaker way of life is progressive and responsive to change. The very name *Shaker* implies a forward movement in the all-important journey they call the Christlife. 🌿

Inspired
Innovations

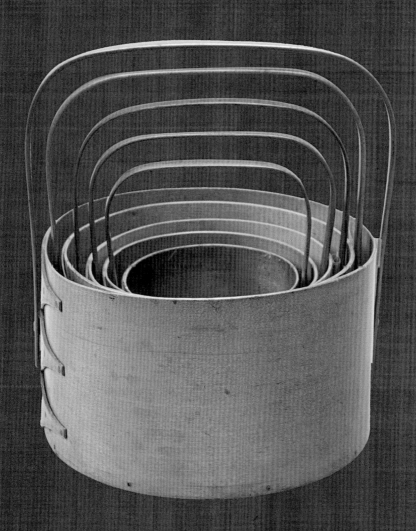

THE FAMILY GARDEN, THE SHAKERS, EAST CANTERBURY, N. H.

(Color lithography on card stock, 3½" × 5¼". Courtesy of Canterbury Shaker Village.)

1
Garden Seeds

M. Stephen Miller

*"Their garden seeds are celebrated for goodness
and find a ready market"* (1819)[1]

WE CAN SAY WITH CERTAINTY that there
was no industry for the sale of garden
seeds in America, on a retail basis, before
the Shakers developed one. David Landreth and Son
of Philadelphia, started in 1784, was a well-known
source for seed sold in bulk. Generally seeds were
available in barrels or in sacks sewn from crude linen.
The packaging and sale of seeds in small quantities—individual paper envelopes, intended for non-
farm use—was wholly a Shaker innovation. Not only
did they develop the concept of providing seeds to
people who wanted to plant small, "kitchen" gardens,
they developed an entire industry to take advantage
of what became a substantial market. The endeavor
included everything from the initial cultivation of
the parent plants that yielded the seeds, to sales in
distant markets.

An industry implies a highly organized and coordinated approach to making or, in this case, growing
a product and then marketing it. Although several
Shaker communities later claimed that they had
been the first among their peers to accomplish these
things, New Lebanon will be used here as the model.
That community certainly developed the largest,
most far-reaching, and longest lasting seed industry
of all the Shaker communities. It is also, by far, the
best documented. Furthermore, the seed industry

at New Lebanon also seems to have been used as a
pattern for success in other commercial ventures,
probably because it was the home of the Lead Ministry for the entire society and the ultimate source of
authority well into the twentieth century.

The garden seed operation was the only major
industry that was ubiquitous across the sect. Whether
in the east or the west, every Shaker community,
had its own version at some time in its history. For
some, such as Enfield, New Hampshire, Hancock,
Massachusetts, and South Union, Kentucky, the
business was an important source of revenue through
most of the nineteenth century. The Civil War
ended Enfield, Connecticut's business by cutting off
access to its vital southern markets. At South Union,
though caught in the crossfire because of its proximity to secessionist Tennessee, the industry resumed
even before the Confederate surrender at Appomat-
tox and continued for another twenty years. Other
Shaker villages gave up their seed businesses after
a much shorter time in order to concentrate on new
products—for Harvard, Massachusetts, it was dried
medicinal herbs and for Watervliet, Ohio, textiles.

Beginning in the early 1790s, New Lebanon
Shakers organized their seed business in such a
way that many hands were concentrated in four specific areas of work: the fields, the barns, the shops,

and the World. In the fields, the soil was cultivated and fertilized in the spring in order to receive the parent seed. A *seeder* was one of the mechanisms made at New Lebanon for the even distribution of seed in the prepared soil. (Shaker blacksmiths also made plows and harrows for breaking up soil, but there is no evidence that these differed from what was already available in the World.) After planting, the new growth had to be watered and thinned, and the soil around it kept free of weeds.

Many plants do not produce seed during their first growing season and must be dug up in the fall and stored in root cellars and barns until the following spring. They are then re-planted for several more months. Although the produce of these plants, which are known as biennials, can be eaten after one growing season, the plants do not set seeds until the second summer. At sprouting time, the younger boys in the community—whose schooling was suspended in summer so they could be called upon for farm chores—assisted in the harvesting. This category of vegetables included onions, cabbages, carrots, beets, radishes, and turnips. All were essential elements of the northern New England diet. They were easy to grow, easy to store (in cool, dry places such as root cellars), were high in nutritional value, and were readily incorporated into soups and stews in the colder months.

In the barns, along with seeing to other wintering-over chores, Shakers sorted, washed, and carefully dried the harvested seeds. Since damp seeds were almost certain to rot or fail to germinate, thorough drying was essential. The Shakers guaranteed customers that their seeds would produce. New Lebanon's guarantee came along with a form of "branding"—probably another of their innovations. Today, almost every conceivable consumer product employs visual devices to make that product instantly recognizable to the public. That was not the case in 1800. Today, branding devices depend on the use of highly specific colors combined with distinctive typography, trademarked names, and corporate logos. The New Lebanon community simply printed "D.M." on each seed envelope, the initials of their venerated first trustee, David Meacham, Sr. So successful was this marketing strategy that New Lebanon employed it to signify trustworthiness, fairness, and quality for more than sixty years following Brother Meacham's death in 1826.

Meanwhile, in Shaker workshops printing presses turned out sheets of tan and orange paper with the names of, and planting instructions for, the many varieties of seed to be packaged. (They reasonably assumed that users would not be as familiar with cultivation methods as farmers obviously were.) These sheets then had to be cut, folded, and pasted—forming envelopes that measured approximately 2½" by 4". Offset chisels were used to trim the edges of the "papers," leaving tabs that were folded over and pasted to enclose three

sides. Smaller numbers of larger-sized envelopes were made up as well. In all, as many as a quarter of a million envelopes were prepared in the peak year of 1860. Additionally, until about the time the Civil War broke out, the Shakers printed most of the other paper materials they needed to support the industry: receipts, invoices, seed lists, labels, and catalogues. After about 1865, most printing was done

SHAKERS' GARDEN SEEDS
FROM THE
UNITED SOCIETY,
NEW LEBANON, N. Y.

for the Shakers by commercial job shops and lithographic firms. It was the only way they could hope to compete with the many retail seed businesses that sprouted after the war.

In other workshops, brethren made wooden boxes to house (and display) the seed envelopes. They used clear pine boards, simply nailed together, with hinges made of wire or leather, and—after about 1850—covered the boxes with a protective coat of red paint. Boxes that were returned from the previous selling season were cleaned, sometimes repainted, and given fresh interior and exterior labels. Recycling, or thrift, was as characteristic of the Shakers as it was of their contemporaries, but for Believers it also had a spiritual dimension. Whatever God provides humankind is a gift and must be used respectfully. Responsible stewardship is part and parcel of Shakerism.

Near the end of winter the boxes of freshly packaged seeds were loaded onto a sled or wagon drawn by a team of horses, and the next phase of the industry—distribution—began. Shakers were the first to sell their garden seeds on a consignment basis. Brethren delivered their loads of boxes to merchants along carefully selected routes. New Lebanon's most profitable route followed the eventual path of the Erie Canal west from the community toward Buffalo and was called the "western load." Other Shaker villages had their own preferred routes, and not infrequently they overlapped, creating competition between two societies As more Shaker communi-

ties diversified their industries after the 1840s, this problem disappeared.

In more rural areas, Shaker seed peddlers often left their filled boxes at general stores, where merchants would display them on counters with their lids open—exposing a printed black-and-white seed inventory. After the Civil War, the inventories were brightly colored—in the hope of attracting the interest of potential buyers. These lists used commercial color lithography and saturated colors that promised abundant yields of gorgeous vegetables for any buyer smart enough to purchase Shaker seeds. The merchant agreed to accept a fixed commission of 33⅓ percent for each seed package sold. When a Shaker brother retrieved the boxes at the end of summer, it was simple to calculate what had been sold and the commission due—for the numbers of seed envelopes of each variety were either hand-written or printed on each interior seed list. Typically, each package— no matter the variety—sold for six cents.

The scale of these innovations taken together, and their importance in supporting their respective communities in the first half of the nineteenth century, cannot be overstated. At just New Lebanon, for example, as early as 1805 seven *tons* of seed were sold with net revenue of $1,240. At the time only twenty-two varieties of vegetable seeds were offered. Thirty years later the New Lebanon catalog expanded to include seventy varieties, the largest being beans (nine types), beets (seven), and cucumber and lettuce (six each). By then net profit soared to more than $6,000 (or approximately $130,000 in 2009 dollars).

Right after the Civil War, many competing seed houses sprouted up in the World. The industry was labor-intensive, and the number of Shaker men was then in steep decline. Other businesses took advantage of cheap labor, locations with more ideal growing conditions—such as in the Genesee Valley near Rochester, New York—and were better capitalized, which enabled them to take advantage of the latest in print technology and railroad transportation. Mount Lebanon, as it was re-named after 1861, was not on a main rail line. In 1888, the seed industry there, the last among the Shaker communities, closed.

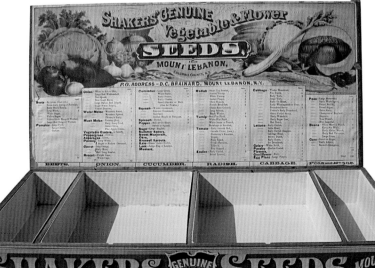

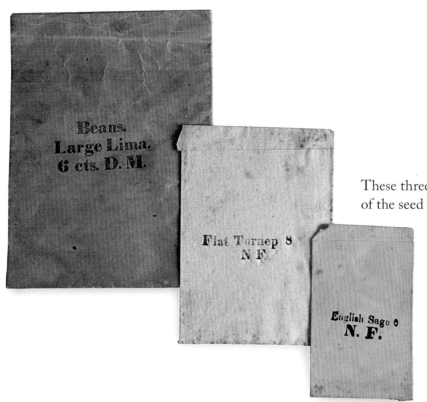

These three envelopes represent the earliest remnants of the seed industry at New Lebanon and may date from any time between 1800 and about 1830. The paper they are printed on has an exceptionally high rag content, a certain indication of their early date. "D.M." stands for David Meacham Sr., the earliest Trustee at New Lebanon.

(Black ink letterpress on heavy tan and gray paper. From the left, 4¾" × 3¾", 3¾" × 2¾", and 3" × 1¾". Miller Collection.)

From about 1830 to the time of the Civil War, the shape, size, and color of seed envelopes changed little. Planting instructions were now included on each, and the New Lebanon family that produced the seed was indicated as N.F. for North, E.F. for East, and S.F. for Second Families. Shakers printed them by the hundreds of thousands in their own print shops.

(Black ink letterpress on stiff orange and brown paper, approx. 3" × 4". Miller Collection.)

These two simple pine or basswood boxes are from a time before the smaller envelopes became the norm. The paper labels on them were changed as needed before the boxes were left with worldly merchants in late winter or early spring. The sides are simply nailed together, and the lids are attached with leather or wire hinges.

(Black ink letterpress on off-white paper. 6¼" × 17" × 8½" and 7¾" × 21" × 10½". Courtesy of the Shaker Museum and Library.)

A rare survivor, this large poster dates from the same period as the two boxes— before the Civil War. It was most likely intended to hang in the window or on the wall of a country general store. Merchants sold the Shakers' seeds on a consignment basis, typically keeping one-third of the selling price as their profit. Through most of the nineteenth century, seeds sold for six cents per envelope.

(Black ink letterpress on heavy white paper. 17½" × 23¼". Miller Collection.)

SHAKERS' GARDEN SEEDS.

FOR SALE HERE.

SHAKERS' GARDEN SEEDS

FROM THE

UNITED SOCIETY,

NEW LEBANON, N. Y.

This two-color poster apparently was printed shortly before the name of the New Lebanon Shaker village changed to Mount Lebanon in late 1861. The large size, complex border style, and use of blue and red inks all point to its having been produced at a commercial "job shop" outside the community. The use of worldly printers for their seed business would soon become commonplace.

(Red and blue ink letterpress on white paper, 10½" × 15". Miller Collection.)

The Shakers at New Lebanon made this ingenious device as they began to mechanize their nascent seed industry in the early 1800s to gear up for greater production. A sliding mechanism inside the hopper can be adjusted to increase or decrease the amount of seed deposited or to take into account the varying sizes of seeds. A detail of one wheel hub shows the finesse that a Shaker wood turner used on a functional object.

(Ash, cherry, maple, pine, and iron with iron hardware, 17¾" × 24" × 48". Courtesy of Hancock Shaker Village.)

The style of seed envelopes remained largely unaltered from 1861 until the early 1880s, the main change being the substitution of Mount Lebanon for New Lebanon after the community was granted its own post office.

(Six envelopes: black ink letterpress on orange papers, each 1¾" × 4". Miller Collection.)

Shakers intended that this seed listing be pasted on the underside of the lid of a seed box. The combination of a much-reduced number of offerings, with black and white printing, indicate that it was used during, or just after, the Civil War. The earliest lists show inventories of almost ninety seed varieties and this one fewer than seventy. Nonetheless, peas and beans were still major sellers with seventeen of the former and twenty-one of the latter offered.

(Black ink letterpress on off-white paper, 10" × 7⅞". Miller Collection.)

The closed and "exploded" views of a "Japan Musk Melon" envelope show how a Shaker-forged chisel was used to trim the sides of a stack of printed papers, resulting in projecting tabs that were folded-over to form a package with three sealed sides.

(Musk Melon [open]: black ink letterpress on orange paper, 5" × 3¾". Miller Collection and Two chisels: Steel, l- 5" and 8¾". Courtesy of the Shaker Museum and Library.)

The standard seed box style after about 1870, and lasting into the early 1880s, was this flat type. The inside was divided into slots where the envelopes were organized according to type. Both the exterior and interior labels were commercially printed with bright colors and eye-catching typography. Boxes were designed to sit atop merchant's counters with their lids open, quietly but boldly promising the results illustrated in their graphics. This example is fitted with four tin trays painted light green; the reason for that unique format is unknown.

(Pine and tin with color lithography on white papers, 3¼" × 23¼" × 11½". Private Collection.)

These two objects from New Lebanon indicate the need for a wide variety of specialized devices in order to effectively conduct a business as an industry, as well as the necessity of labeling them to assure their being returned to their proper place. On top is a seed riddle or coarse sieve with a wire rather than horsehair mesh. It was used to separate seeds from soil and other extraneous matter. The stenciling on the side also tells us that there were at least eleven garden sites. Below is the bottom of a seed-sorting tray; the top has sides with an opening (to the right) for removing either the discards or the "keepers."

(Ash and metal mesh with iron hardware: 4" × 19⅞" and pine with iron hardware: 2¾" × 27¼" × 14½". Courtesy of Hancock Shaker Village.)

This remnant from New Lebanon's early years selling seeds is a reminder that not all of their output was sold in small paper envelopes. From an early but unknown date the

community was selling seed in bulk—shipped in tight crates or barrels of different sizes. This metal stencil would have been used for identifying the source of the seeds being shipped: New Lebanon.

(Sheet iron, 5¼" × 20". Miller Collection.)

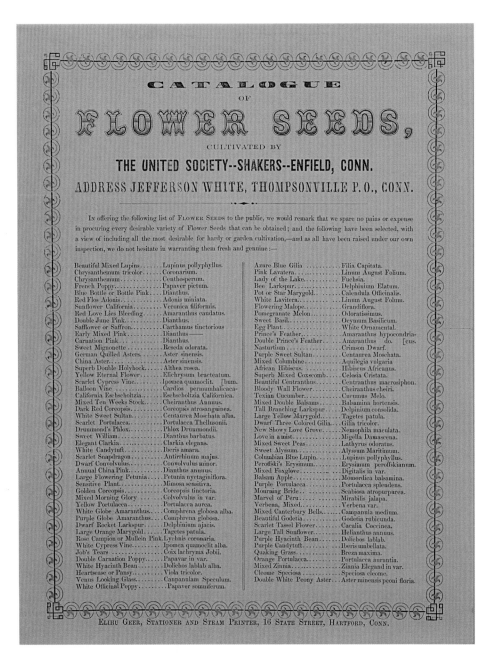

Although the focus here has been on New Lebanon—the largest and longest surviving of the Shaker seed industries—it should be kept in mind that *every* community grew and sold seeds. In the case of Enfield, Connecticut, there is reason to believe their claim that they were the first. The problem is that the evidence is anecdotal. Nonetheless, they did have a very early and very large business, one that was especially strong in two areas: flower seeds and southern markets.

Flower seeds were also sold at New Lebanon, but most of their seeds were used for growing vegetables. Shaker leaders considered ornamental plants and flowers "worldly" and "superfluous" until their medicinal properties came to light. In true Shaker fashion this fact (and the potential profits that it presented) allowed them to change their minds. Only these two communities marketed flower seeds. This list offers ninety-five, and Enfield assured that they "spare[d] no pains or expense in procuring every desirable variety of Flower Seeds. . . . as all have been raised under our own inspection, we do not hesitate in warranting them fresh and genuine."

(Black ink letterpress on pale gray paper, 10¾" × 8⅛". Miller Collection.)

GARDEN SEEDS,

FRESH AND GENUINE,

RAISED BY THE UNITED SOCIETY--SHAKERS--ENFIELD, CONN.

Address JEFFERSON WHITE, Thompsonville P. O., Connecticut.

[On or before July, annually,]

SEEDSMAN AND AGENT.

For Sale by

Papers.		Dolls.	Cents.
ARTICHOKE—Green Globe,			
ASPARAGUS—Giant,			
BEANS—Early Red-eyed China Dwarf,			
— Early black-eyed China Dwarf,			
— Early Six Weeks, do.			
— Early Mohawk do.			
— Early Rachel, Dwarf, 6 wks.			
— Extra Early Victoria,			
— Refugee, or thousand to one,			
— Royal White Kidney, Dwarf,			
— White Marrow Demy, do.			
— *White Cranberry, Dwarf,*			
— *Red Cranberry, Dwarf,*			
— Red Marrow or Valentine.			
— Red French or Warrington,			
— Rob Roy, Dwarf.			
— Horticultural do.			
— *Dutch Case Knife Dwarf,*			
— Horticultural Pole,			
— Dutch Case-knife Pole, White,			
— Large Lima, do. do.			
— Carolina do. do. do.			
— Dutch Runners, white,			
— Large do. scarlet,			
BEETS—Early Extra Bassano,			
— Early Blood Turnip,			
— Early Orange do.			
— Early Half Long Blood,			
— French Amber Sugar,			
— White Silesia do.			
— Long Blood,			
— Long Mangel Wurtzel,			
— Swiss Chard Silver, for greens,			
BENE PLANT,			
BROCOLI—Large Purple Cape,			
— Large White do.			
CAULIFLOWER—Early,			
— Large Late,			
CABBAGE—Early Sugar Loaf,			
— Early Dutch,			
— Early York,			
— Early Drumhead,			
— Early Ox Heart,			
— Large York,			
— Large Bergen,			
— Large Drumhead,			
— Mammoth,			
— Cromwell's Superb,			
— Flat or Late Dutch,			
— Green Globe Savoy,			
— Drumhead Savoy,			
— Green Glazed,			
— Turnip Rooted above ground,			
— Red Dutch, for pickling,			
COLEWORT or Collords,			
CARROT—Early Horn, dark orange,			
— *Early Half Long,*			
— Large Altringham,			
— Large White Field,			
— Long Blood,			
— Long Orange,			
CELERY—Large White Solid,			
— Red Solid,			
— Silver Giant,			
CHERVIL—Curled, for Sallad,			
CORN—Early Canada,			
— Early Smith's White,			
— *King Philip,*			
— Early Tuscarora,			
— Early Sugar, 12 rowed,			
— Early Red Cob Sugar,			
— White Flint or Chinese,			
CORN SALAD or Fetticus,			
CRESS—Curled or Peppergrass,			
— Broad Leaved,			
— Extra Curled,			
— Water, (biennial,),			
CUCUMBER—Early Green Cluster,			

Papers.		Dolls.	Cents.
CUCUMBERS—Early Frame,			
— Early Short Green,			
— *Extra Early White Spanish,*			
— White Spined,			
— Extra Early Russian,			
— Long Green Turkey,			
— Long Green Prickly,			
— Small Gherkin, for pickles,			
MARTYNIA, or Markeroes,			
EGG PLANT—Large Purple,			
— White, (ornamental,)			
ENDIVE—Green Curled,			
— Broad Leaved,			
KALE—Green Curled Scotch,			
— Sea,			
LEEK—Large Scotch or Flag,			
— Large London,			
LETTUCE—Imperial Head,			
— Early White Head,			
— Early Curled Silesia,			
— Large Green Head,			
— Large Drumhead,			
— Ice Head,			
— Ice Coss,			
— *White Mammoth Head,*			
— Royal Cabbage Head, early,			
— Extra Cabbage or Cape Head,			
— Brown Dutch,			
MELON—Large Musk, rusty coat,			
— Large Cantelope, yellow,			
— Green Citron,			
— Fine Nutmeg,			
— Ward's Nectar,			
— Pine Apple or Persian,			
— Skillman's Fine Netted,			
— *Beachwood,* extra fine,			
— Water, Imperial, scarlet flesh,			
— do. Early Apple Seed,			
— do. Long Island,			
— do. Carolina,			
— do. Black Spanish,			
— do. Mountain Striped,			
— do. *Mountain Sweet, extra,*			
— do. *Mountain Sprout,*			
— do. *Ice Cream,*			
— do. *New Orange,*			
— do. Citron, for preserves,			
MUSTARD—White,			
— Brown,			
NASTURTIUM,			
OKRA—Long White,			
— Short Green,			
ONION—White Portugal,			
— Yellow Dutch,			
— *Danvers Yellow,* new,			
— Large Red,			
— *Early Red,* extra,			
PARSNIP—Guernsey or Cup,			
— Long White,			
— Hollow Crown,			
PARSLEY—Plain or Single,			
— Curled,			
— Dwarf Curled,			
PEAS—Early Cedo Nulli,			
— Early Prince Albert,			
— Early May, extra,			
— Early Washington or JUNE,			
— Early Charlton,			
— Early Champion of England,			
— Large White Marrowfat,			
— Large Black-eyed do.			
— Dwarf Marrowfat,			
— Dwarf Blue Imperial,			
— Dwarf Sugar, eatable pod,			
PEPPER—Squash,			
— Bell or Ox-heart,			
— Bull Nose,			
— Long Cayenne,			
— Cherry,			

Papers.		Dolls.	Cents.
PEPPER—Sweet Spanish,			
— Sweet Mountain,			
PUMPKIN—Mammoth,			
— Large Yellow,			
— Large Cheese,			
RADISH—Long White Summer,			
— Early Scarlet Short Top,			
— Long Salmon,			
— Long Scarlet or Early Frame,			
— Scarlet Turnip,			
— White Turnip,			
— Large Yellow do.			
— White Fall Spanish,			
— Black do. do.			
ROQUETTE—For Salad,			
RHUBARB—Early Tobolsk,			
— Myatt's Scarlet Victoria,			
SORREL—English Broad Leaved,			
SPINAGE—Broad Leaved Savoy,			
— Round Leaved,			
— New Flanders Prickly,			
SALSIFY or Vegetable Oyster,			
SQUASH—Bush Crookneck Summer,			
— Dutch Summer Scollop, white,			
— Dutch Summer scollop, yellow,			
— Boston Marrow,			
— Bergen Striped Bush,			
— Crookneck Winter,			
— Canada Crookneck,			
— Lima Cocoanut or Porter,			
— Sweet Potatoe,			
TOMATO—Large Smooth Red,			
— Small Yellow,			
— Cherry or Cuba,			
— Pear Shaped,			
— Large Yellow,			
TURNIP—Early Dutch or Spring Flat,			
— Early Snow Ball,			
— Early Garden Stone,			
— Large White Norfolk,			
— Large White Globe,			
— Red Top Flat, strap leaved,			
— White Flat,			
— White Flat, extra, white top,			
— Yellow Aberdeen or Bullock,			
— Dale's Yellow Hybrid,			
— Rutabaga, Swedish, yellow,			
— Long French, white,			
— Long French, yellow,			
— Long White,			

HERB SEED.

Caraway,
Coriander,
Dill,
Fennel,
Lavender,
Lemon Balm,
Rosemary,
Saffron,
Sage,
Summer Savory,
Sweet Basil,
Sweet Marjoram,
Sweet Thyme,
Marygold Pot,
Rue,

FLOWER SEEDS,

description and mode of culture.

GARDENERS' MANUAL.

GRASS SEEDS.

Red Clover,
White Dutch Clover,
Lucerne or French,
Blue Grass,
Herds or Red Top,
Timothy,
Millet,
Canary Seed,
Broom Corn Seed,
Top or Button Onion,

ALSO:—Articles manufactured by the Society, viz: SWIFTS, OVAL SUGAR BOXES IN NESTS, WHISK BRUSHES, BROOMS, &c. We can furnish GARDEN SEEDS per lb. and bushel, at reasonable prices. Our Garden Seeds are put up in papers with directions, stating time of planting, mode of culture, &c., printed on them.

N. B.—Some SEEDS, such as can not be successfully raised in this climate, are procured from the best sources. HERBS used for MEDICINAL purposes, put up in pressed packages from one ounce to one pound each.

Enfield's decision to invest nearly all its effort in southern markets proved to be disastrous. With the onset of the Civil War, those markets were cut off, and the business had to be closed down completely. Earlier they had an agent in Americus, Georgia, who acted as their distributor in the South, but their entire list of offerings, including herb, grass and flower seeds, could not endure a five-year hiatus.

(Black ink letterpress on white paper, 18½" × 12¼". Miller Collection.)

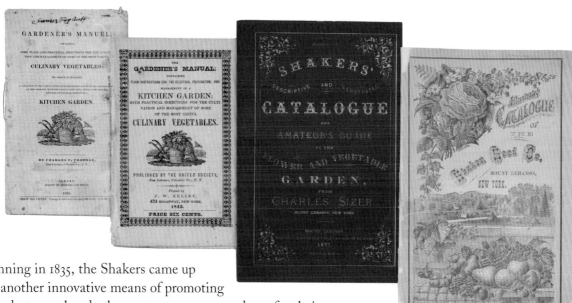

Beginning in 1835, the Shakers came up
with another innovative means of promoting
this industry—already the greatest revenue-producer for their community; they began issuing "Gardener's Manuels." The first was a simple
affair, twenty-three pages long, that provided detailed descriptions for planting seeds from A (asparagus) to Y
(yellow rutabaga). It also gave a recipe for making "catchup or Catsup" from tomatoes, in and of itself an innovative idea, for many Americans still regarded the tomato plant with Old World suspicion. Because it was part
of the nightshade family, some thought it might be toxic. This no doubt prompted the Shakers to describe the
tomato as "a very harmless and wholesome vegetable." They themselves began cultivating the plant in 1830 and
offered seeds for the first time through this manual.

A second, now called *The Gardener's Manual*, was published in 1843. It included many more recipes for processing vegetables: pickling, preserving, and cooking. In general format it was similar to the first. From the mid-1870s
until 1888 they issued seed catalogs frequently—perhaps every year—and with time these became increasingly elaborate. The books' dimensions and number of pages expanded, covers became more colorful, often printed in bright
blue with gold type and decorative borders, and pages were replete with line drawings of the plants that their seeds
would produce. Almost half of the listings now were for flower seeds, and some of the interior plates were two- and
three-color affairs. It seems that unlike the first two, these were given away rather than sold.

(Black ink letterpress and lithography with wood or metal engravings. From the left: 7" × 4¼"; 7" × 4⅝";
8¾" × 5¾"; and 9" × 6". Miller Collection.)

By the late 1880s the seed business at (now) Mount Lebanon was in desperate
straits. The loss of able-bodied brothers continued and even accelerated. At a
time when competition from the World was increasing exponentially, they grew
ever more dependent upon hired help from the outside. The pink order form was
a concession to worldly tastes that had become inclined toward more colorful
papers and fancier typography for even the most mundane uses—in this case, an
order form. (Its accompanying envelope is bright orange.)

In 1883 the entire business was reorganized from one still identified with
individual families into a single entity—the Shaker Seed Company. After this
date most sales were wholesale, rather than using the now-traditional system of
individual seed envelopes sold on consignment. The catalog on the right is an 1886
wholesale price list "For Market Gardeners." On the back it reads: "Our Terms
to Grangers" (an organization of farmers founded in the United States in 1867).
Clearly the Shakers' target audience was one that would buy in bulk.

(Black ink letterpress on off-white paper, [unfolded] 11" × 13¼". Miller Collection.)

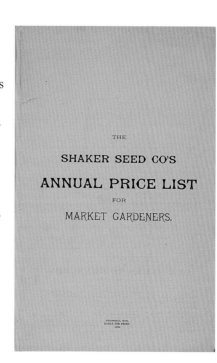

This label would have been used on the interior lid of the final style of seed box, which was taller and narrower than its predecessor. The colors are richly saturated and the fruits and vegetables take on an almost too-good-to-be-true look. Unfortunately, in spite of their most valiant efforts, the Shaker Seed Company only lasted for a few years, and the entire industry folded in 1888. New Lebanon's seed business had been active for nearly one hundred years—the first major income producer for the community and a transforming force for the way that garden seeds were produced and marketed in the United States. Even resorting to bulk sales, indicated on this order form [below] for "pints, pounds" as well as "ounces papers," was insufficient. Ultimately, it succumbed to the challenges of too few resources and too much competition.

(Label: color lithography on white paper, 8½" × 21¼". Miller Collection.)

(Order form [detail]: black ink letterpress on pink paper, 11" × 8½". Miller Collection.)

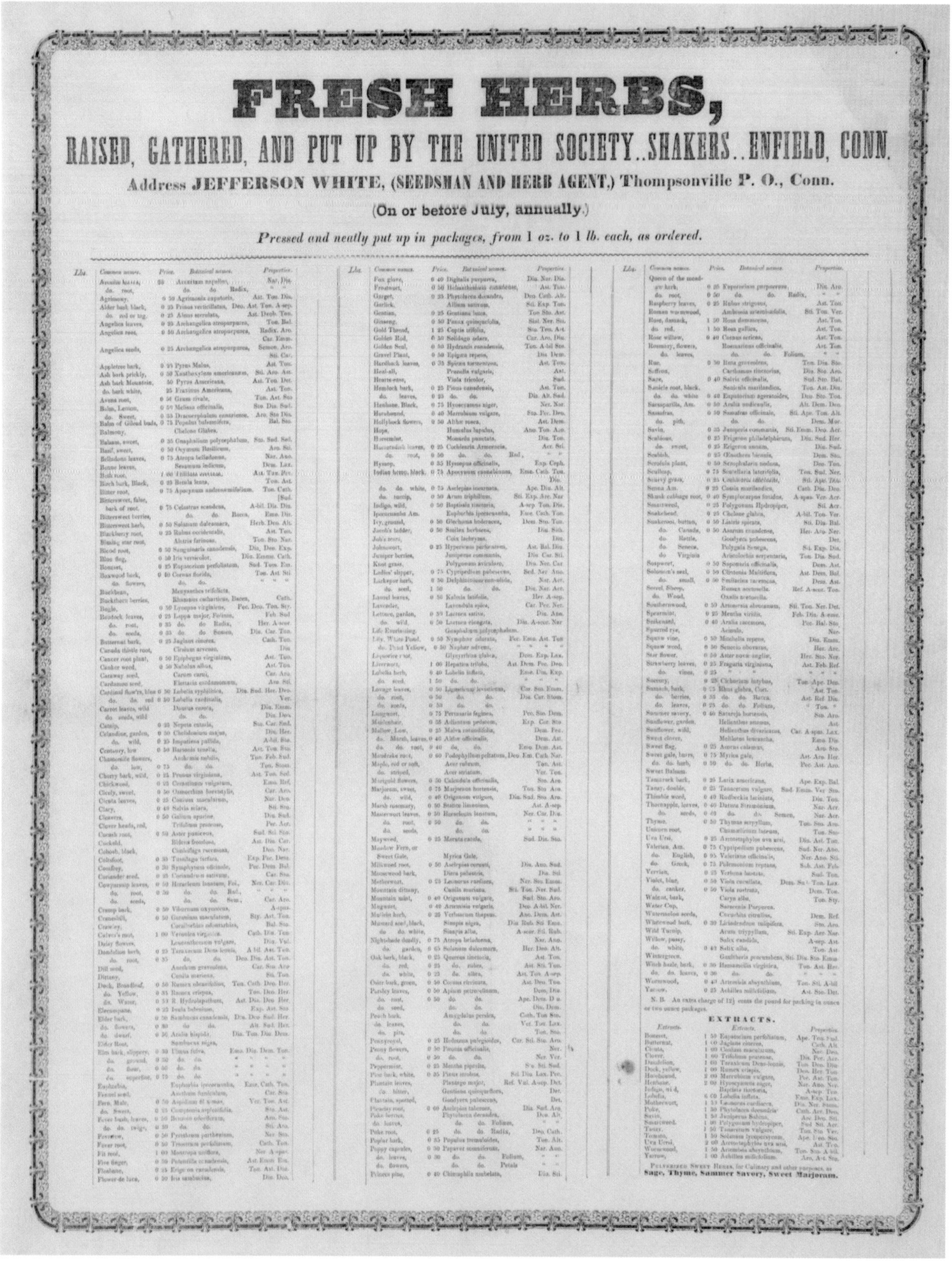

FRESH HERBS,

RAISED, GATHERED, AND PUT UP BY THE UNITED SOCIETY..SHAKERS..ENFIELD, CONN.

Address **JEFFERSON WHITE, (SEEDSMAN AND HERB AGENT,)** Thompsonville P. O., Conn.

(On or before July, annually.)

Pressed and neatly put up in packages, from 1 oz. to 1 lb. each, as ordered.

This huge herb list from Enfield, Connecticut, is the largest of any of the known broadsides used by the Shakers to sell medicinal (and other) herbs. Issued about 1854, it was meant to be sent to customers who would fill in their order and return it "On or before July, annually," which seems to indicate that it was used for more than a single year. However, only two other copies have been located (in Richmond's *Bibliography of Shaker Literature*, R-195), one of which is trimmed and filled out with the date 1857. More than 300 varieties of dried materials are offered here along with nineteen extracts and four culinary herbs—sage, thyme, summer savory, and sweet marjoram. In some instances, such as with Burdock and Lovage, a buyer had their choice of plant parts: leaves, roots, or seeds. (Black ink letterpress on white paper, 22¼" × 17¼". Miller Collection)

2
Medicinal Herbs and Preparations

GALEN BEALE

MANY INNOVATIVE SHAKER DOCTORS
rose to prominence in their communities
and in the larger medical world because
of their abilities to cure the sick and to compound
medicines. Village nurses initially cared for the sick
by using a combination of "spiritual healing" (such as
the "laying on of hands"), wild gathered herbs, and
simple medicines (or "simples") produced in their
distilleries. As they witnessed the aging and failing
health of the first generation of founders, who by
the 1820s were into their seventies and beyond, the
Shakers steadily improved their medical care and
accelerated their efforts. They also may have recognized the fact that in order to attract and hold new
members, they had to create a healthy environment
in which to live and work.

The resulting medicinal preparations—essential
oils, tinctures, and ointments—produced throughout the society led to the parallel development of
an entire medicinal industry, one they designed to
serve those living outside their insular communities. This was the realm of their medicinal herbs and
preparations. Examples of the numerous health care
devices Shakers developed for their own use—mainly
in their infirmaries—will be discussed in Chapter
10. Here we take a look at some of the early Shaker
physicians from the two Shaker communities in New

Hampshire—their education and practices, and their
success in marketing medicines to the outside World.

In the late eighteenth century, orthodox medicine
as practiced by trained physicians was called "heroic."
This often meant that an empirical approach (trial
and error) as well as aggressive treatment that frequently included removing what was believed to be
the offending agent or afflicted part. Purging, bleed-
ing, and surgical removal of diseased parts (including amputation) was customary. What was accepted
as "medical" care in the first half of the nineteenth
century would be called surgical treatment in the
twenty-first. In addition to these drastic procedures,
physicians dispensed medicines such as calomel
(mercury chloride) and opiates for ingestion that
often had serious and lasting side effects.

As the Shakers organized their communal health
care, they looked for alternatives to "heroic" methods
and began by combining existing botanical practices.
They learned the medicinal properties of indigenous
plants from local Native Americans while their
European-born converts contributed the lore of their
own families' herbal cures. Herbal medicine was
already an ancient art. Over the centuries people had
discovered that certain plants contained one or more
chemical compounds that can act on the human body
to treat disorders and restore or maintain health.

Once therapeutic substances had been isolated through infusion, extraction, or distillation, herbal remedies could be targeted at particular organs or tissues to produce the desired result.

This largely grassroots, nontraditional approach appealed to the Shakers, whose very lives were nontraditional. Another important self-taught advocate in the herbal movement in New England was a New Hampshire native named Samuel Thomson (1769–1843), many of whose formulas are found in the Shaker's recipe books. Altogether the Shakers offered no fewer than sixty of his sixty-eight recommended herbs for sale. In 1822, Thomson published *A New Guide to Health; or, Botanic Family Physician*, which turned out to be extremely popular and was eventually reissued in several editions. Thomson's simplistic premise (thirty-five years before Louis Pasteur published his work on germ theory) was that bodily functions obstructed by "cold" were the root cause of all human disorders and diseases. This naive approach found a ready audience in an American populace who were skeptical about the remedies offered by trained physicians.

The world too was ready for an alternative to heroic medicine, and the Shakers—who had begun selling herbs by 1812 and were looking for an additional source of income to support their communities —were ready. In 1821, New Lebanon formed the Shaker's Physicians Orders and they, along with their communities in Watervliet, New York, Harvard, Massachusetts, and Canterbury and Enfield, New Hampshire, began to apply the most current scientific knowledge to the cultivation, harvesting, and processing of medicinal herbs. By 1830 each had developed an industry in which Shakers not only raised their own herbs but also developed the means to package and market them.

Early Shaker medical care was initially quite rudimentary but still well advanced compared to that of their neighbors. With the building of a distillery in 1797, the Canterbury Shakers began creating medicines from individual herbs such as goldenrod, wormwood, and wild ginger. The packaged medicine industry, based on compounded herbs, would not develop until after the

first quarter of the nineteenth century. A full inventory of the Canterbury, New Hampshire, infirmary in 1802 effectively illustrates the simplicity of their early medicinal approach:

3 gal. Brandy
2 gal. Rum
3 lb. white sugar
1 pt. Gin
2 pt. Alcohol
11 lb honey
29 lb brown sugar[1]

New Hampshire's Physician's Orders came to exemplify the creative and innovative spirit found throughout the society. The most notable physicians from these communities were Thomas Corbett of Canterbury and Enfield's Samuel Brown and Jerub Dyer. All three successfully improved their villages' existing medical care and also created very profitable businesses that went well beyond dried herbs into the realm of "finished" medicines. Each man received recognition in the World from established, university-trained physicians, and each also enjoyed successes in the arena of non-traditional botanic practice.

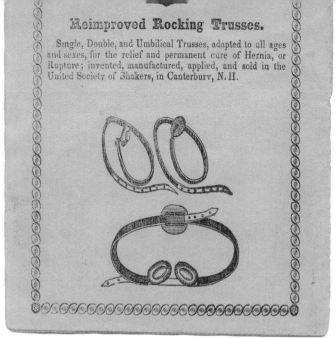

When Thomas Corbett arrived at Canterbury in 1794, nurses were taking care of the sick in the Church Family Dwelling House, using a small recipe book sent by the physicians of New Lebanon. Shaker historian Henry Blinn described Corbett as "spare in form, decidedly erect, medium height, light hair, a thin sharp visage, penetrating hazel eyes and a very active brain . . . a man of deep religious feeling and scrupulously honest in all his business relations"[2] That he had an "active mind" was an understatement. By the time Corbett matured he had already designed a new flax wheel and Canterbury's first fire engine, and was also known to have built several tall clocks. Born in 1780, his interest in medicine began nearer to mid-life. In 1809 he designed a variety of hernia-relieving "Rocking Trusses" that were widely advertised for sale by the community, and the following year, after experimenting with electricity, he built an electrostatic machine.

Finally, in 1813 when he was thirty-three, he undertook the serious study of medicine. By reading and by apprenticing himself to a local physician, he qualified to become the community's doctor. Soon, following the example of New Lebanon, he established Canterbury's "physic garden." While the community continued to gather the wild herbs that grew all around them, this garden provided an area for the cultivation of scarce and non-native plants. Most importantly it became the foundation for soon-to-be thriving medicinal herb industries in dried material and compounded preparations.

Once the herbs were harvested, Shakers used presses powered first by horses, then water, and finally steam, to compress them into "bricks" or small "cakes" that were then wrapped in paper for sale. The papers, along with bound catalogs, carried the common as well as Latin names. The cakes weighed one ounce each and bricks one pound. The non-Shaker medical community had previously received their herbs dried in loose bunches, and Shaker physicians had to personally introduce this new means of packaging and preserving them. Corbett found that "when they were first introduced and left at the apothecary stores in Boston, they were the food of merriment to some of the regular physicians. Gradually, however, Dr. Corbett . . . succeeded in their introduction until the prejudice of the doctors has been so far conquered that many of the faculty are constantly apply[ing] for them."[3]

Corbett next began to focus on developing a line of finished or compounded medicines, and by the 1840s many of his creations bore his name. Both the Enfield and Canterbury Shakers had developed a close relationship with the physicians at the Dartmouth College Medical School, and Corbett consulted freely with them on his new medicines. In 1841, Canterbury's distillery was moved and enlarged for the production of what would become their best-known and largest selling product, Corbett's Compound Concentrated Syrup of Sarsaparilla. It sold for the next seventy-five years.

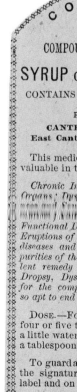

Canterbury's early entry into the herbal medicine market enabled the community to secure a foothold in this competitive industry. By 1850 ten other brands of sarsaparilla were being sold, and by 1880 the number exploded in a market that remained unregulated until the Pure Food and Drug Act took effect in 1906. Meanwhile, Shaker medicines were submitted to the competitions of the day. Corbett's Sarsaparilla won a medal at the 1850 Massachusetts Charitable Mechanic's Association in Boston, a distinction that catapulted Corbett's Sarsaparilla Syrup into the public's awareness.

To further promote this product, Shakers appealed to the public by claiming to be both the originators of Sarsaparilla and knowledgeable botanical physicians. "The Shakers feel that they do not exceed the bounds of propriety when they claim to have originated Sarsaparilla, and request the public, as matter of justice, to discriminate between this time honored blood purifier and remedies called Sarsaparilla, but which bear no relation to it in the variety, quality, and quantity of its ingredients. . . . Our claim to superiority is based on the growth, curing and selection of its several roots and berries, and the care with which they are compounded."[4]

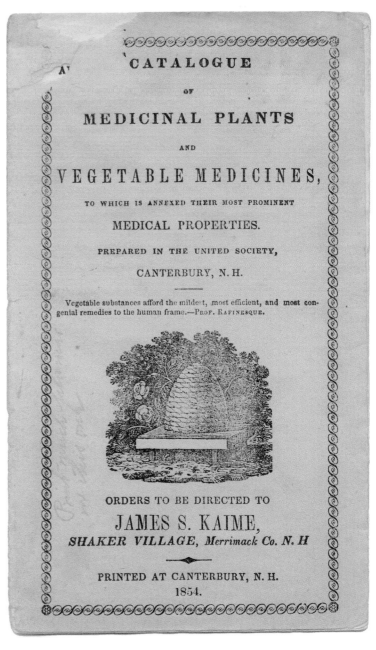

Corbett introduced a number of other medicines and promoted them in partnership with the Trustees and Canterbury's print shop. Labels, brochures, broadsides, and catalogs were created and distributed. In trying to reach a broader audience, the community published its first medicinal herb catalog in 1835; it listed 150 herbs for sale. In his second catalog, Corbett introduced four culinary or "sweet" herbs (sage, thyme, summer savory, and sweet marjoram), and by the 1850s the Canterbury Shakers were selling over $3,000 worth of herb products annually.[5] They would continue to refine and expand their advertising techniques as they competed in an arena where the quantity of advertising was becoming more important than the quality of the product.

The physicians of the Enfield community also created significant medicine brands. Brother Samuel Brown rose to prominence because of his work with the plant English valerian, *Valeriana officinalis*. Although the medicinal qualities of valerian as a sedative had been known throughout history, the herb was available locally only in dried form, and the large amount of the dried root necessary to effectively cure cholera and "nervous debility" caused many unpleasant side effects. By the mid-nineteenth century it had been largely abandoned in favor of opium or morphine with their attendant ill effects. Brown developed a method of extracting valerian's essential oil without using heat— which deactivates it—and created a line of medicines for "the cure of Nervousness, Lowness of Spirits, Debility, Hypochondria, Neuralgia, Hysteria."[6] Brown's Shakers' Pure Fluid Extract of English Valerian was heavily advertised, using the same techniques found in Corbett's Sarsaparilla advertising—pamphlets, medal competitions, and testimonials from leading physicians, all of which emphasized the Shakers' medical and marketing acumen. Brown's medicinal products provided a secure income for Enfield into the early twentieth century.

Jerub Dyer, a family physician at Enfield's Church Family, had a more formal education than most of the early Shaker physicians. A man with a "fine intellect," he "attended medical lectures at Dartmouth, and it is said was prepared to receive a diploma but the Shakers' rules deemed that [act] a worldly honor and would not allow it."[7] Returning to Enfield, Dyer created a long list of family medicines that included a Canker Cure, Catarrh Snuff, and Vegetable Pills. Shaker physicians studied the newspapers and journals of the day and both Corbett and Dyer's product promotions reflected an awareness of current events and a keen advertising sense. While Corbett promoted his Vegetable Rheumatic Pills for seamen going to the tropics, Jerub Dyer targeted his cholera cure, Arnica of Tannin, to those going west to join the California gold rush. Even with an increased dependence on outside physicians for their own care after Corbett and Dyer's deaths, the Shakers continued selling their medicines to the World into the early twentieth century.

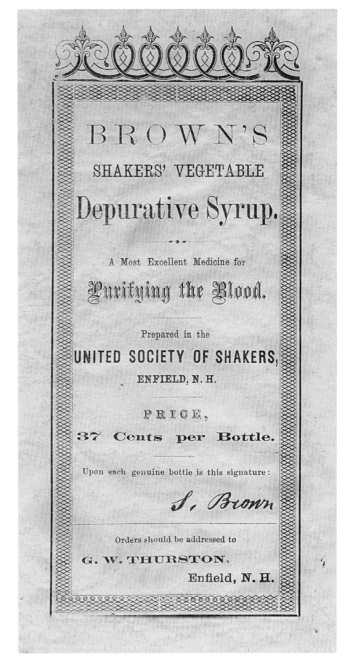

An innovative spirit helped these early doctors succeed in their labors as guardians of their communities' health and enabled them to securely establish Shaker medicines as reliable and honest remedies in the larger medical community and in the world of non-traditional treatment. The public's romance with the Shakers' abilities continued through the nineteenth century. "What the Indian has been supposed to be," an 1880 endorsement claimed, "the Shaker has been in reality—the Custodian of Nature's secrets."[8]

As the ranks of Believers continued to grow through the first quarter of the nineteenth century, and the need for other income grew with it, it happened that a coincidental interest in herbal medicines arose among non-Shakers. At New Lebanon and Watervliet, the garden seed businesses were thriving, with the annual harvest of seed measured in *tons*. Still, the Shakers at both villages needed to expand their economic bases and the production of medicinal herbs was the "natural" answer. Each had the few elements necessary to transform a communal enterprise into a large-scale industry: abundant land, good growing conditions (soil and weather), a large labor force, and a few individuals who were knowledgeable about medicinal herbs and their uses.

Several Shaker villages claimed to have been the first to package dried herbs for sale. Among these were New Lebanon and Watervliet. Their industries, separated by only about thirty miles, were started in 1820 or 1821. The processes used were nearly identical and the products are, not surprisingly, nearly identical as well so they can be considered together. This group of 10 herb "cakes" weigh one ounce each and were put up at both villages. The colored wrappings were always stamped with the common and botanical name of the contents and the name of the village from which they came. They were actually sold when packaged in one-pound groups of sixteen— "blocks"—that were wrapped in plain tan papers with a separately printed label affixed to one end.

(Cakes: black ink letterpress on thin colored papers, each approx. 1½" × 3¼" × ⅞". Miller Collection and Blocks: tan papers with labels of black letterpress on colored papers, 3¾" × 3¼" × 10⅝". Courtesy of the Shaker Museum and Library.)

This herb press could be from either village, but since it was once part of the famed Andrews' Collection, New Lebanon is more likely. It is from the period before large steam presses—each capable of exerting pressure of three hundred tons—were installed at both communities in the early 1850s. This hand-operated press, activated by turning the handle, could only compress one cake at a time. When the industry was at full strength at New Lebanon, for example in 1855, seventy-five *tons* of dried plant material was processed. The consumer used the product by nipping off small pieces of dried herb and adding to boiling water, making a tea or "infusion." Their initial major innovation—dried herbs, roots, and barks put up in a form that was convenient for the general public to use—brought enormous profits to both communities.

(Ash, maple, and iron. 49½" × 11⅜" × 36¼". Courtesy of Hancock Shaker Village.)

New Lebanon and Watervliet issued a number of catalogs that listed their offerings, with prices per pound and a description of their pharmacological effect. The earliest was issued in 1830, and continued until 1874. The four illustrated here date, from left to right, 1851, 1845, 1837, and 1861–62. The two outer ones are from New Lebanon, the two inner—Watervliet. Commercial printing houses produced all of these catalogs. Several Shaker brothers, trained to be physicians in the World, oversaw the herbal medicine industry. This added a definite measure of credibility to the entire enterprise.

In addition to dried products, these catalogs listed fluid extracts for hundreds of herbs; the example on the far right had 135. Included in it were the herb's common name, price per bottle, and dose. The Shakers' foray into this hitherto unknown area—unknown on an industrial scale at least—was another major innovation that led to

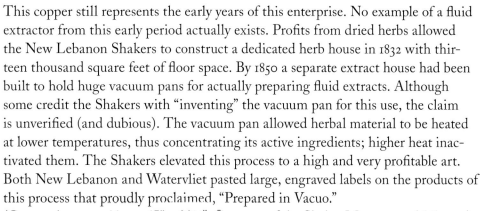

medicinal herbs, in all forms, overtaking garden seed as the largest revenue producer at New Lebanon by the mid-nineteenth century.
(Four catalogs: black ink letterpress on variously colored papers. From the left: 6¾" × 4½"; 7" × 4¼"; 6¼" × 3⅞"; and 3⅞" × 2⅝". Miller Collection.)

This copper still represents the early years of this enterprise. No example of a fluid extractor from this early period actually exists. Profits from dried herbs allowed the New Lebanon Shakers to construct a dedicated herb house in 1832 with thirteen thousand square feet of floor space. By 1850 a separate extract house had been built to hold huge vacuum pans for actually preparing fluid extracts. Although some credit the Shakers with "inventing" the vacuum pan for this use, the claim is unverified (and dubious). The vacuum pan allowed herbal material to be heated at lower temperatures, thus concentrating its active ingredients; higher heat inactivated them. The Shakers elevated this process to a high and very profitable art. Both New Lebanon and Watervliet pasted large, engraved labels on the products of this process that proudly proclaimed, "Prepared in Vacuo."
(Copper, brass, and iron, 45" × 23¼". Courtesy of the Shaker Museum and Library.)

One form in which extracts were sold was a squat glass bottle, packaged within a cardboard cylinder that was covered in bright green paper. Though a number of these cardboard packages survive in several sizes and with labels from both communities, the bottle and cylinder on the right have always been together and are the only such combination known. This makes one wonder if most cylinders once held only dry herbs and no extract bottle, but it would have been odd for a sect that valued efficiency to have routinely made up an elaborate system of packaging without good reason. (Cardboard, green and yellow papers, black ink letterpress and stone engraving on white paper. Taller examples: 3¾" × 2⅜". Shorter examples: 3" × 1¾". Miller Collection.)

SHAKERS' PRICE LIST

OF

MEDICINAL PREPARATIONS,

Mount Lebanon, Columbia Co., N. Y.

HERBS, ROOTS, BARKS AND POWDERS, NET PRICES.

FLUID AND SOLID EXTRACTS, DISCOUNT ACCORDING TO THE AMOUNT PURCHASED.

Discount on Fluid and Solid Extracts.—On $10, 25 per cent.;—$20, 30;—$40, 35;—$50, 40;—$75, 45;—$100, 50.

Common Names.	Botanical Names.	Herb Price	Pulvrized Price	Fluid Price	Solid Price
Abscess Root.......	Polemonium Reptans.......	25			
Aconite Leaves......	Aconitum Napellus.......	25		1 90	
Do. Root.....	" " Radix...	22	30	2 00	4 50
Agrimony..........	Agrimonia Eupatoria......	20		1 75	
Alder Bark black,..	Prinos Verticillatus.......	20		1 50	
Do. Berries, black.	" " Bacca..	30			
Do. red or tag,.....		10		1 25	
Aloes............				2 75	
Angustura..........				4 00	
Aromatic Comp.....	Alnus Rubra...........			2 25	
Alum Root........	Heuchera Pubescens........	22			
Angelica Leaves,....	Archangelica Atropurpurea.	15			
Do. Root.......	" "	25		1 25	
Do. Seed......	" "	25			
Anise Seed........	Pimpinella Anisum........	30			
Apple-Tree bark....	Pyrus Malus...........	20			
Archangel.........	Lycopus Sinuatus........	25			
Arnica Flowers......	Arnica Montana..........	30		1 75	
Do. Root...	" Radix...	30			
Ash Bark, Mountain,	Pyrus Americana.........	20			
Do. Prickly......	Xanthoxylum Americanum..	20	25	1 75	
Do. White......	" "	20		2 00	
Ash Berries, Prickly,	Fraxinus Americana......	40			
Asparagus Root.....	Asparagus Officinalis......	30			
Avens Root........	Geum Rivale...........	25		1 50	
Backache Brake,....	Asplenium Filix-fæmina..	30			
Balm, Lemon......	Melissa Officinalis........	20			
Do. Sweet......	Dracocephalum Canariense.	20			
Balm of Gilead buds..	Populus Balsamifera......	60			2 50
Balsam, Sweet.....	Gnaphalium Polycephalum.	14			
Barberry bark......	Berberis Vulgaris........	20	25	1 25	
Basil, Sweet.......	Ocymum Basilicum........	25			
Basswood bark......	Tilia Americana.........	16			
Bayberry bark......	Myrica Cerifera........	13	10	1 25	
Beech bark........	Fagus Ferruginea........	14			
Do. leaves.....	" Folium...	20			
Belladonna leaves ...	Atropa Beladona........	30	36	2 50	6 00
Bellwort...........	Uvularia Perfoliata.......	30			
Benne leaves.......	Sesamum Indicum	30			
Beth Root.........	Trillium Pendulum.......	25	30	1 75	
Betony Weed.......	Pedicularis Canadensis.....	25			
Birch Bark, black,...	Betula Lenta...........	13			
Black Pepper.......	Capsicum Baccatum.......			1 50	
Bitter Root........	Apocynum Androsæmifolium	25	30	2 00	3 00
Bittersweet, False bark				3 00	
of Root,......	Celastrus Scandens.......	35			
Do. Berries........	" " Bacca..	20			
Do. Herb.......	Solanum Dulcamara......	20		1 50	
Blackberry Root,....	Rubus Villosus.........	10		1 50	
Blackberry Root bark		16			
Blood Root........	Sanguinaria Canadensis...	16	20	1 75	6 00
Blue Flag.........	Iris Versicolor	20	25	1 60	5 00
Boneset...........	Eupatorium Perfoliatum...	10	16	1 25	3 00
Borage...........	Borago Officinalis.......	20			
Boxwood bark......	Cornus Florida........	16	20	1 25	4 00
Do. Flowers......	" "	24			
Brooklime.........	Veronica Beccabunga				

Common Names.	Botanical Names.	Herb Price	Pulvrized Price	Fluid Price	Solid Price
Buchu leaves	Diosma Crenata	60		2 50	
Do. Comp.......				2 50	
Buck Bean	Menyanthes Trifoliata	36			
Buckthorn Brake	Osmunda Spectabilis	36			
Buckthorn berries	Rhamnus Catharticus......	45		1 50	
Bugle	Lycopus Virginicus........	18		1 25	
Burdock leaves	Lappa Major, Folium......	13			
Do. Root	" " Radix...	17	22	1 50	3 00
Do. Seed	" " Semen...	18	24		
Butternut Bark	Juglans Cineria...........	13		1 25	3 00
Canada Thistle Root,	Cirsium Arvense.........				
Cancer Root Plant,..	Epiphegus Virginiana......	22			
Canker Weed.......	Nabalus Albus..........	25			
Caraway Seed.......	Carum Carui...........	20			
Canella	Canella Alba			1 50	
Cardinal Flrs, Blue,	Lobelia Syphilitica	30			
Cardamom.........	Eleterium Cardamomum ...			3 00	
Do. Comp....				3 00	
Carduus, spotted, ...	Cnicus Benedictus	20			
Cassia............	Cinnamomum..........			3 00	
Cascarilla..........	Croton Eleuteria			1 25	
Carrot Seed, wild,....	Daucus Carota	25			
Catnip............	Nepeta Cataria..........	12		1 25	
Cayenne Pepper,....			50	3 00	
Celandine, Garden,	Chelidonium Majus.......	20		1 50	
Celandine, Wild,..	Impatiens Pallida........	14			
Centaury, low,...	Sabbatia.............	25		1 50	
Chamomile Flowers,	Anthemis Nobilis........	40		1 75	
Do. low...		30			
Cherry Bark, wild,..	Prunus Virginiana.......	12	16	1 50	2 00
Do. Comp...	" "			1 50	
Chickweed.........	Cerastium Vulgatum......	25			
Cinchona Pale				2 50	
Do. Calisaya...				4 25	
Do. Comp...				2 50	
Do. Red...				4 25	
Colchicum Root.....				2 00	
Do. Seed				2 75	
Cloves...........				1 75	
Colocynth	Cucumis Colocynthis			2 25	6 00
Cicely, Sweet......	Osmorrhiza Brevistylis				
Cicuta Leaves.......	Conium Maculatum......	13	20	2 00	3 50
Do. Seed.......				2 50	
Clary............	Saliva Selara.........	20			
Cleavers	Galium Aparine........	18		1 25	
Clover Heads, red,.	Trifolium Pratense......	25		2 00	
Cocash Root.......	Aster Puniceus.........	25			
Cuckold..........	Bidens Frondosa.......	25			
Cohosh, Black,....	Cmicifuga Racemosa......	12	18	2 00	1 25
Do. Do. Comp.				2 00	
Do. blue.........	Leontice Thalictroides.....	14	20	1 50	3 00
Do. red.........	Actæa Rubra..........	25			
Do. White........	" Alba	14	28		
Columbo Root......	Cocculus Palmatus......	20		2 50	3 00
Coltsfoot Herb,.....	Tussilago Farfara.......	18			
Coltsfoot Root		25		1 50	
Comfrey Root.......	Symphytum Officinale.....	16	22		

As happened so often when the Shakers innovated in a field, imitators soon followed. In the case of medicinal herbs at New Lebanon (now named Mount Lebanon), the by now "usual" combination of dwindling resources in manpower and increased competition from the World doomed the industry. This "Price Sheet," issued in 1874, was the final printed publication for the industry. It is a bi-fold listing exactly 400 herbs with medicinal properties. Some of these, such as cayenne pepper, cloves, dill seed, ginger, mustard seed, sweet marjoram, sage, summer savory, thyme, and watermelon seed are better known for their culinary uses. The back page actually lists sage, thyme, summer savory, and sweet marjoram as: "For Culinary and other purposes."

(Blue and red ink letterpress on white paper. 11" × 8½". Miller Collection.)

Harvard also laid claim to being the first to undertake, in 1820, a large-scale medicinal herb business though almost two hundred years after the fact it is impossible to establish priority. Still, they certainly could have challenged any other Shakers for the size of this industry relative to the size of the community. While New Lebanon had almost 400 members in 1820 when the business started, Harvard had fewer than half that number. By the time of the Civil War, Harvard had only one-fifth

the number of members and an even smaller proportion of males (who did the heavy work). The comparison between Harvard and Watervliet is less striking but still lopsided in favor of the latter.

The Harvard Shakers nevertheless managed to keep their business going into the twentieth century. In fact, aside from some small crafts such as brooms and sieves, nearly all of their resources went into producing dried herbs. Unlike the other large herb-growing Shaker communities of Canterbury, New Lebanon, and Watervliet, Harvard never became involved in putting up finished medicines or other medicinal products. Like the two New York societies, they packaged their herbs in one-ounce "cakes" but compressed their one-pound sizes into one-piece "bricks" or boxes. Shredded leaves and roots were wrapped in heavy papers while barks and berries were placed in cardboard boxes and wrapped.

(Paper, some with cardboard, and black ink letterpress on paper labels. Each approx. 1½" × 4¼" × 8¼". Miller Collection.)

Since almost all of Harvard's products were in dried form—there were few extracts, oils, tinctures, or ointments—the main use for bottles was for powders. Below is a bottle of "Golden Seal Root, Pulv[erized]" from after 1858—the patent date embossed on the glass—but before 1862, when the community's post office changed from South Groton (printed on the label) to Groton Junction. In *Shaker Medicinal Herbs*, author Amy Bess Miller writes of this product: "The powder may be boiled in water and sniffed up into the nostrils for nasal congestion." In addition to the traditional paper-wrapped ounce cakes (here peppermint, used medicinally, and lobelia, a mainstay in the Thomsonian System) there are one-ounce boxes of "Prickly Ash Berries" and "Wahoo Bark." This format mimics the one-pound forms above where barks and berries are boxed. Finally, they put "sweet" or culinary herbs in tins—one for sweet marjoram and one for sage.

(Bottle: glass and tin, 5¾" × 3⅛"; Cakes: paper, 2" × 2" × ¾"; Boxes: cardboard, 2" × 2" × 1⅜"; Tins: 3¼" × 2⅜" and 2" × 2". All have labels with black ink letterpress on off-white papers. Miller Collection.)

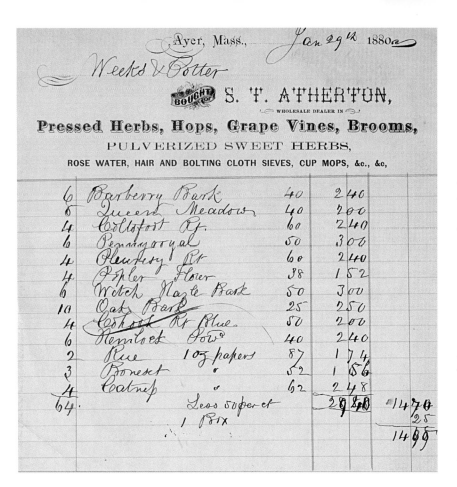

6	Barberry Bark	40	2 40
5	Queen Meadow	40	2 00
4	Coltsfoot Rt.	60	2 40
6	Pennyroyal	50	3 00
4	Pleurisy Rt	60	2 40
4	Popler Flower	38	1 52
6	Witch Hazle Bark	50	3 00
10	Oak Bark	25	2 50
4	Cohosh Rt Blue	50	2 00
6	Hemlock Bow	40	2 40
2	Rue 1oz papers	87	1 74
3	Boneset "	52	1 56
4	Catnep "	62	2 48
64	Less 5 per ct	29 30	14 70
	1 Box		25
			14 95

One element in the "paper trail" that was necessary to keep track of sales were billheads. Collectively, all of the printed papers that were intended for one-time or short-term use and seen throughout this volume are referred to as "ephemera." This billhead, dated 1880, documents the sale of thirteen varieties of dried herbs to a worldly distributor named Weeks and Potter. Simon T. Atherton, whose name is printed here, was a Trustee overseeing the herb industry for fifty years until his death in 1888.

(Black ink letterpress and manuscript on red ruled pale blue paper: 7" × 6⅞". Miller Collection.)

Of course, there had to be a means for marketing these dried herbs in the World and so a series of catalogs were issued over the years. The earliest one, shown in the background, was a single very large sheet, printed about 1830. It demonstrates how well developed the industry was at this early date; nearly 180 varieties were offered, many in multiple forms—seed, root, leaves, etc. This format was followed by a succession of bound catalogs over the following fifty or more years. Three of the bound versions are depicted here—from the left: 1845, 1854, and 1873. The number and type of herbs that Harvard raised for sale remained remarkably consistent over the course of the century from 1830 until at least the 1890s.

(All black ink letterpress on variously colored papers: background, 19½" × 11¾". From the left: 6⅞" × 4"; 6¾" × 4½"; and 7" × 4½". Miller Collection.)

Moving from the cultivation of dried herbs to "simples"—medicines derived from individual plants—was another innovative leap for the Shaker communities, primarily those at Canterbury and New Lebanon. Moving then from simples to compound medicines was an inspiration. Once again the Shakers had the plant material, the manpower, and the expertise in trained chemists and medical doctors to carry this out. Those in the World who were interested in non-traditional herbal medicine were also interested in products that went beyond herbal teas and infusions. This presented a previously unrealized opportunity for the Shakers in an entirely new market.

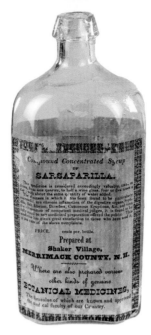

Brother Thomas Corbett of Canterbury was the most important Shaker physician when it came to developing a medicinal *industry*. The first product that he, or any other brother, developed for "mass marketing" was called "Compound Concentrated Syrup of Sarsaparilla." It also turned out to be one of the best- and longest selling of all Shaker medicines—beginning about 1843. His method of promoting the product is quite familiar to us today but was innovative for its time—he received endorsements, many of them, from respected medical doctors in the World and relied upon them as his major form of advertising.

In addition to seven herbs—the main ingredient being the roots of the wild sarsaparilla plant— *Aralia nudicaulis*—several types of berries were also used to make the syrup. It took several weeks to soak, boil, strain, distill, then repeat these steps, and finally allow the mix to settle-out before large quantities of sugar, a few inorganic substances plus alcohol (to 10 percent by volume) were added. This bottle, seen front and back, is the earliest remnant from the enterprise. The many endorsements on the label are dated 1843 and the contents were probably put up about that time. It is interesting that one doctor whose recommendation is included on the label is a worldly physician with whom Corbett himself trained in about 1813—Dr. Richard P. J. Tenney of nearby Pittsfield, New Hampshire. (Glass and black ink letterpress on tan paper: 6¾". Private Collection.)

This group of Corbett's products dates to the later nineteenth and early twentieth centuries. The label on the Syrup of Sarsaparilla bottle [far right] announces that it is "Guaranteed under the Food and Drug Act, June 30, 1906," which only meant that its alcohol content, 10 percent, was listed on the label. It also shows that the medicine was sold at least as late as that date. The other products shown—Wild Cherry Pectoral Syrup, Dyspepsia Cure, and Medicated Lozenges were less successful but nonetheless marketed through the second half of the nineteenth century.

(Box: cardboard and black ink letter press on white paper, 7¼" × 8¾" × 6½" and Bottle [right]: glass with black ink letterpress on tan paper, h= 7¾". Miller Collection.)

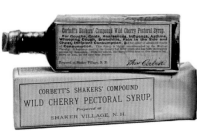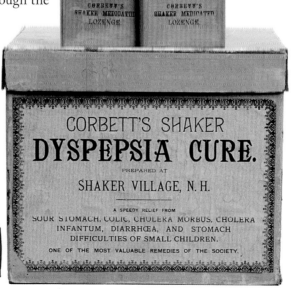

This possibly unique, four-sided advertising piece
was intended to sit on a counter or tabletop. Beyond that, nothing
is known about when it was made or for whom. Clearly, a good deal of
careful woodworking (with a scroll saw) and hand-painting were required.
It probably dates to about 1880 when this ad was placed in an Augusta,
Maine, newspaper—promoting the syrup as "The Great Blood Purifier."
(It is unclear whether the caricature of a Shaker brother depicts him before
or after he used the product.)

(ABOVE: Walnut with paint: 6" × 22" [each side]. Courtesy of Canterbury
Shaker Village and RIGHT: Black ink on newsprint, detail, approx. 3½" ×
2½". Miller Collection.)

While one almost never encounters instances of boasting among Shakers,
there are many instances where "quiet" pride is found. Corbett's Syrup
was submitted to the many competitions held in the middle years of the
nineteenth century, where medicines were judged, presumably for their
efficacies. Corbett's Syrup of Sarsaparilla was a frequent winner. The
Massachusetts Charitable Mechanic Association awarded this medal in
1850 to Trustee David Parker, who oversaw the initial development of its
formula and worked tirelessly to promote it.

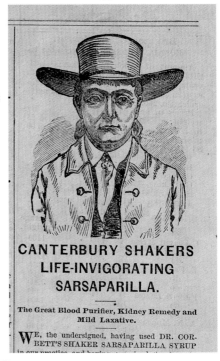

CANTERBURY SHAKERS
LIFE-INVIGORATING
SARSAPARILLA.

The Great Blood Purifier, Kidney Remedy and
Mild Laxative.

WE, the undersigned, having used DR. COR-
BETT'S SHAKER SARSAPARILLA SYRUP

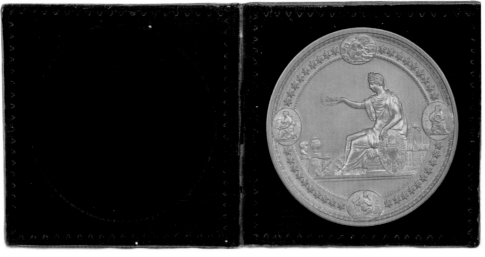

(Bronze, velvet, and unknown
wood: 3" × 6½". Courtesy of
Canterbury Shaker Village.)

A curious offshoot of the many, many medicines developed by the Shakers is the Shaker Extract of Roots or, abroad, Mother Seigel's Syrup. It is worth examining this product because although the Shakers at Mount Lebanon did not develop the formula for it or market it, they were the makers and beneficiaries of it. In fact, after the disastrous fires at their Church Family in 1875, this enterprise proved to be an economic boon. Trustee Benjamin Gates and A. J. White, a drug purveyor (and physician) from the World forged the joint venture in 1875.

Andrew Judson White was born in the town of Canterbury, Connecticut, in 1824 and, after being educated locally, graduated from Yale Medical College in 1826. His career over the following fifty years involved him in various aspects of the proprietary or "patent" medicine business. After his partnership with the Mount Lebanon community was formed, White went on to develop a system of agents around this country and eventually throughout the world who sold his preparation on a consignment basis—similar to the innovative system that the Shakers themselves had pioneered for garden seeds seventy-five years earlier! Mount Lebanon supplied him with the raw product—essentially herbal roots and extracts plus salt and borax—and the labor force to prepare, bottle, and label it. White promoted it as a "blood purifier," a common belief being that dyspepsia (indigestion) allowed foreign substances to enter the bloodstream and caused most diseases. By the time he died in 1898, White was a very wealthy man.

This grouping of some of White's products includes bottles and packaging labeled as Mother Seigel's Syrup and intended for markets in the British Empire that, at the time, included South Africa, Australia, and India. With the help of Shaker Brother Gates, White established a plant in London by 1880 to manufacture the product for worldwide distribution. The Shakers continued to supply the raw products—at least while they had the manpower to do so. Mother Seigel was a wholly fictitious character, supposedly a kindly but elderly German woman who "discovered" a combination of local roots that were capable of curing most diseases—a panacea. White used her "story" as his major marketing strategy, and it worked better than anyone anticipated. There is good reason to believe that his preparation, in the last quarter of the nineteenth century, was the largest selling medicinal preparation in the world.

(Box: wood and color lithography on off-white paper, 7¾" × 9½" × 8" and Bottle [far left]: glass and black ink letterpress on white paper, h- 4¾". Miller Collection.)

What the Shakers of Mount Lebanon know more about than anybody else, is the use of herbs and how to be healthy.

They have studied the power of food. They nearly all live to a ripe old age.

The Shaker Digestive Cordial is prepared by the Shakers from herbs and plants with a special tonic power over the stomach.

It helps the stomach digest its food, and digested food is the strength-maker.

Strong muscles, strong body, strong brain, all come from properly digested food.

A sick stomach can be cured and digestion made easy by Shaker Digestive Cordial.

It cures the nausea, loss of appetite, pain in the stomach, headache, giddiness, weakness and all the other symptoms of indigestion, certainly and permanently.

Sold by druggists. Trial bottle 10 cents.

This ad copy is part of a large sheet filled with differing texts, each numbered, which was sent to an advertising agency (Dauchy & Co., New York City) for insertion in consecutive issues of an unnamed publication. White did not always use his close working partnership with the Shakers to market his products as he does here. Although the sheet is not dated, the stamp on the accompanying envelope was issued only between 1894 and 1902.

(Black ink letterpress on white paper: detail, 2½" × 2¼"; full sheet 12½" × 7¾". Miller Collection.)

The entrepreneurial White went to great lengths to market his products and was not above gimmicks such as sample sizes of the extract, sewing thimbles embossed with Mother Seigel's Syrup, and these clocks encased in silver- or gold-colored metal that were in all likelihood designed to sit on the counters of pharmacies. He also published a huge number and array of pamphlets, almanacs, and four trade cards— all as giveaways (and, for Victorians at least, collectibles).

(Unknown metals and glass: h- 7¾"; h- 7¼". Miller Collection.)

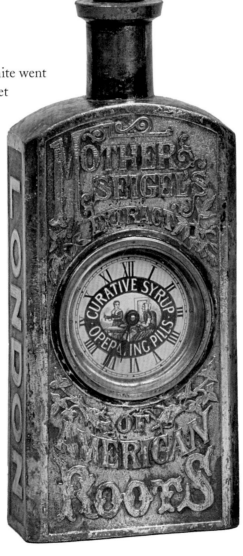

White established a manufactory in Lille, France, in 1883; this in addition to plants in London and Montreal. By 1893 that branch was earning more than ₣100,000 annually. These labels are "die proofs"—the first trial printings of labels that, if approved, were archived by the Waterlow firm (and numbers of labels printed for the client).

(Steel engravings on off-white papers, 5⅛" × 3" and 5¼" × 3⅛". Miller Collection.)

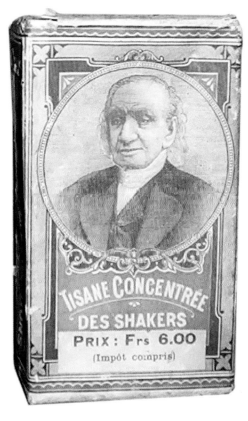

This box and bottle are rare survivors of White's French manufactory.

(Printed papers on glass and on cardboard, box: 11-5¼". Private Collection)

It is not likely that the Shakers supplied much of the herbal material to White beyond the turn of the century. These two colorful display cards are from indeterminate dates—the vertical format displaying the same style of packaging seen on the previous page, perhaps from before 1890. Its sailor is saying: "Do as I do."

(Display card: multicolor letterpress on card stock, 14½" × 7⅜". Miller Collection.)

The horizontal format shows a slightly later type of label. This style was steel engraved—an elaborate, expensive process—by the prestigious firm of Waterlow & Sons in London, beginning in 1888 and lasting until at least the late 1920s.

(Display card: color lithography on card stock with string, 10¾" × 15½". Miller Collection.)

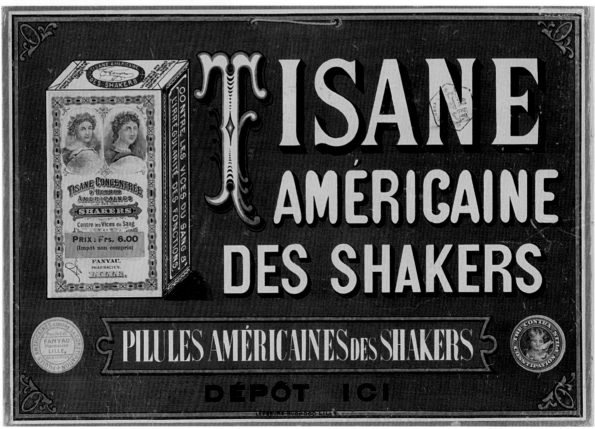

Lyman Brown and A. J. White had a very close but still not fully explored relationship; one that lasted until White's death in 1898. And as they were with White's, the Shakers at Mount Lebanon were an integral part of Brown's business. Born in upstate New York, and eighteen years White's junior (although he died only eight years after him, in 1906), Brown was a pharmacist. He marketed a liquid extract that was called Seven Barks—supposedly based on its being made from the seven layers of the hydrangea plant. He attributed this discovery to a Franz Gauzwein. Herr Gauzwein, like Frau Seigel and the story of Seven Barks, were all elaborate fictions. According to the Shakers at Mount Lebanon who actually made the preparation, it was made from *eight* plant ingredients (and none of them hydrangea). Unlike the Shaker Extract, which claimed to be all vegetable but contained 10 percent dilute hydrochloric acid and other non-plant matter, Seven Barks had no inorganic ingredients.

Although none of the contents came from the *bark* of hydrangea, Brown insisted on using a Latin name for his medicine: *Acetum Hydrangea* (Vinegar of Seven Barks). *The root* of the hydrangea plant is a diuretic, capable of removing tiny stones (here called "gravel") from the urinary tract. Like nearly all proprietary and patent medicines of the nineteenth century, it was mainly a laxative. This billhead advertises it as such while the pamphlet with Franz Gauswein (later, Gauzwein) is the earliest known, ca. 1874. The pink sheet gives instructions (on the inside) for agents to order on a consignment-commission basis.

(Billhead: black letterpress and manuscript ink on red and blue ruled white paper, 7¼" × 8½"; Pamphlet: black ink letterpress and wood engraving on off-white paper, 8½" × 5½"; Pink sheet: black ink letterpress on pink paper, 8" × 11". Miller Collection.)

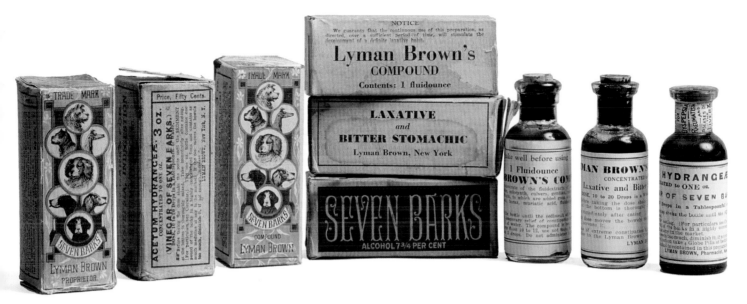

The packaging for the product changed little over the years: corked, three ounce bottles in cardboard boxes. Each box included instructions for use ("10 to 20 drops in a wine glass of water") as well as a tiny corkscrew for removing the stopper. The earlier bottles had labels with the Latin name, later ones Lyman Brown's Compound. The price throughout was sixty cents per bottle.

(Boxes: color lithography on paper on cardboard, 3½" × 1⅜" × 1⅜". Miller Collection.)

Lyman Brown also employed a variety of advertising gimmicks to promote his product, using the visual puns of seven (*bark*-ing) dogs or seven sailing ships (*bark*-entines) on booklets, almanacs, and display cards. These three cards, with nearly identical imagery, were intended to be hung (the two larger) or to perch on a countertop.

(All—color lithography on card stock: 6½" × 4¼"; 11" × 8¼"; and 14½" × 10½". Miller Collection.)

Shaker thoughts and lifestyle are incongruous with the concept of vanity, and a product whose only recommendation is an appeal to self-image, therefore, may appear to be a bit jarring. One should never forget that the profit motive was certainly not incompatible with Shakerism—not when that profit has been earned honestly. This idea of the "rightness" of every financial transaction included selling products that were pure, fresh, fairly presented and, when appropriate, of honest weight or ingredients. It carried over to crafted objects as well; they had to be well made, using the best available materials, and, usually, displaying their surfaces and details of construction. This is why, for example, woods were often varnished or stained with thinned paint—the need to protect the wood was realized and the grain of the wood was allowed to show. Shaker craftsmen preferred solid woods rather than veneers and laminates, and generally favored open mortise and tenon joints and exposed dovetails over concealed joinery.

Finally, there is Shaker Hair Restorer, which took its place among products that were intended to both profit the New Lebanon community and appeal to vanity in the World. None other than the energetic entrepreneur of the Shaker Extract of Roots, A. J. White, provided New Lebanon with the formula for this product, one that "Restores gray hair to its original color, beauty, and softness." This came about in early 1885 and a year later the Second Family at the community launched the business with a flurry of marketing strategies—pamphlets, post cards, and broadsides. Unfortunately, in spite of their vigorous approach, the product faltered and was terminated by New Lebanon in 1890. Subsequently, the Phenamido Chemical Co. in Albany, New York, offered it in the 1890s. The record of a transfer of rights to the formula, from either the Shakers or White, has not been located. Illustrated here are a colorful package, unopened; a brass stencil used on shipping crates; a simple broadside with endorsements dated 1889; and a package insert from the succeeding company.

(Box: Color lithography on cardboard, h- 8" and Stencil: brass, 10⅛" × 10½". Courtesy of Hancock Shaker Village. Broadside: black ink letterpress on tan paper, 9½" × 6" and Insert [detail], black ink letterpress on white paper, full size 9½" × 4". Miller Collection.)

SHAKER HAIR RESTORER

Restores Gray Hair to its Natural Color, Beauty and Softness, and is an Excellent Toilet Dressing.

THE well-known Society of Shakers, located at Mount Lebanon, N. Y., has for a century past been engaged in the cultivation of medicinal herbs and in the preparation of various essences, extracts and compounds, that are largely used in medical practice by the public at large. The Society takes great pleasure in offering to the public a

HAIR RESTORATIVE,

Feeling assured that it will supply a long-felt want, and hoping that it will receive the same generous reception that has been accorded to all articles of Shaker manufacture.

Gray Hair may be Honorable, but the Natural Color is Preferable.

In a great majority of cases gray hair is the result of disease, necessitating the employment of some remedial agent, which is found in the SHAKER HAIR RESTORER.

IT IS NOT A DYE,

But when used according to directions it will restore gray hair to its original color, imparting that beauty and softness which is natural to hair in a healthy state.

Baldness is prevented by the application of the HAIR RESTORER, as it renews the activity of the torpid glands and causes the falling out of the hair to cease.

Dandruff, which injures and destroys the roots of the hair, is thoroughly removed by applying the HAIR RESTORER.

Irritation, Itching and Disease of the scalp it readily cures, and it keeps the head clean and agreeably cool.

SHAKER HAIR RESTORER.

For BALDNESS, LOSS OF HAIR, DANDRUFF, and all SCALP DISEASES, by directly fertilizing the hair follicles, stimulates, and promotes the growth of a good healthy head of hair.

IF USE IS PERSISTED IN WILL GROW HAIR ON ANY BALD HEAD NO MATTER FROM WHAT CAUSE OR HOW LONG STANDING. THIS IS A STRONG STATEMENT BUT WE ARE CONFIDENT IT IS A TRUE ONE.

HERBS AND PREPARATIONS 61

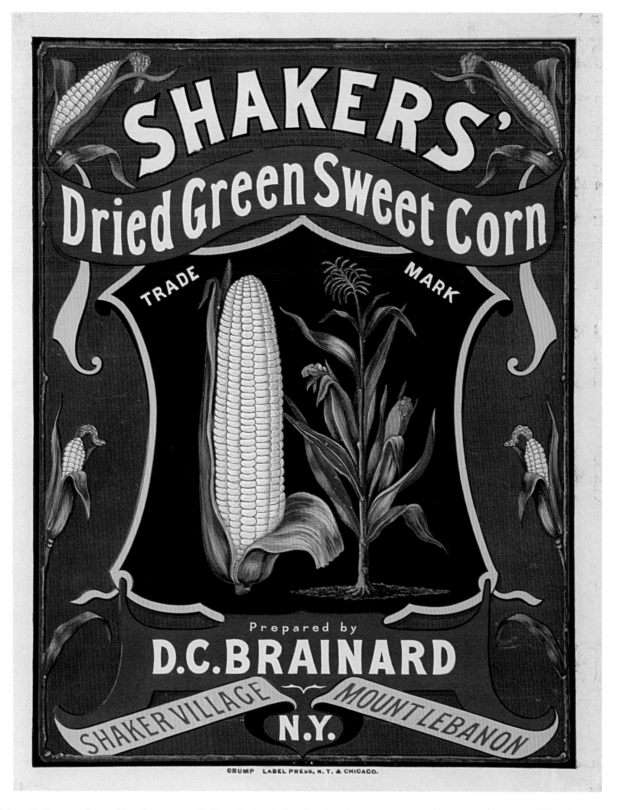

New Lebanon first offered corn seeds for sale in their *Gardiner's Manuel*, initially printed in 1835. The description there reads: "The sweet or sugar corn is the best for cooking in its green state, as it remains much longer in the milk, and is richer and sweeter than any other kind." A dedicated corn-drying house was built there in 1840, some forty years before this colorful display sign was printed by Crump Label Press in New York City (1879–1882). D[ewitt] C[linton] Brainard (1828–1897) was the trustee who oversaw this and other industries at Mount Lebanon. (Multicolor letterpress on white card stock, 14" × 11". Miller Collection.)

3
Planting Perfection
The Shakers As Horticultural Innovators

DARRYL THOMPSON

THE SHAKERS HAVE ALWAYS BEEN visionaries and continuous experimenters who early on developed a doctrine of stewardship which asserted that everything humankind possesses is a gift from God, who holds men and women accountable for how they use His gifts. Believers, therefore, must fully develop each gift: they must use it creatively, wisely, and without waste while employing it to serve one's fellow human beings. One was following a directive from God when using selective propagation to breed plants with qualities that gave them maximum utility. This work represented man cooperating with God in the act of creation. It should come as no surprise then to learn that in their quest for horticultural perfection the Shakers developed over twenty new fruit, vegetable, and herb varieties.

Little was known about hybridizing during the years when the Shakers developed their plant varieties so the brethren developed them by observation and selection. They carefully observed both their gardens and the plants that grew wild in woods and fields. When they found a naturally occurring cross or mutation that worked well, they selected it out and perpetuated it as a distinct variety. A good example of a Shaker innovation is the Union Village Grape,

hereafter referred to as the Union Village, developed by the community at Union Village, Ohio.

The evidence seems to indicate that the Shakers first developed this variety prior to the mid-1850s although exactly when cannot be determined. Ulysses Prentiss Hedrick (1870–1951), the renowned horticulturist who served at the New York Agricultural Experiment Station at Geneva from 1905 to 1930 and his colleagues investigated the history of the Union Village (sometimes known simply as the "Union"). They compiled a chronological list of references to the grape in nineteenth- and early twentieth-century agricultural literature. The list claims that the earliest printed reference to it appeared in *Elliott's Fruit Book*, or the American Fruit-Grower's Guide in Orchard and Garden, by F. R. Elliott in 1854.[1] The U.S. Commissioner of Patents Report for 1856 shows that the Union Village grape was also known by the alternate name "Shaker."[2] The 1860 edition of Andrew Jackson Downing's *The Fruits and Fruit Trees of America* notes that "this very attractive grape originated among the Shakers at Union Village, Ohio, and was introduced [i.e., first made commercially available] by Mr. [Nicholas] Longworth of Cincinnati."[3]

To understand how the Ohio Shakers developed the Union Village, it is necessary to trace the grape's

ancestry. All sources are in agreement that Union Village's "parent plant" was a grape called Isabella. Hedrick and his colleagues wrote: "Isabella is generally classed as a pure Labrusca but there are many who think there is a strain of Vinifera present." Such a cross would have been the result of natural forces rather than human intervention because grapes were not being artificially hybridized when Isabella first arrived on the scene in the eighteenth century.

Between the seventeenth century and the middle of the nineteenth, various attempts were made to grow Vinifera grapes in the New World. Climate and other factors caused these attempts to fail in the eastern United States, but the effort must have resulted in Vinifera grapes and Labrusca grapes growing in proximity to each other at some point and cross-pollinating, resulting in what would become known as Isabella.

Grape growers today generally propagate by cuttings, but in the nineteenth century they sometimes obtained their vines by planting grape seeds. A seedling (the term is used here to mean a plant grown from seed) possesses greater genetic variability than a plant from the same species grown from cuttings or by other means. A number of nineteenth-century grape varieties arose from horticulturists' practice of planting grape seeds and selecting from among the varied offspring the vines that possessed the qualities they wanted to perpetuate. That is exactly how the Shakers created the Union Village variety from Isabella.[4]

This is how Ulysses Prentiss Hedrick and his colleagues at the New York Agricultural Experiment Station at Geneva described the Union Village:

> Vine vigorous to rank, usually productive, somewhat tender, subject to attacks by fungi. Canes large, long; internodes short. Leaves coarse and large. Fruit ripens about one week before Isabella. . . . Clusters large to very large, often shouldered, compact. Berries large to very large, roundish, dark purplish-black covered

ABOVE: Wine Bottle (ca. 1895) Color lithography on white paper on amber glass, H-13⅞" Private Collection.

with heavy bloom, shell badly. Skin moderately thin. Flesh tart, resembling Isabella somewhat in flavor, quality fair to good.[5]

The Isabella grape, by contrast, was described as having flesh "inclined to foxiness." Some understand this to mean that the aroma of the grape smells like a fox, but in fact writers have employed a whole range of adjectives to describe the fox grape's taste, including "musky," "earthy," "acid," "astringent," "tart," "sprightly," "biting," "bracing," "cloying," "refreshing," "spicy," and "mouth-puckering." Foxiness is not necessarily a fault, however. It is entirely a matter of individual taste. Some people adore the foxy flavor while others despise it. The popularity of the fox grape diminished significantly as sweeter varieties were developed, sometimes by selection from seedlings and in other cases by crossing the European and American species to create hybrids. Nevertheless, a part of the American public continued to enjoy the foxy flavor of the Labrusca varieties and eagerly bought them.[6]

Several qualities attracted growers to the Union Village. The variety's earlier ripening date appealed to some. Fuller reckoned that it achieved ripeness anywhere between the "first to middle of October."[7] Hovey wrote: "Of all the grapes that have been recently introduced, there is none, that for size, beauty, and flavor, is superior to the Union Village."[8]

ABOVE: "Premium Wine Grape" (1859) Black ink letterpress and wood engraving on white paper, 22" x 8". Collection of the United Society of Shakers, Sabbathday Lake, Maine.

Finally, as to the health of the plant, it possessed a "vigor of vine and showiness of fruit attracted the attention of the viticulturists of a half century ago."[9]

Interestingly, the distinguished viticulturist T. V. Munson thought the Union Village's chief value lay in making jelly.[10] Although several other viticulturists expressed a good deal of skepticism about the variety's worthiness as a wine grape, there is a surprising entry in a section of the book *Facts for Farmers* entitled "Culture of Grapes for Wine": "*Union Village*—A beautiful, dark-colored wine; not much body or strength; will make a fine, light, summer drink. Alcohol, 5½ per cent."[11]

Union Village's vulnerability to pests and disease was a major reason for its decline. A second was that some raised questions about its susceptibility to mildew. These controversies over the grape's flaws eroded public confidence in it. In 1858 it was placed on the American Pomological Society's list of grapes that "promise well," but it was dropped in 1883. The striking of Union Village's name from the catalog marked the beginning of its decline. Nevertheless, in 1908 Hedrick still expressed the hope that "it might prove of some value in breeding for the characters for which, even among the largest and most vigorous grapes of to-day, it is distinguished."[12] The emergence of Shaker-originated fruit, vegetable, and herb varieties was a logical outgrowth of the Shaker interpretation of the doctrine of stewardship. Eldress Antoinette Doolittle (1810–1886) wrote: "We perceive it was not in the divine economy to instantly evolve a perfected plant . . . but to vivify, and give time . . . to develop and consummate the original plans of the great Master builder . . . [through] . . . supernatural agencies combined with human skill and labor."[13]

Among the other better-known fruit varieties developed by the Shakers were the Wachusett Blackberry, Austin Seedling Strawberry, and Ohio Everbearing Raspberry. The most prolific developer of Shaker plant varieties was Brother Philemon Stewart, a member of the New Lebanon, New York, community (and, for a short time, a member of the small Shaker family at Poland Hill in Maine). His Mountain Seedling Gooseberry was the first known cultivated gooseberry variety to be developed from a naturally occurring cross between *Ribes cynosbati*, the eastern North American species of wild gooseberry,

"Premium Wine Grape" (1859) Black ink letterpress and wood engraving on white paper, 19" x 11¾". Collection of the United Society of Shakers, Sabbathday Lake, Maine.

and *Ribes grossularia*, the common species of European gooseberry. It only lost popularity when gooseberries in general fell into disfavor in the United States because of widespread fears that they were carriers of the white pine blister rust, a fungus that threatened one of the U.S. lumber industry's most important species of timber.[14]

Of course the Shakers were involved in many other facets of food production and processing, some of which will be addressed in the pages ahead. For one thing, they had hundreds of their own members to feed in each community, and they had to feed them three times daily—on an industrial scale. For another, they turned a host of their new approaches in consumables into marketing successes that provided additional income for Believers for more years than any other area of endeavor. The foregoing is a brief summary of their efforts in cultivating new plant varieties—a relatively unknown facet of this indefatigable group of innovators. 🌿

Other than the development of several new plant varieties, the Shakers made two major innovations in the area of foodstuffs: finding efficient ways to feed up to one hundred Believers at a time and developing ways to process comestibles for sale. Regarding the latter, products made for sale came largely from two crops, apples and corn. Most of what follows will pertain to them.
—M. Stephen Miller

In 1828, the New Lebanon community once again set a standard for a profitable business among Shakers by preparing the corn grown on their lands for sale. In his landmark 1933 book, *The Community Industries of the Shakers*, Edward D. Andrews wrote of the early corn industry: "At first the process consisted merely of boiling the cobs in great iron kettles, cutting the kernels off with hand knives, usually three-bladed affairs screwed to a vise . . . and then drying them."[15] The device illustrated here is one of those three-bladed knives; whether the Shakers invented it is unknown. Cobs would be passed across the extremely sharp blades and dislodged by the duller one at the end. The blades were screwed into their retaining arm so that they could be easily removed for sharpening. One Shaker brother, I. N. Youngs, wrote: "A corn sheller (very valuable) was introduced about 1830."[16] This is what he was referring to.

(Iron and steel, 8" × 3¼" × 5½". Miller Collection.)

By the 1870s, either as the result of increased demand or reduced capacity, Mount Lebanon was compelled to buy additional corn from outside sources. This agreement states that the provider will "raise, sell, and deliver at the Kiln of said D. C. Brainard . . . during the year 187_, _____ acres of Sweet Corn . . . Such corn is to be picked just after it is 'out of the milk.' "

The formality of this agreement is evidence of the importance of this business to the community and of the extent to which the Shakers went to be assured of a high-quality product.

(Black ink letterpress on white paper, 10" × 8". Miller Collection.)

AGREEMENT.

This Agreement, made this   day of
            in the year of our Lord eighteen hundred and seventy-
                , by and between
of   in the County of
and State of   and D. C. BRAINARD, of the
United Society, called Shakers, of New Lebanon, in the County of Columbia, and State of
New York :

WITNESSETH, That the said   hereby
agrees to raise, sell, and deliver at the Kiln of said D. C. Brainard, in said New Lebanon,
during the year 187   ,   acres of Sweet Corn ; all corn delivered at
said Kiln to be good, sound, and clean ; and to be delivered within twenty-four hours after the
same shall have been picked from the hill. Said Corn is to be picked just after it is "out of
the milk," and is to be delivered at such times, and in such quantities, as said D. C. Brainard
may direct ; and said   not to deliver any ears of
Corn which are " in the milk," or soft, or damaged, or in any way injured by smut, frost, or
animals, or that are less than four inches in length, or that is unsuitable for drying for food.
All corn delivered shall be properly "husked" and "silked," and the stems or cobs cut or
broken off close up to the kernels, the ears to be kept nice and clean. And said
                            is to deliver the same as aforesaid, for the sum or price
of
for each and every hundred pounds of ears of Corn, to be weighed at the Kiln on delivery,
and to be paid as follows, viz :

And said D. C. Brainard hereby agrees to purchase and receive of said
                                    acres of Sweet Corn, of the quality
aforesaid, during the Summer and Autumn of the year 187   , at the price aforesaid, and to
pay for the same as above stated.

And it is mutually agreed by the parties hereto, that they, and each of them, will well
and faithfully carry out and perform the stipulations herein written, according to the true
intent and meaning thereof—and the party failing so to do will pay to the other the sum of
dollars as liquidated damages.

This post card image shows Elder Robert Valentine (1822-1910) using a powered machine that stripped kernels from their cobs. It is postmarked October 29, 1906. Behind him are several younger workers and baskets of corn. A similar device is on display at Hancock Shaker Village.

(Photograph on card stock, 3½" x 5¼". Courtesy of Hancock Shaker Village.)

Although New/Mount Lebanon led the way in the production of dried sweet corn for sale, there is no evidence that the community ever packaged it in individual containers.[17] The Enfield, Connecticut, and Hancock, Massachusetts, communities, however, did so. At Enfield, Shakers had instructions for cooking printed on the cardboard boxes: "Put the corn to soak four hours previous to cooking, in tepid water, place it to cook in the same water one-half hour before eating, where it will heat gradually until it comes to a scalding heat . . . then add a little butter, and season to taste." The larger, two-pound containers from Hancock were formed of thin bent wood with tin bands on the top and bottom and paper labels. These instructions were virtually the same as Enfield's.

(Blue letterpress on tan cardboard, 6¼" × 3" × 2¼", and unknown wood with multicolor letterpress on yellow and green papers and tin, 6½" × 4½". Miller Collection.)

A curious but ingenious byproduct of raising corn, a crop that is appealing to birds—especially crows—is this device developed by the Shakers to keep these nuisances at bay. It is a "clacker," an innovation that generates a very loud sound when twirled. Over the centuries farmers have developed many strategies for dealing with this problem but perhaps none quite so elegant as this one. It is made from several types of wood, each chosen to best serve its specific task. The handle is cherry, a wood that turns well; the body is walnut, a heavy and sturdy wood; the gears are hard maple; and the actual clackers are ash, a wood that is both strong and pliant. A steel plate is precisely fitted to add weight to the end and shaped to help the sound resonate. In short, it is a perfect crow-scaring machine. (Mixed woods and steel, 6¾" × 1" × 8¼". Miller Collection.)

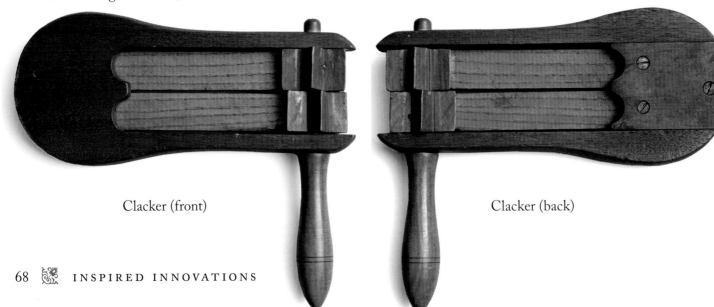

Clacker (front)   Clacker (back)

Several Shaker villages were involved in the production of wines—using grapes, fruits, and berries—but none undertook it with the entrepreneurial energy of the Union Village, Ohio, community. In 1890, as the fortunes here along with the other three Shaker communities in Ohio were in decline (one, North Union, had already closed in 1889), a new source of income was desperately needed. The Lake Erie shoreline was a productive one for viniculture. Here, in 1892, in the village of Wickliffe, Union Village established a one-thousand-acre vineyard.[18] Their first crop was harvested in 1897 for sale as grapes, but the operation was soon converted to producing grape juice and wine. The broadside dates to the first year of grape sales—1897. It begins with the following assertion: "We are planning now to handle what is probably the largest crop of grapes ever raised in an American vineyard—that of the United Society of Shakers at Wickliffe, Ohio." The bottle would date from within a few years after this. The Shakers abandoned the project by 1900.

(Broadside: green ink letterpress on light tan paper, 11½" × 8¼". Miller Collection and Bottle: color lithography on white paper on amber glass, h- 13⅞". Private Collection.)

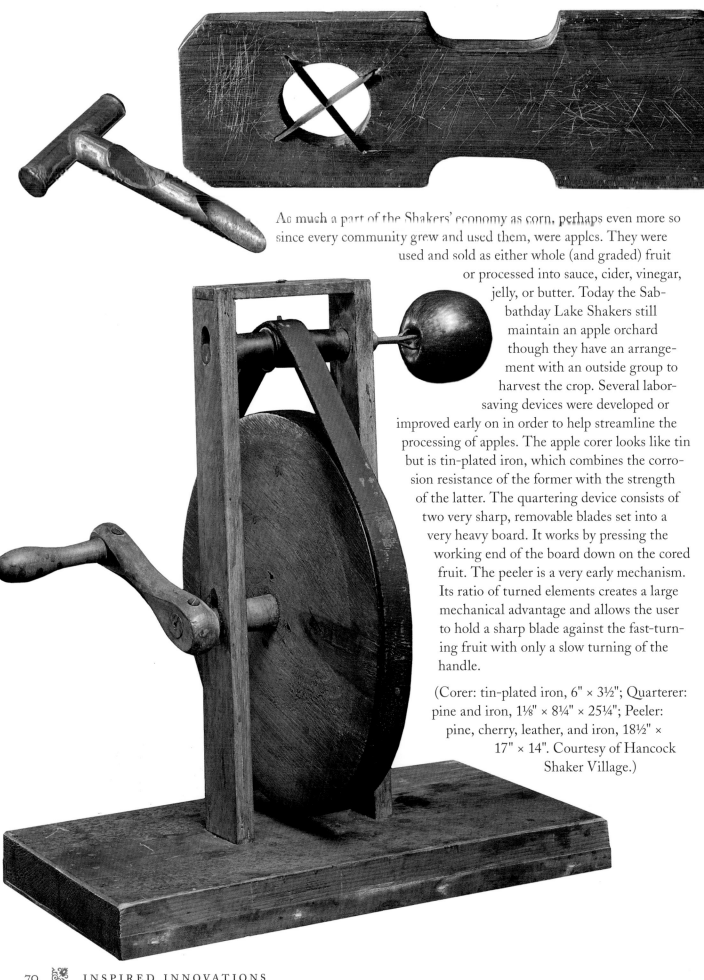

As much a part of the Shakers' economy as corn, perhaps even more so since every community grew and used them, were apples. They were used and sold as either whole (and graded) fruit or processed into sauce, cider, vinegar, jelly, or butter. Today the Sabbathday Lake Shakers still maintain an apple orchard though they have an arrangement with an outside group to harvest the crop. Several labor-saving devices were developed or improved early on in order to help streamline the processing of apples. The apple corer looks like tin but is tin-plated iron, which combines the corrosion resistance of the former with the strength of the latter. The quartering device consists of two very sharp, removable blades set into a very heavy board. It works by pressing the working end of the board down on the cored fruit. The peeler is a very early mechanism. Its ratio of turned elements creates a large mechanical advantage and allows the user to hold a sharp blade against the fast-turning fruit with only a slow turning of the handle.

(Corer: tin-plated iron, 6" × 3½"; Quarterer: pine and iron, 1⅛" × 8¼" × 25¼"; Peeler: pine, cherry, leather, and iron, 18½" × 17" × 14". Courtesy of Hancock Shaker Village.)

This rare postcard view of the apple orchard at the North Family of Enfield, Connecticut, is postmarked 1909. Below are three wooden firkins that were the standard size for selling applesauce on a retail basis. These cooper wares were not made by the Shakers; rather they were furnished to them by a worldly source, George Lane & Son of East Swanzey, New Hampshire. We do not know who printed the labels for them, but it was also a non-Shaker firm. From left to right these rare survivors were sold by Canterbury; Enfield, Connecticut; and Enfield, New Hampshire.

(Post card: photoengraving on card stock, 3½" × 5½". Miller Collection.)

The Shakers at New/Mount Lebanon often seemed to trump the efforts of the other communities when it came to the use of bold colors and eye-catching graphics in their printing. This was probably the result of their greater relative wealth. The firkin illustrated here was put up there in the 1880s. The label's printer, Hinds, Ketcham, & Co., existed from 1880–1890.

(Firkin: pine and wire with color lithography on paper, 6½" × 6½". Courtesy of the Shaker Museum and Library.)

(Firkins: pine and iron wire with black ink letterpress on off-white papers, 6½" × 6½". Miller Collection.)

The exact use for the two sizes of rectangular labels remains a mystery since no container, wood or glass, with one of these types is known. The round example would have been placed on the head of a cask or small barrel of sauce, one that would have been sold wholesale—perhaps to a restaurant or institutional food service.

(Round label: gold ink letterpress on deep blue paper, diam. 8¾" and Rectangular labels: red and blue ink letterpress on white papers, 4¼" × 8¼" and 4⅝" × 10". Miller Collection.)

This display card from the Shirley Shaker community is one of the few remnants of their very large and important applesauce business. When reporter Charles Nordhoff visited Shirley in 1874 he wrote, "The society owns two thousand acres of land . . . and their main business is to make apple sauce."[19] It probably would have hung in a small village food store where their firkins were sold.

(Red and blue ink letterpress on white card stock, 11" × 14". Private Collection.)

One of the last food industries at any Shaker community—Sabbathday Lake still puts up dried herbs, herbal teas, rose- and other flavored waters, and candies (seasonally)—was the canned vegetable business at Watervliet, New York, carried on under the guidance of the last eldress there, Anna Case (1855–1938). This can, rusted and somewhat battered, is the only known surviving example—it dates from sometime between the late 1920s when Eldress Anna took over the responsibility for this business from Elder Josiah Barker (see label below), and ran it until she died (and the community closed) in 1938.

(Color lithography on white paper on tin, 6¼" × 4¼". Courtesy of Canterbury Shaker Village.)

These two never-used labels, and the brass stencils used to mark shipping crates of cans, date from the 1920s and/or 1930s. The Shakers were among the earliest in America to popularize eating tomatoes, especially, in an uncooked state. Although the plant originated in the Western Hemisphere, as a member of the nightshade family, it aroused superstitions of a toxic potential in Europe that were carried back to this country with the early settlers. Beginning in 1835, the Shakers promoted its virtues as a foodstuff. Eventually, the World came to love and cherish it, and by 1880 Mount Lebanon was offering tomato seeds in eight varieties for kitchen gardens.

(Labels: color lithography on white papers, 4¼" × 12⅛" and 4¼" × 14¾"; Stencils: brass, 7½" × 12" and 6½" × 13¾". Miller Collection.)

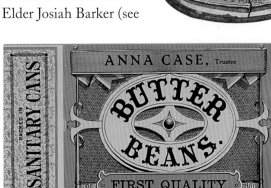

The challenge of feeding large numbers of people—and, indeed, feeding them well—was met in a variety of ways. Though many of the kitchen devices associated with the Shakers were innovative, it is not possible to know which ones they invented, or adapted and improved upon, or simply borrowed. The Shakers do have a strong tradition of caring for the various products made and used in the past by Believers. We are privileged today to have many of these artifacts, in good condition, from a much earlier time. The slicing device would have been clamped to a tabletop, allowing vegetables to be cut up as fast as the operator could raise and lower the handle. Likewise, the "chopper," set on a Shaker-made table, was fashioned by a Shaker blacksmith and fitted to a heavy block of pine. It was fitted with a pivoting hinge that facilitated chopping from side to side. Finally, the double rolling pin was in all likelihood a Shaker invention. Sheets of dough could be rolled thinner and faster than was possible with the traditional form.

(Slicer: cherry and iron, 12" × 6¼" × 20"; Chopper (without table): pine and iron, 1⅞" × 25¼" × 15¼"; Rolling pin: maple and cherry, 2½" × 20⅝" × 3⅝". Courtesy of Hancock Shaker Village.)

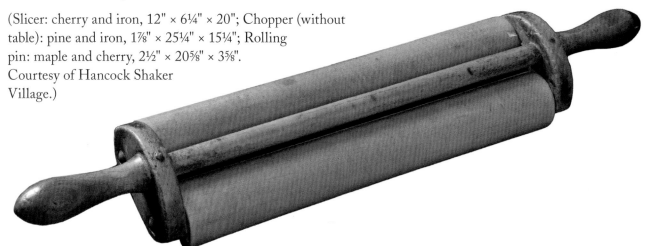

In *The Community Industries of the Shakers*, Andrews attributes the invention of the oven with revolving shelves in the basement of the dwelling house at Canterbury to Sister Emmeline Hart (1834–1914) but the editor has not been able to substantiate this. In any event, this innovation allowed heat to be evenly distributed during cooking, a great improvement where a large oven was required to heat food for the hundred-plus members three times daily. In the 1930s and 1940s, when their numbers here were reduced to dozens, several sisters put the oven to good use by creating a small industry of preparing baked beans (and brown bread) for sale. The business ended in 1952.

(Containers: black ink lithography on off-white cardboard, 3¾" × 3½" and Card: 2" × 3½". Miller Collection. Photograph on card stock, 3½" × 5¼". Courtesy of Canterbury Shaker Village.)

Sisters Eleanor Parmenter, Evelyn Polsey, and Aida Elam (left to right) pose with the truck used to bring the baked beans and brown bread to Concord, ca. 1940. This superstructure is now located at the Shaker Museum and Library. (Photograph on card stock, 3½" × 5¼". Courtesy of Canterbury Shaker Village.)

(Oval boxes from New Lebanon: maple, pine, and iron,
l- 10½", 12", 13½" and 15". Collar box from New Lebanon:
Ash, pine and brass, 3¼" × 6½" × 5¼". Miller Collection.)

4
Woodenwares
Oval Box Making at Mount Lebanon, New York

JERRY V. GRANT

ABOUT 1850, Brother Isaac Newton Youngs began compiling notes on the trades practiced by the Brethren living at New Lebanon from the time the church was gathered in 1787. He incorporated these notes into a manuscript history of the church at New Lebanon that eventually was edited and serialized in the pages of the *Manifesto*.[1] Youngs opened his section on the making of oval boxes by remarking that its history "is greatly hid in obscurity," an interesting choice of words implying that the history was there but hard to find. The following sketch of the oval box–making business at New Lebanon, with some passing comments about similar work at other Shaker communities, relies more on information retrieved from obscure comments in Shaker records than from boxes themselves. It is nevertheless fortunate that many boxes remain to inform and corroborate the written record.[2]

This essay addresses oval box–making as an industry and business rather than as the "fireside craft" of the colonists so charmingly described by Mary Earle Gould in *Early American Wooden Ware*.[3] There is no particular mystery associated with bending thin strips of wood into round or oval boxes. Americans

have been employing the technique since the seventeenth century, and much earlier in Europe. It is entirely possible that any Shaker brother from any Shaker community made a quantity of oval boxes. Yet, only a few Shaker communities made boxes on an industrial scale. Among them were Canterbury, New Hampshire; Alfred and Sabbathday Lake, Maine;[4] Union Village, Ohio;[5] and New Lebanon, New York, which produced the greatest quantity of boxes over the longest period of time. The history of New Lebanon oval boxes provides the greatest insight into this Shaker industry.

An undocumented assumption persists to the effect that a number of Shaker industries evolved out of their need to make items for their own use and in doing so created the means to make a surplus for sale. But it is highly unlikely, for example, that Shakers just decided there was profit to be made in growing garden seeds to package in pre-measured portions since no one had ever tried that. It is far more likely that in growing seeds for their own use, they found that a market existed for their surplus. The same is probably true of the oval box business. By the time the tools, jigs, templates, forms, materials, and machinery had been set up to make boxes to supply the community, it only made sense to make more of them to sell, for they soon found that the World was eager to buy these products.

Preparations to make boxes for sale began at New Lebanon in 1799. Youngs writes that it was Elder Brother John Farrington—the Elder of the First Order of the Church Family—along with Brother Joseph Green who first had charge of the business. Records show that it was Farrington who in January 1799 "Gits the Body of a larg[e] Maple tree for Box Timber from the Smith p[lace]," and in April of that year Brother Jethro Turner was "Shaving Boox Timbers for John." In 1801, Jethro Turner wrote that he and Brother Stephen Markham were sawing "Box heading," that is, the pine boards used for box tops and bottoms, and planing box "hoops," the thin maple boards that were bent to form the body and rim of a box.[6] In April 1806, Ebenezer Cooley, elder of the North Family, retired from that duty and moved to the Church Family, where he worked on boxes until 1816. He was joined in 1812 by Ministry Elder Abiathar Babbit, who previously was a maker of bent wood dippers. Elder Abiathar moved the box business into the Ministry Shop. When Babbitt moved to Watervliet in 1821, Elder Brother David Meacham Jr. took the box business back to the Elders' Shop, where it remained until 1880. Daniel Boler began working in the box business in 1832, around the time he was appointed Second Elder. As a result of failing health, Meacham gave the box business over to Brother Daniel Crosman, who kept at it until 1880 when the whole business was moved to the Second Family and into the hands of Brother Ransom Gillman.

Making an oval box required a number of discrete steps. The hardwood rims and pine "heads" were rough-sawn from logs. The craftsman then cut the top and bottom rims to the right size for a particular box, planed them to the right thickness, and smoothed them by hand or machine. The ends of the rims were tapered to create a smooth overlap. He then traced distinctively shaped "swallowtails" on the rims using a template and cut them to shape with a knife. Rims were steamed, bent around an oval form, and secured with copper tacks. The bent rims were placed on oval "followers" as they dried. Pine heads of the proper thickness were cut into ovals and sized to fit securely in the bent rims. Finally he fastened the heads to the rims with small headless copper tacks called "points." Everything was sanded and finished with paint, shellac, or varnish. Any of these steps that could be made more efficient with jigs, fixtures, templates, or machines made boxes a better business for the Shakers.

Oval box production increased dramatically with technological innovations. In 1829 the Church Family built a new Machine Shop with a twenty-six-foot diameter water wheel that greatly increased the power available to operate machinery. In the early 1830s the Shakers purchased a relatively new invention, a Smith's Revolving Timber Plane, to make rough-sawn boards the proper thickness for bending into box rims. That work had previously been done with hand planes. At the same time Shakers developed a planing machine of their own design to smooth and regulate the thickness of boards used for box heading. Brothers David Rowley, Luther Copley, and Daniel Boler made a succession of improved machines for cutting out the oval heads.

All of these innovations facilitated an increase in annual production from 1,308 boxes in 1830 to 3,650 boxes in 1836. As the likely result of several factors soon after—the economic crisis of 1837, demands on the leaders during the Era of Manifestations (see Chapter 13), Elder David Meacham Jr.'s illness, and the increased availability of tin and glass containers—oval box production never again rose to the peak it achieved in 1836. During the tenure of Elders David Meacham, Daniel Boler, and Daniel Crosman, Mount Lebanon's oval box business had its "golden age" in the number of boxes made and in improved machinery for making them. For example, between 1822 and 1865 Mount Lebanon produced nearly 77,000 boxes.[7] By the end of the Civil War, annual production had fallen from thousands of boxes to hundreds.

Sales recorded in accounts kept by the Office Deacons beginning in 1805 provide some insights into the business. Boxes were sold individually as well as in "nests." Prices were given in pounds, shillings, and pence for many years. The smallest examples sold for one shilling two pence and the largest for four shillings. (A shilling was equal to twelve and a half cents.) Nests of boxes usually sold for thirteen shillings, but variations in price suggest that the number of boxes in a nest was not standardized. Account books do not refer to boxes as "oval" until the spring of 1814, and even after that the term is rarely used. For that matter, Youngs, in his history of trades, consistently uses the term box, never oval box.

Just before Brother Ransom Gillman became box maker at the Second Family, the sale of boxes began to be promoted in much the same ways Shaker chairs were marketed at Mount Lebanon. An illustrated insert advertising eleven sizes of "Fancy Oval Covered Wooden Boxes" was produced in the mid-1870s to accompany chair catalogs. The fanfare of this advertising piece suggests a growing business when, in fact, business was probably shrinking in the severe economic depression of those years. Brother Ransom Gillman died in 1886 and it is unclear which Shaker, if any, took his place as box maker. Within a decade, the illustration of the nest of boxes was altered to eliminate the two largest and two smallest boxes making, instead, a nest of seven. The advertisement was included in *An Illustrated Catalogue and Price-list of the Shakers' Chairs* probably published in the early 1880s.[8]

By 1900 the box business at Mount Lebanon had definitely passed from the hands of Shakers to those of hired men, and there it remained except for the relatively brief period of box-making in the twentieth century by Brother William Perkins and Sister Lil-lian Barlow at the Second Family. The best known among the hired woodworkers was George Roberts of Lebanon Springs, New York, who began working for the Shakers in 1916. He had been taught by "Daddy" Sharpe, another hired man who was already making oval boxes for the Church Family Store. Roberts supplied boxes to Sister Sadie Neale. The boxes he made, like those of other hired men, suffered over time from a shortage of materials. Properly sawn and planed wood, copper tacks, and the copper points that held tops and bottoms in the bent rims had become hard to find. Roberts made some boxes with tops of different hardwoods laminated together like a fancy cutting board. During the last years of his box-making career he used plywood for tops and bottoms and shaped the swallowtails with a jigsaw rather than a knife, leaving them rough and not nearly as elegant as earlier boxes.[9]

Roberts worked at the Shakers' Machine Shop until 1943, at which time he purchased the box-making tools and machinery from Mount Lebanon and set up shop at his home. For the first time since the late eighteenth century, boxes were no longer made at Mount Lebanon. In 1945, Sister Sadie Neale answered a request for boxes from Mrs. L. J. Peterson in Cincinnati by writing, "We have had to stop making boxes of late for we could not get the burrs and rivets, and three ply boards; also many other things needed to work with, so I just keep still in my cozy corner and wait results."[10]

The box business had "run out" at Mount Lebanon, but boxes were still being made at Sabbathday Lake, Maine. Most boxes made during the nineteenth century were used in the kitchen for storing flour, sugar, spices, and baking soda. Then in 1894 sisters at Sabbathday Lake began lining boxes with cloth and furnishing them with sewing necessities. The result was a rejuvenated oval box industry in which thousands of "sewing carriers" were produced for the tourist trade. Brother Delmer C. Wilson was the best-known of the carrier makers, but the business quickly spread to Alfred, Maine, and even back to Mount Lebanon. Brother Delmer continued making boxes and carriers through the mid-1950s. In the late 1990s the Sabbathday Lake community revived the oval box business once again, and it continues on a limited basis today. ❧

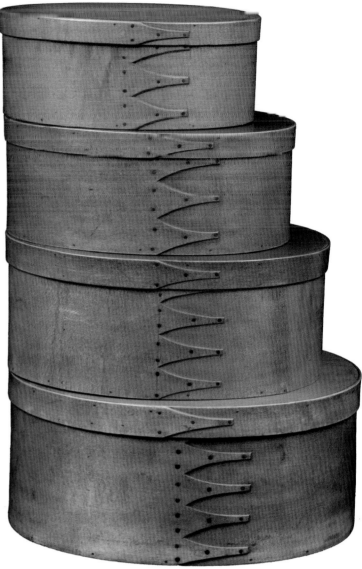

These three solid wood box forms were used to wrap the steamed sides around. The sheet iron inserts are there to bend or "deaden" the tips of tacks that were hammered into the fingers from outside in order to hold the box in its oval shape. Deadening tacks prevented them from pulling out over time. Once the wood dried, a Shaker-made box held its perfect oval shape indefinitely.

(Wood forms: pine and iron, l- 9", 10⅜", and 11¹¹⁄₁₆". Courtesy of the Shaker Museum and Library.)

These four oval boxes are typical of the types made at New Lebanon during the middle decades of the nineteenth century: maple sides, pine tops and bottoms (headers) held with tiny iron "points," and iron tacks securing the joints. The "fingers" form sharp, symmetrical (but horizontally oriented) Gothic arches; these shapes are more evident when the boxes are held in a vertical position. The fingers and especially finger's tips are in intimate contact with the body or the box.[11] The edges of the fingers are finely beveled and the top fits equally well when placed frontwards or backwards. Most boxes were left unpainted and achieved a rich, nut-brown patina over time. Many boxes found today have painted surfaces, though the Shakers applied paint to relatively few of them. (How the paint found its way on the majority is a matter of speculation.) This "stack" of oval boxes was made at New Lebanon; it is impossible to know whether or not they are the work of the same brother.

(Maple, pine, and iron: l- 10½", 12", 13½" and 15". Miller Collection.)

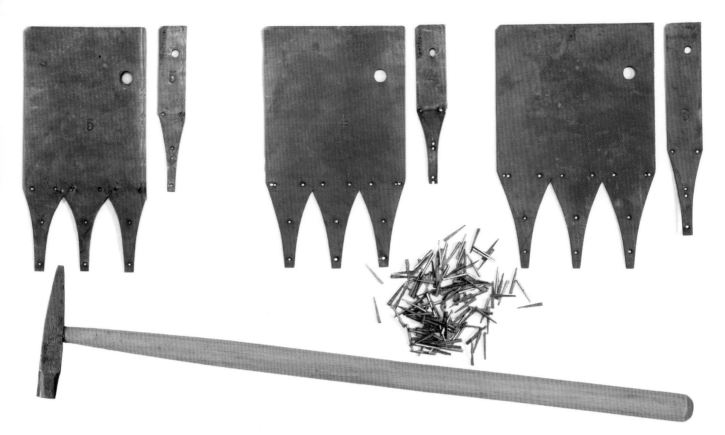

The Shakers used these tin patterns to trace the shape of the sides and lids on thin sheets of planed maple wood before steam-bending them. The copper tacks and tack hammer were used to secure the fingers to the sides of the boxes after bending.

The thin disk below is a form used to shape the rim piece after steaming. It was later tacked to a header to make the lid of the box. The exact function of the holes is not known. Perhaps a series of these were stacked in some sort of holder that had parallel rods.

(Tin patterns—for body: 1- 6⅜", 6⅞", and 6¹⁵⁄₁₆"; Copper tacks. Courtesy of the Shaker Museum and Library. Rim former: pine, ⅝" × 13" × 8¾". Courtesy of Hancock Shaker Village. Tack hammer: maple and iron, 1- 15¼". Miller Collection.)

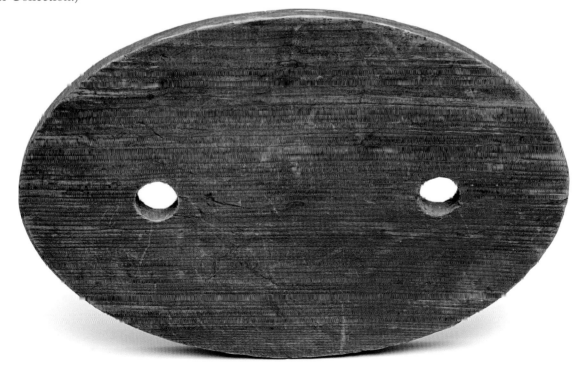

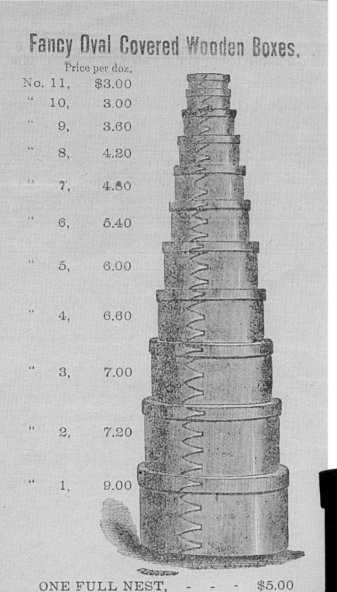

Fancy Oval Covered Wooden Boxes.

Price per doz.

No. 11,	$3.00
" 10,	3.00
" 9,	3.60
" 8,	4.20
" 7,	4.80
" 6,	5.40
" 5,	6.00
" 4,	6.60
" 3,	7.00
" 2,	7.20
" 1,	9.00

ONE FULL NEST, - - - $5.00

This is the only stand-alone broadside the Shakers at Mount Lebanon issued to advertise oval boxes (although as Jerry Grant points out, they did include box advertisements within chair catalogs from the 1870s to the early 1880s). The illustrated nest, numbered from 1 (largest) to 11 (smallest), is priced at $3.00 to $9.00 per dozen.[12] "One Full Nest" depicted here was $5.00. The nest of three boxes below is a "natural" one, that is, they were made together and have always been together. It is extremely rare to find this in the twenty-first century. The use of dome-headed copper tacks indicates a late date of manufacture, possibly after 1875.

(Broadside: black ink letterpress and metal plate engraving on off-white paper, 5½" × 3⅛" and maple, pine, iron [points], and copper [tacks]: l- 4½", 5¼", and 6". Miller Collection.)

A corollary to the oval box industry at New Lebanon was their dipper-making venture. According to Andrews, sales of dippers began as early as 1789, only two years after the community was fully organized.[13] By 1806 they recorded making more than two hundred of them, and sales continued for decades. Although at some point they were made in three sizes, the editor has seen only the two sizes illustrated. Several refinements in their construction set them apart from worldly examples: the virtual ribbon of tacks holding the seam that insured against warping and consequent opening of the joint, and the careful shaping of the square nut that secures a bolt holding the handle in place. This nut, located on the outside, was filed to smoothly conform to the concave portion of the handle. While this style of dipper was made for handling dry materials such as grains, at some point dippers were also turned and carved from single blocks of maple for wet uses [below]. No history for those shown here has been found.

(Dry dippers: maple sides and handles, pine bottoms, 3" × 4½" and 3½" × 5¾". Miller Collection. Wet dippers: maple with paint, 3" × 5". Courtesy of Hancock Shaker Village.)

Virtually every room in every Shaker dwelling built before about 1840, as well as in the Meeting House, laundry, and shops, had one or more small cast iron stoves in it. They will be discussed in Chapter 11; suffice it to say here, each stove needed a source of fire-starting material nearby. Additionally, many Shakers chewed tobacco in the nineteenth century and needed a convenient place to "deposit" the juices and saliva that resulted from this practice. Hence, the ubiquitous appearance of "spit boxes," also called shavings boxes, throughout their villages. One visitor to Watervliet, New York, in 1820 commented: "The meeting room . . . was a large rectangle in which pine spittoons filled with sawdust were distributed at regular intervals."[14]

The spittoons noted as "pine" were actually another extension of the oval box industry. The sides were always made of thin, steam-bent maple and the bottoms of clear (knot-free) pine. The joints were secured with either a straight ribbon of tack or tacked fingers. Occasionally, a room number or other designation was painted freehand or stenciled on the side. The "M" here may stand for Meeting House or Ministry. Usually a narrow reinforcing band of maple wood was placed around the rim to help maintain its round shape. At some point, the Shakers began to adapt the form to other uses with the addition of a handle. This could have facilitated the transport of a spit box but also could have allowed for a variety of other functions.

Finally, they refined a humble spit box into its ultimate form, this large round "carrier" [left] with a finely carved, fixed handle, similar to those found on large fruit baskets made at New Lebanon. Its body is painted bright yellow inside and out, and its handle brick red.

(Boxes at top: maple and pine with paint and iron hardware: left to right, 4⅛" × 10½"; 3⅜" × 10¼"; 11¼" × 11½"; 10½" × 11½" and Carrier, 12½" × 13¾". Miller Collection.)

Although we do not intend to suggest that carrier designs developed in a direct, linear sequence from one to another, general patterns of progression are discernible. As a rule, carrier bodies changed in shape from round to oval—with or without tops—over time. The carrier [right] is a singular example of a round body with a top. Its handle is also similar to those used on some New Lebanon baskets (see the next chapter)—flat on the outside and quarter-round on the inside with both surfaces having a silky, "machined" look and feel to them. This piece is covered in clear varnish, the protective coating used by the Shakers as a frequent alternative to paint.

(Maple, pine, and ash. 9½" × 10½". Miller Collection.)

The best-known shape of carriers is the oval, a sure evolution from earlier oval boxes. These two examples, formerly in the Andrews Collection, are the earliest adaptations of box-to-carrier forms seen thus far. The Shakers took New Lebanon–made oval boxes and added wood "shims" to either side so that when a fixed handle was secured, there was space for the top to be raised and lowered.[15] The bottom finger on the carrier to the right was cut short for some unknown reason. Shaker craftsmanship was not always perfect.

(Maple, pine, and ash, 7½" × 10½" × 7" and 11¾" × 15" × 11½". Miller Collection.)

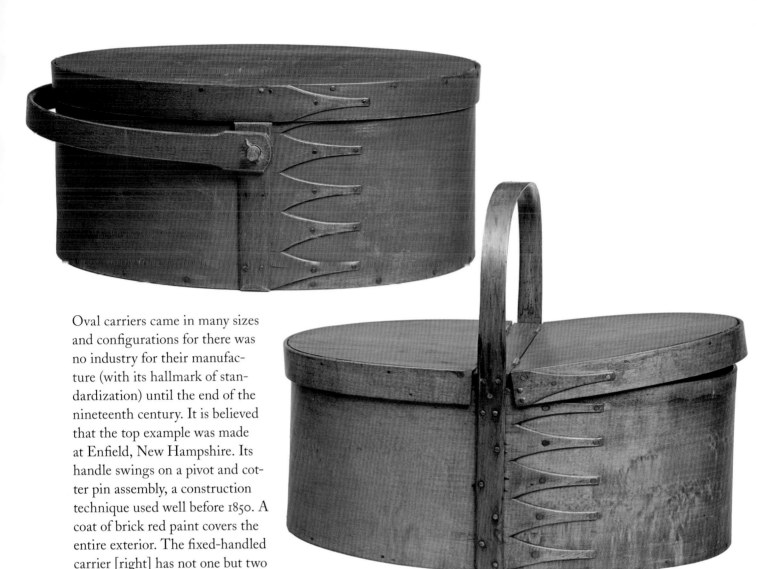

Oval carriers came in many sizes and configurations for there was no industry for their manufacture (with its hallmark of standardization) until the end of the nineteenth century. It is believed that the top example was made at Enfield, New Hampshire. Its handle swings on a pivot and cotter pin assembly, a construction technique used well before 1850. A coat of brick red paint covers the entire exterior. The fixed-handled carrier [right] has not one but two lids, hinged to a fixed centerpiece, a rare if not unique example of this form. It too has a New Lebanon–style handle. The Shakers left the outside wood, made from figured maple, unfinished in order that the grain might show—a subtle but effective means of "decoration."

(Maple, pine, and hickory, 13" × 15" × 12" and maple and pine, 13" × 15" × 11". Miller Collection.)

New Lebanon and Enfield were not the only makers of carriers before the 1890s. This example is from Canterbury, where many of this same form were made in the middle years of the nineteenth century. Nearly all Canterbury carriers are this length, eleven inches although some have interior rather than exterior handles. A feature shared by all of their carriers is the distinctive way in which the tacks fix the handle to the body in a pattern of 2:1:2. This one is covered in bright chrome yellow paint, inside and out.

(Maple, pine, and ash or hickory, 7⅝" × 11" × 8¼". Miller Collection.)

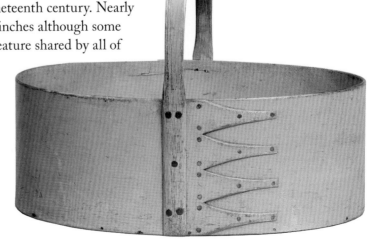

The Shakers made square and rectangular carriers in addition to round and oval shapes but in much smaller numbers. They are, therefore, highly prized today. This example is curious for several reasons. It almost surely started as a rectangular box without a handle and is dated "1798" underneath. In about 1880 a handle was added, along with some sewing accessories and two exquisitely fine, woven poplar baskets. Stamped into the top of the handle are the initials "J A" for Sister Janette Angus (1810–1894) of Watervliet, New York. This sewing carrier was not made for sale—today it would be called a "one off"—but it shows how the Shakers were thinking several decades before a sewing carrier industry developed at any of their villages.

(Pine and ash with silk, wax, and poplar, 9" × 12½" × 7". Miller Collection.)

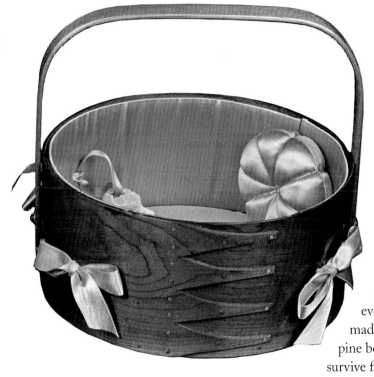

Throughout this book the question arises: what exactly did the Shakers invent and what did they modify in some fashion by adaptation, improvement, or refinement? The next section addresses this question directly, for the Shakers took the simple idea for a sewing box and then adapted, improved, and refined it. In the 1890s, sisters at Sabbathday Lake took some plain oval carriers that had been made at Mount Lebanon, lined them with cloth, and added some sewing accessories. When they found them to be quite saleable in the World, they approached a very clever and energetic brother, Delmer Wilson (1873–1961) and asked if he would make more boxes for them to outfit for sale. In 1896, Brother Delmer (his preferred title, even after he became an elder) took up the challenge and made his first thirty carriers, all with cherry sides and handles, pine bottoms, and all of them round.[16] Few if any other examples survive from his first year's output today.

From this modest beginning a new and very profitable industry was spawned at Sabbathday Lake and, soon after, their sister community in Alfred. Every one of the tens of thousands of outfitted sewing carriers that followed after 1897 from both communities was oval-shaped—round ones were never made again. Sisters lined each with silk of varying colors (and later with floral patterns) and attached four sewing accoutrements to the sides of the box with matching silk ribbons: a wax (to strengthen the thread), an emery bag in the shape of a strawberry (to sharpen needles), a small "book" of felt leaves covered with woven poplar (to store needles), and a tomato-shaped pincushion. (Cherry and pine with silk, wax, emery powder, felt, and poplar, 7⅝" × 7½". Miller Collection.)

Some years Brother Delmer made more than one thousand carriers, using jigs and machinery that he modified or built himself. The carriers were available in the four sizes illustrated and sold for between $1.50 and $3.25 in the first decades of the twentieth century. Different woods were used in constructing these carriers: maple, quarter-sawn oak, and Brother Delmer's apparent favorite—because he also had charge of the orchards—apple wood. The business effectively came to an end in the 1950s when he was the sole brother at Sabbathday Lake and was in his mid-seventies. (Mixed woods with silk, wax, emery powder, felt, and poplar, from left to right l- 10⅞"; 6¾"; 9⅞"; and 7⅞". Miller Collection.)

A brief diversion from carriers as an industry will be used here to illustrate a different facet of Shaker organization—their interest in consecutive sizing. The idea of numbering their oval boxes and offering different sizes of essentially identical dippers and sewing carriers has already been discussed in this chapter; here we get an even better look at just how precise the progression of sizes could be. Excepting the largest carrier seen here, the other four have numbers stamped into the underside of their bottoms; from smallest to largest, #8, #7, #6, #5, and no number. These were made at Mount Lebanon around 1875 and are the only five of this type the editor has ever seen. The precision of their sequencing clearly demonstrates a seldom discussed attribute of Shaker craftsmen: not only were they meticulous in their work, they could be almost obsessive about their sense of order.

(Maple with pine or cherry bottoms: l- 5¾", 6¾", 8⅛", 9¼", and 10½". Miller Collection.)

It is a bit of a surprise to those who have investigated the Shaker industries in the twentieth century that Mount Lebanon did not become seriously involved in the lucrative sewing carrier business until the 1920s. Sister Lillian Barlow (1855–1947) and Brother William Perkins (1861–1934) teamed up to manufacture a style of sewing carrier quite different from those made in Maine. The most obvious distinction was that all Mount Lebanon boxes had covers while none of the Maine ones did. The former were generally made from a tree that was not otherwise used by the Shakers—gum. The sides, top and handle are gumwood, the bottoms are pine, and a thin coat of varnish covers them. Since they have lids, the handles had to be shimmed, which the Shakers did using flattened wooden beads. As in Maine, each box was outfitted with the four standard sewing accessories, and they were offered in four sizes. The open box shows its furnishings—in this example brocaded silk lines the interior.

(Gum and pine with silk, wax, emery powder, felt, and poplar, l- 7½", 8½", 9½", and 10½". Miller Collection.)

One of the industries at New Lebanon, Canterbury, Sabbathday Lake, and perhaps elsewhere, was making sieves for sale. The wooden portions were usually formed from steam-bent ash, and the mesh was horsehair. In order to facilitate the binding procedure, the Shakers at New Lebanon came up with the simple device illustrated: a three-legged stool with round top, surmounted with a second lead-weighted disk. This upper disk would be removed and an open woven mesh of horsehair laid atop the stool. The heavy disk would be placed over the mesh to prevent it from moving as a previously made wooden hoop was slid over the two disks. Finally, a second, wider hoop was fitted around the first one, pinching the mesh and stretching it taut. It is not known if the Shakers were the first to use this type of device.

(Ash and horsehair: 4½" × 14½" and pine, birch, and lead: 25½" × 14⅞". Courtesy of Hancock Shaker Village.)

A more ambitious project was the attempt of the Shakers at Sabbathday Lake to anticipate the World's use of the Metric System. Beginning in 1877, Brother Granville Merrill (1839–1878) made a series of patterns for the manufacture of dry measures in sizes that ranged from a tenth of a liter up to twenty liters. Twice in the nineteenth century Congress authorized the use of metric measurements, and, progressive thinkers that they were, Shakers found the concept appealing. We do not know how many of these measures ultimately sold, but it is clear that the non-Shaker world, at least in this country, has yet to "convert" to metrics. The billhead (detail) illustrates the promotion of these measures (as well as sieves, etc.) by Sabbathday Lake.

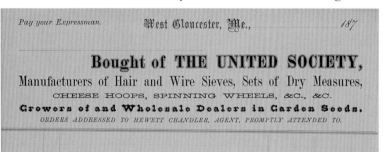

Pay your Expressman. **West Gloucester, Me.,** *187*

Bought of THE UNITED SOCIETY,

Manufacturers of Hair and Wire Sieves, Sets of Dry Measures,
CHEESE HOOPS, SPINNING WHEELS, &C., &C.
Growers of and Wholesale Dealers in Garden Seeds.
ORDERS ADDRESSED TO HEWETT CHANDLER, AGENT, PROMPTLY ATTENDED TO.

(5-Liter—birch and pine: 7¼" × 7½"; 10-Liter—oak, pine, and iron: 9½" × 9¾"; and 20-Liter—oak, pine, and iron, 12" × 12". Black ink letterpress on white paper with red and blue lines, full size 13¾" × 8½". Miller Collection.)

The Shakers at New Lebanon devised these quirky but useful little devices for snapping lines, chalk line safes, in the 1850s. Builders and paperhangers still use lengths of string coated with a colored chalk, which are stretched tautly across an expanse—usually a floor—and "snapped," leaving a straight (chalk) line behind. The safes shown here are essentially large, encased spools with a rewinding mechanism. A label on the back of one reads: "ALSO FOR LADIES' FLOWER BEDS OR ROOM LINE, FOR HANGING SMALL ARTICLES TO DRY." Two of these examples still retain their old reddish-color chalk.

(Unknown hardwoods with paint and string, 3" × 3". Courtesy of Hancock Shaker Village.)

5
Shaker Basket Making

MARTHA WETHERBEE

The Shakers and their "working baskets"

MUCH CONFUSION has been created over the years between the baskets the Shakers made and those they purchased. Shaker-made "working baskets" were used in every one of their villages on a daily basis, alongside those made by Native Americans and even other, locally made, farm baskets.

The Shakers began making baskets around 1813. Most were made for field, dwelling, or shop use. For the most part, these working baskets were large, heavy, and limited

Working Basket

to simple forms. The forms were often repeated, but their heights may have varied, as did the handle styles. The same basket shapes were used for different tasks. Some were made from heavier gauge splint for use in the orchards while others, woven from lighter cut splint, were for use inside such as transporting goods from ironing rooms to dwelling houses or from carpenter's shops to carriage barns. Most were made without the benefit of a coordinated system, each being the work of an individual maker who fashioned it from start to finish, just as baskets were made in the outside World. The Shakers, though, soon refined their craft by utilizing a variety of splint weights and differing basket heights, changes that reflected their adaptation of vernacular basket design for specific uses.

The tools they used were at first similar to those used by itinerant basket makers and Native Americans because indigenous materials and hand tools made for the farmstead were common. The drawknife, the shaving horse, and the froe were used to "work up" the wood, the splints being painstakingly released with the heavy hand blows of a sledgehammer. It was tedious, backbreaking work.

Drawknife

The Shakers and "fancy baskets"

By 1830, Shaker basket making had taken a new direction with the production and sale of "fancy baskets." When the need to produce a greater volume of these arose, a division of labor was established within a Shaker community. In this innovative and organized approach to task specialization, different people carried out the various phases of basket making so that the final product was the work of several hands. Work could be performed with greater speed and ease.

Innovative tooling was introduced when Shaker basketry evolved into an industry. New Lebanon, New York, for instance, was probably the most productive basket making community. Shakers here were richly endowed with the proper "raw materials"—abundant wood and a committed labor force of brothers and sisters—and began making baskets by the hundreds, quickly and efficiently.

No. 9   No. 8   No. 7   No. 6   No. 5   No. 4   No. 3   No. 2   No. 1

Nest of New Lebanon, NY "Fancy Baskets"

They had an ingenious brother at the helm, Daniel Boler, who established standards of creativity and resourcefulness.

Along with the Industrial Revolution in the United States came a concurrent decline in Shaker membership, particularly among men. For sales to continue, the Shakers had to find new product designs that better reflected the styles of the times, along with a more streamlined means of producing them. The need for heavier workbaskets also declined as more of the population moved to towns and cities. The newer baskets were comparatively tiny, what the Shakers called "diminutive." They simplified the designs and made them from finer-cut splints, making them much more practical to manufacture than their larger predecessors. The Shakers were quick to recognize that large profits could be realized by marketing these baskets to this new, mainly urban audience, with its steadier means of income.

Hand Plane

"Tooling-up" for the new industry

Basket making demonstrated the astonishing versatility and skills possessed by individuals in the Shaker order. In their new system, basket bodies, rims, and handles were shaped over wooden molds, while the pattern makers—those who first created the designs and later checked the outcomes—attested to the fact that these baskets met their specifications. Shaker baskets were becoming standardized. This uniformity itself would have pleased the Shakers' sense of "right order," but it also meant different people could make the bodies and other parts in stages and in volume. The Shakers had created a kind of assembly-line operation. After various parts were fashioned separately, they were assembled together with little further work needed.

Shaker communities had on average three hundred members—New Lebanon actually had 615 Believers in 1842—and among them were knowledgeable woodsmen who managed the forests and harvested its trees. The essential material for the construction of Shaker baskets is black (also called "brown") ash. This tree flourishes in swampy areas and was readily available in parts of New Lebanon's more than six thousand acres of land. In addition to woodsmen, Shaker villages also contained cabinetmakers whose work was known for precision, delicacy, and durability. A tradition for fine work was established early on at all of the communities.

Under the guidance of Brother Boler, who had charge of New Lebanon's basket shop, innovations continued. Shaker blacksmiths cleverly adapted an 1816 mechanical trip hammer to pound the ash logs. The hammer, previously used to forge iron door latches and hinges, was adapted so that it would free-up splint material from the ash log. A swage (pronounced "swedge") block of steel was attached to the wide face of the anvil. This had a depression in it similar to that of a spoon that cradled the log. The log was rolled into the cradle and with each blow of the hammer the annual growth rings were loosened.

Nest of Cat Head baskets, woven of ash with bent wood bonnet handles.

Nest of three fingered oval boxes,
bent from quarter-sawn maple

This basket splint or, as the Shakers called it, "basket stuff," was pulled up and off the log quickly. Basket production greatly increased with the use of this labor-saving device.

The Shakers' early adaptation of the circular saw permitted them to cut wood for basket handles directly from a sawn board. With this "spinning arbor," wood could be quarter-sawn for a straighter grain so that rims and handles could be steam-bent with ease and accuracy. Splitting timbers by hand became a thing of the past. Other new tools were brought into the basket shop for this new, burgeoning industry. Hand planes proved to be far more sophisticated shaping tools than drawknives, and when applied to basket making this simple innovation resulted in a far superior way to dress rim and handle stock. The workbench replaced the old shaving horse, providing a larger platform on which to perform related tasks. Each new tool brought more refinements.

Spinning Arbor

The surface planer was another tool brought from the cabinet shop to the business of basket making. An earlier Shaker-made device (*See page 100*) used hand power to draw splints through a blade attached to an adjustable yoke. Now the basket shop took advantage of a power-driven machine that was normally used to dress lumber. Shakers fitted an adjustable table to the planer bed so it could be brought to extremely low levels, enabling them to reduce the splints until they were almost paper thin without being "chewed up" by the knife. It was now possible to attain consistent thickness with a "satiny" finish, and to easily grade the splints by width and weight. By the time the Shakers had finished re-configuring

the surface planer into a splint planer, the tedious task of hand-scraping splint was out of fashion.

Well into the nineteenth century, most worldly basket makers continued to be satisfied with what they achieved using the drawknife and shaving horse. Yet for Shakers, basket making was no longer a one-person occupation; it was shared with others, each of whom learned to become highly skilled in specific phases of the business. Inventiveness and striving for perfection were part of Shaker culture—even when it came to making baskets for the outside World.

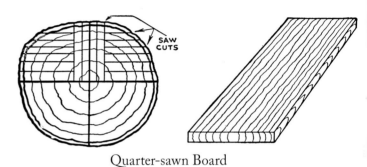

Quarter-sawn Board

After the middle of the nineteenth century, many more aspects of the Shaker basket industry became mechanized. Brothers Daniel Boler and Daniel Crosman (who was also in charge of the oval box industry) now worked together, sharing shops and sharing tools. The manufacture of oval boxes was a very profitable business venture at New Lebanon, dating from the earliest years of the nineteenth century, and it shared many traits with basket making. In the oval box industry, increasing use was made of power machinery as it became available. Basket making, however, still required a high degree of handwork, for there was no mechanism for actually weaving splints around uprights—the basic process for making a basket. Yet the baskets now had a new and more sophisticated look. The body, rims, and handles all fit snugly and precisely because of the exacting system by which they were made. They also had a smooth, polished appearance, the result of both the planing machine that left the splints with a satin-like surface and the use of fine hand files to finish rims and handles. Shaker baskets displayed a delightfully delicate, "stylized" appearance. While non-Shaker-made basket rims have a squared or "blocky" profile, theirs were smoothly, evenly rounded. And while non-Shaker-made basket handles have a squared or irregular profile in cross-section, theirs usually have flat outer and half-rounded inner contours, and a very fine, polished finish.

Soon, the Shakers had a flourishing business on their hands. Their baskets were in great demand as a decoration in stylish Victorian homes. Their gift baskets became very saleable, as no others in the marketplace could compare to their quality. Although almost every Shaker community made baskets, New Lebanon appears to have been the site of the major basket making *industry*. As this billhead clearly shows, they were also providing their sister communities—in this case Canterbury, New Hampshire—with various types of "sale" baskets. Their journals show them making as many as three thousand baskets per year. Unfortunately, some baskets

that the Shakers sold alongside their own—imported German split-willow skein baskets of high quality—are sometimes confused with their ash splint examples. The error is reinforced by early postcard images of Shaker gift stores that show both types on display. The imports allowed the Shakers to offer a greater selection and volume of items to sell at a time when membership had seriously declined and fewer skilled craftsmen were available to continue this labor-intensive craft.

The business of making fancy baskets lasted for more than sixty years at New Lebanon. Although it never produced income on the scale of the soil-based industries—garden seeds and medicinal herbs, for example—skilled Shaker hands and innovative technology allowed it to flourish on its own terms. 🌿

Mount Lebanon, N. Y., August 2th 1874

1	Work stand at 2,00, 1, at 2.50	4	50	
2	Oval shape at 3.00, 1, at 2.00	5	00	
1	Heart shape 1.30	1	30	
3	Square Oval at 1.00 each	3	00	
3	Cover'd Spoon baskets at 3.00	3	00	Various types
3	Spoon with tails 1.50	1	50	
3	Spoon with Ears 1.50	1	50	
3	Round Box baskets 2.75	2	75	
3	Saucer shape 2.75	2	75	
4	Tub Shape 4.25	4	25	
6	Cat head shape at 35c each	2	10	
6	Mullen heads shape at 25c each	1	50	
		33	15	
	Loop 12½%	4	15	
		29	00	
1	Pendant 3.75	3	75	
		32	75	

This 1874 billhead documents the sale of a large number of baskets (40) to Canterbury. Sister Polly Lewis (1815–1898) was office deacon at New Lebanon's South Family for many years, in charge of business matters (including sales to other Shaker villages). The baskets sold were of many varieties, all of them in the category of "fancy baskets." The smallest were sold for twenty-five cents, the largest, one dollar.

(Black ink letterpress on red and blue lined pale blue paper with lavender manuscript ink [photo-enhanced]: 8¼" × 7". Miller Collection.)

In their book, *Shaker Baskets*, where this example is illustrated, Wetherbee and Taylor have this to say: "The 'knife' basket was the most popular style in the Shaker fancy line . . . all have rectangular bottoms, straight sides and rectangular tops.[1] The sides may rise perpendicular to the bottom or they may flare out a little (as in this one)." This style of basket is deceptively small with some splint less than one-sixteenth inch wide.

(Black ash, 5¼" × 6½" × 3½". Miller Collection.)

The above was made on a solid wooden form, similar to this. The hole in the top was meant to hold a dowel that would have fitted into a heavy wood block. This allowed the form to be inverted, elevated, and rotated for the convenience of the maker.

(Pine, 2½" × 5⅛" × 3". Courtesy of Hancock Shaker Village.)

The Shakers devised this handle former so that once a black ash blank was cut to length, trimmed in width, thinned, smoothed, and steamed, it was held in a curved shape while it dried.

(Pine with iron hardware, 8 × 8⅛ × 1 ½. Courtesy of Hancock Shaker Village.)

RIGHT: We do not know where this simple clamp, activated with a thumbscrew, was used, but its small size suggests that it could have been used in basket making.

(Ash and maple 2⅝" × 1⅜". Courtesy of Hancock Shaker Village.)

ABOVE: There is scant evidence for basket making at either of the two Enfield villages—Connecticut or New Hampshire—yet there is good reason to believe that these came from one or the other, for both have convincing provenances. The rectangular basket is unusual for any Shaker basket because its rims are made from cane rather than black ash. Written in pencil in several places on the bottom are the following: "Shoe Makers Shop," "1852," "Enfield, N.H.," and "Herb . . . 1860." At one time it had a cloth lining on the bottom; retaining threads remain. It was formerly in the collection of the town historian for Lebanon, New Hampshire, Robert Leavitt.

(Black ash and cane, 9½" × 16⅞" × 12". Miller Collection.)

RIGHT: This square-to-round basket was part of the Copley-Lyman Family collection that passed on to Clarissa Stow. Her grandparents, Clarissa Kezia Lyman and John W. R. Copley, were long-time members at Enfield, Connecticut, who departed in order to marry only days after each left separately. Naturally, that caused quite a scandal.[2] The basket's openwork bottom indicates it would have been used to gather and hold lightweight material, such as field herbs, which require air circulation.

(Black ash, 12⅝" × 9⅝". Miller Collection.)

Also illustrated in *Shaker Baskets* (Fig. 327) is this large utility basket from Sabbathday Lake, Maine. It was constructed with all but one of the uprights split at the bottom, thereby making for an odd number. When the the horizontal splints—"weavers"—were woven from the bottom up, a twilled pattern resulted. While this might add a measure of overall strength (and beauty) to the basket, it was not a usual Shaker practice. The initials "PAS" penciled on the bottom stood for Eldress Prudence A. Stickney (1860–1950).

(Black ash, 12" × 19". Miller Collection.)

Perhaps the most "classic" shape for a Shaker basket is the so-called "cat's head." It is a square-to-round basket and when inverted, the corners are said to resemble a cat's ears. These were made in large numbers at New Lebanon for decades during the mid-1800s. Wetherbee and Taylor refer to them as "utilitarian art." The handles have a sculptural quality with tight curves at the top, sharp edges, a smooth underside, and a satin-smooth finish. The rims are generally double-wrapped to firmly secure the handle.

(Black ash, 15⅝" × 15". Courtesy of Hancock Shaker Village.)

This fan straddles two Shaker worlds—basketry and fancy goods. It is considered here because it is made of black ash splint rather than woven poplar. The pattern used is called "quatrefoil," a form based on the four-leaf clover. Among Shakers, this form was unique to New Lebanon. Again quoting from Wetherbee and Taylor: "The quatrefoil was emblematic of the Shaker vision of a radiant heavenly sphere; it was a graphic signature. [It] is the embodiment of what made the Shaker system 'Shaker.' It united system and soul."[3] (These are the concluding words of their definitive *Shaker Baskets*.) Here, a quatrefoil-centered round is affixed to a maple handle to make an attractive fan.

(Black ash and maple, 11" × 7⅞". Miller Collection.)

This ingenious device shaved black ash basket-making splint to any desired thickness. As long as the blade was kept razor sharp, the silken finish that Shaker baskets are known for was assured. In order to attain this smoothness on both sides, the splint had to pass through twice—top and bottom. The sides of the two threaded screws are flattened to allow for a better grip when adjusting.

(Cherry, pine, and ash with iron, 11⅛" × 5" × 9". Courtesy of Hancock Shaker Village.)

6
Cooperage

M. STEPHEN MILLER

THE SHAKERS' MAJOR CONTRIBUTION to the broad arena of cooperage—staved and bound vessels—was in their refining of these products rather than in the field of invention. For the most part, they took advantage of available craft practices and technologies, adapted and improved some of them, and developed the fine details of construction and finish that distinguishes their work from that done in the World in the nineteenth century.

The earliest production of coopers' ware at New Lebanon took place by 1790, only a few years after that community was formally organized. It is very likely that men who had been coopers in the World continued their trade at the other Shaker communities that were gathered at around the same time but only New Lebanon's output is well documented. The forms that were made there included pails, firkins (whose bottom is wider than its top), tubs, keelers (shallow tubs), churns, casks, and barrels. Large quantities were made into the 1830s after which time most cooperage there was made for "home use" rather than for sale. (The Shakers generally used the term pail rather than bucket for this familiar form, preferring to call vessels for applesauce and maple syrup buckets: but, this distinction was not consistent.)

What is significant about early Shaker coopering is that it was not easily distinguishable from that made in the World though not enough of either survives to say this definitively. The Shakers did add some refinements that were probably not found in worldly cooperage. For example, the top edges of the two longer staves, to which the handle was attached, had their outer edges heavily chamfered (or beveled) to prevent the end grain from splitting-out. Also, the handles were carefully finished with fine wood files, with a flat outer surface and a smooth half-round inner surface, making pails more comfortable to carry when filled.

The more notable refinements took place at the two New Hampshire communities, Canterbury and Enfield, a decade or two after New Lebanon's production ceased in the early 1840s.[1] Canterbury only made pails and, other than modest variations in size, the only real difference in their output was that some pails had lids and some did not. Pails made there *always* have staves whose edges are shaped into a "v." (This is called "matching" the edges.) Earlier cooperage, both Shaker and non-Shaker, had staves with flat or butted edges. Cooper ware is made watertight by the simple principle that when wood comes in contact with moisture it expands across its grain. Thus, staves are always formed with the grain of the wood running vertically, insuring that when they will swell laterally, the piece will be tighter. Shaping the edges of staves allowed them to be interlocked. This increased the surface area of contact and made then even more watertight (or, where the piece was intended to hold dry material, airtight). It also made them more dimensionally stable for the bottoms also swell and shrink across the grain and over time, older pails tend to become elliptical in shape as the staves warp to follow the shape of the bottom.

Canterbury, like New Lebanon, was also making pails in the 1790s, using first horse- and later water-powered turning mills. It is not clear who made the first barrel-stave sawing machine or the first flat and stave planing machines, the Shakers or the World, but all were in use there and at Enfield before 1850. The earlier craft of riving staves from "blanks" of heavy oak or cedar and shaping them with hand tools was extremely labor intensive. With the introduction of commercially made tub lathes at both communities soon after 1850 resulted in cooper wares of pine that today are distinguished for their machined, ultra-smooth finishes. This was not only the result of a mechanical device but was also due to the grade of lumber used for most—clear (knot-free), tight grained, first-growth white pine. Other improvements were introduced for commercially made cooperage but they were all designed to speed-up production rather than to refine the products themselves.

Refinements in hardware, finishes, and handles set Canterbury's pails apart from others. The hoops are of heavier gauge strap iron than was common and they are secured with two rivets rather than the usual one. Also, their ends are always shaped into a "V" rather than cut across on the diagonal and are less likely to snag on clothing. (Diamond-shaped bail plates—metal pieces that are used where the handles are attached to the side of pails, intended to prevent the wood from splitting there—that are often pointed to as an indication of Shaker origin in cooper wares, are not. They are simply the result of a long strip of strap iron that is cut on the diagonal and rotated 90° and are commonly found on worldly pails.) The outsides of all Canterbury pails were covered with a protective coating of paint; the insides sometimes were, too. These paints were deep red, blue, or, most often, some shade of yellow/ocher. Handles were always made from birch wood and turned in either a concave or convex form, chamfered along their outer edges to prevent the splitting-out of the end grain, and often incised with a decorative scribe mark or two. They were also painted in a color that was different from the color of the body of the pail. (Yes, contrary to the myth, Shakers *did* use decoration. The scribe marks on handles were completely non-functional, a subtle and refined form of decoration, and while the use of paint was protective, the use of contrasting colors was purely a decorative flourish.)

Canterbury's coopering output actually declined after its mid-century heyday and by the 1870s was no longer a significant factor in the community's economy. Enfield's business, meanwhile, was on the upswing. One family there, the Second or South, reported making twelve thousand pails in just one year, 1860. A map of the South Family made that year shows a "Pail Factory and Machine-Shop," the only one of the nine buildings to be identified by name.[2] That year, under the leadership of first William Wilson and then Henry Cumings, also marked the ascent of the North Family's cooperage industry.[3] Most of the cooperage that can be identified today as coming from Enfield was made under the latter's leadership, and much of it has impressed into the bottom "N.F. Shakers/ Enfield, N.H." Among the Shaker communities that produced cooper wares, only here was brass occasionally used to bind the staves and as straps and bail plates. Also, only here were enormous quantities of sap buckets made for sale. These had a metal strap fixed to one stave, rather than a handle, so the bucket could be suspended from a spile—a combination of spout and hook—driven into sugar maple trees.

By 1870, cooper wares earned $1,460, twice as much income for the North Family as the next most profitable business, medicinal herbs. In 1876 this number ballooned to five thousand dollars—the equivalent of about $97,000 in 2009 dollars. In 1881, however, Cumings left the Shakers. Pails and other cooperage made from wood were soon to be replaced by ones that were cheaper, more easily stacked and stored, and made from more durable materials—primarily galvanized (tin-coated) steel—and in 1892 the North Family's coopering business closed. It was the last remnant of a Shaker industry started at New Lebanon almost one hundred years earlier. ❧

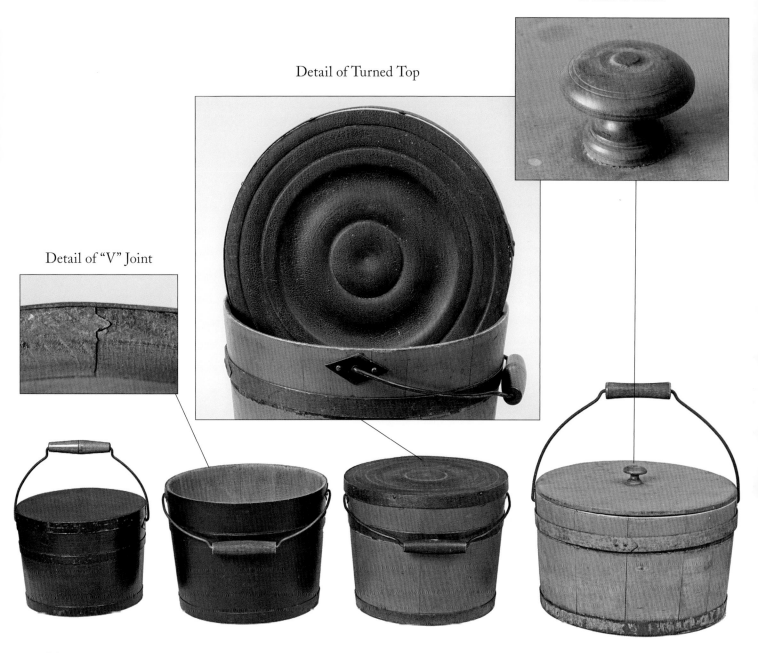

Detail of Turned Top

Detail of Knob

Detail of "V" Joint

These four pails were made at Canterbury in the middle of the nineteenth century. While each has somewhat differing dimensions, colors, and varying features, they all have certain elements in common: heavy gauge iron hoops whose ends are clipped into a "v" shape, clear white pine bodies with birch handles, and v-shaped, tongue-and-grooved staves—most of which is distinctive to Canterbury among the Shaker villages producing cooperage.

The finely turned birch wood knob on the lid of the right pail and the concentric, lathe-turned circular pattern of the lid next to it are but two examples of how the Shakers used refined decorative flourishes on utilitarian woodenwares. The small red pail on the left has the initials "B. H. S." painted under the lid and on the bottom. These stood for New Hampshire's Ministry Elder Benjamin Harrison Smith (1829–1899) and indicate that this pail was a gift to him.

(Pine, birch, and iron, from left to right, 10" × 8¼"; 13" × 10½"; 13¼" × 10¼ "; and 14¼ " × 12¼". Miller Collection.)

Detail of "U" Joint

Enfield, New Hampshire's cooperage industry played a much greater role in the economy there than did Canterbury's. Washtubs were made only at Enfield and, on occasion, brass hardware was substituted for the more usual strap iron. All of the cooper wares from this community have a distinctive u-shaped joint as seen in this detail of the tub's bottom. Also, only at the North Family there did the Shakers identify their work with a stamp impressed in the bottoms of tubs, pails, and sap buckets, such as that seen here.

One thing that nearly all of the cooperage at both communities had in common—except for Enfield's sap buckets, which were relatively inexpensive and turned out in huge quantities—was a highly polished surface. After their wares were assembled, the Shaker coopers placed them on lathes and turned their outsides and insides in order to achieve a smoother, more polished finish. Today, well over one hundred years after these pails and tubs were made, their surfaces often retain a "machined" appearance. (Pine and brass, 12" × 20". Miller Collection.)

Detail of
"NF Shakers/
Enfield, N.H."

Although these four objects *look* like pails, an argument can be made that they are fancy goods instead. They all have staves, a solid bottom, iron hoops, bail plates, and a handle or "bail," just as do those pails made in New Hampshire, but they are of little use as pails. For one thing, most of the few dozen surviving examples are too small for household functions. Even more important, the use of thin strips of hard wood as staves, butted together without the benefit of shaped joinery, renders them incapable of holding liquids.

This genre of cooperage was made at Mount Lebanon sometime after 1875. That was the year that fire destroyed the huge Church Family dwelling house and eight other structures there—all the result of arson. This form of cooperage may have developed as a response to the fire and other financial setbacks the community suffered about that time. A photograph of the gift shop at Mount Lebanon from the last quarter of the nineteenth century shows similar fancy pails suspended from the ceiling, suggesting that they were sales items and were made in some quantity. On the other hand, it has been suggested that they were intended as gifts from one Shaker to another—a practice that became more common as the century wore on.

The woods used include figured maple, walnut, cherry, birch, cedar, and perhaps others that cannot be identified because they are in such small strips. The pails are varnished on the outside and have turned wood handles with identical features: two concave halves separated by a router-formed center groove, heavily beveled ends, four deeply incised lines, and four black-painted lines. All these features are on handles that are only a few inches in length. Shaker manuscript sources attribute their manufacture variously to Brothers Rufus Crosman, Daniel Boler, Giles Avery, all members of the Church Family, and even to "Ministry Sisters." The fact is that we still do not know enough about this genre and its significance to the larger canon of Shaker cooperage.

(Mixed woods and iron, 4" × 6¼"; 4½" × 6½"; 5" × 7½"; 5" × 8¼". Miller Collection.)

Detail of Fancy Pail Handle

This detail from a billhead for the cooperage industry records the sale of 6 sap pails in 1879— two years before Henry Cummings [sic] left the community for the World. It is thought that the term "Second-Growth Pails" referred to the lower quality sap pails.

(Black ink letterpress and manuscript ink on white paper with blue and red linings. Full size 4¾" × 8½". Miller Collection.)

Cooper ware that looks like an upside-down pail is commonly called a firkin. This firkin was made either at New Lebanon or Watervliet, New York, probably the former. The cooperage industry there was developed before 1800 and continued into the 1830s. Although individual wares continued to be made for decades more, wherever they were needed in the community, the Shakers no longer pursued cooperage as an industry. From the beginning, it combined the talents of barrel makers, wood turners, and blacksmiths. This firkin exhibits the best of early Shaker work in this genre; particularly noteworthy are the knob and handle. The knob is a finely turned hardwood that is threaded into the lid, insuring that it will not pull out over time. We have seen similar handles in the chapters on basketry and woodenwares made at New Lebanon. The outer surfaces are flat and the inner ones half-rounded; the surfaces also have an even, dense, "machined" feel that craftsmen achieved by using fine hand tools to finish them. These methods differed from those of the World, where drawknives were used to shape handles.

(Pine, ash, unknown hardwood, and iron, 15" × 12". Courtesy of the Shaker Heritage Society.)

7
Shaker Textiles
Cloak Making

SHARON DUANE KOOMLER

JUST AS THEY HAVE BEEN in other commercial endeavors, Shakers were inventive, creative, and economical in their textile industries. Nowhere were these traits more evident than in the cloak industry. Men and women have commonly worn cloaks as outerwear for centuries, but in the hands of Shaker sisters they were refined in design and construction and became, for worldly buyers, "special."

Many of the Shakers' communal industries were initiated as a result of interest from the World in products that the Shakers made and used themselves. Shaker sisters commonly wore cloaks as the weather required and, during much of the nineteenth century, they also produced the fabric used in making those cloaks. Their cloak industry began as women from the World admired the sisters' cloaks and requested that similar ones be made for them. Although Shaker sisters did not regularly mingle with non-Shaker women, they had many opportunities to be seen by or interact with them. Certainly those coming to do business with the Shakers or to attend a Sunday worship meeting saw the sisters in their own villages. During the last quarter of the nineteenth century, sisters often traveled to resorts along the eastern seaboard and in the mountains of New England, as well as to hotels in larger cities, to offer their "fancy goods" for sale. These were just a few of the ways in which the World's women could encounter the sisters, and their clothing, especially outerwear.

As interest in acquiring Shaker cloaks grew, their cloak-making became more stylized and standardized. Oral history indicates that the cloak industry began at Canterbury, New Hampshire, where Eldress Dorothy Durgin created the well-known cloak design around 1890 and had it trademarked under the "Hart & Shepard" name in 1903. That design became commonly known as "The Dorothy," and by that time the industry was already well-established. Records of cloak sales at Mount Lebanon, New York, date from as early as 1888.[1] At Mount Lebanon the Shakers applied for a trademark for "Long Cloaks" in the name of E. J. Neale & Co. on September 20, 1901. That trademark was granted on November 26, 1901.[2] Shaker enthusiasts commonly refer to *all* Shaker cloaks by the generic term "Dorothy" cloaks.

At Mount Lebanon, sisters worked at cloak-making for themselves as the community's needs required. It is likely that the cloaks made for their own

4 silk bookmarks. (Silk on cardboard with gold letterpress printing, overall 8" x 4¼". Miller Collection)

use did not reflect the wider range of colors, or the flourish of detail, used in later versions produced for the World. A record of wool processed and what it was used for includes a notation in 1856 for forty-one pounds of "cloaking — stained in the butternut dye," a reddish-brown color commonly used in nineteenth-century Shaker clothing.[3] Similar amounts of woolen cloth in that color were listed annually during that decade. In the absence of any accounting records for cloak sales during that period, it is probably safe to assume that cloak material made around mid-century was for crafting cloaks worn by the sisters.

Mount Lebanon's cloak-making became an economic endeavor beginning in the late 1880s, first under the direction of Sister Clarissa Jacobs (1833–1905), and after 1899 under the leadership of Trustee Emma J. Neale (1847–1943). So significant was the activity there that the work was regularly noted in Church Family domestic records. ". . . Sisters driving the cloak building or making nearly day & night . . ." "Sisters driving the cloak business" "Sisters driving away on cloaks"[4] In 1894 the Deaconess's Journal of the Church Family noted at the end of the year that 237 days had been devoted to cloak-making; in 1895 three sisters worked 112 days on cloaks; in 1896 the end-of-year notes commented that the sisters continued working "on the cloaks which are now in demand." The only time cloak-making was not mentioned was during months of activity requiring intense labors from everyone in the community. For example, in October 1892 there are no entries for cloak-making but almost daily comment on the sisters' attention to working at the apple harvest.[5] Although Mount Lebanon's cloak industry was centered at the Church Family, the business was sometimes so brisk that North Family Shakers were hired to make cloaks for the Church Family.[6]

An order book, begun in 1888, recorded cloaks shipped from Mount Lebanon to more than twenty states from Maine to Colorado, and to England.[7] From the beginning, Eldress Emma J. Neale was actively involved in the industry at Mount Lebanon, traveling to the Russell Woolen Factory in Pittsfield, Massachusetts, to acquire fabric in 1892, promoting sales in 1894, and securing exhibition space for the Shakers to display their work at the Woman's Industrial Exposition in Madison Square, New York City, in 1902.[8]

Many observers believe that Shakers kept their personal appearance drab and uniform, yet nothing

Six colors of cloaks (Courtesy of The Shaker Museum and Library)

could be further from the truth. Witness the array of colors used in the cloaks—reds, blues, greens, browns, grays, purple, black, tan, and white. The Russell Woolen Factory was the source for much of the fabric used in Mount Lebanon's commercial cloak-making.[9] Cloaks were most often made to order from information submitted on printed forms that allowed specific measurements to be considered. Requests for repairs to cloaks were honored "from January to September only." [10]

Those beautiful, elegant cloaks were worn by women from many walks of life. Probably the most famous cloak story is that told by Mrs. Eloise Myers in her unpublished 1966 manuscript, "Recollections of My Friends, The Shakers." Eloise recalls a visit with Eldress Emma Neale during which she asked if the Eldress had a cloak available for sale. The Eldress produced a "beautiful grey Shaker cloak" and told Eloise its history. The cloak had been made by Sister Clarissa Jacobs for Mrs. Grover Cleveland to wear to her husband's inauguration as president of the United States.[11] Once it was finished, a flaw was discovered—a small, barely noticeable scorch in the fabric. Eldress Emma explained that they could not sell an imperfect cloak, so another was quickly made for Mrs. Cleveland. Nevertheless, at Mrs. Myers' urgent request, the Eldress agreed to sell her the imperfect Cleveland cloak.

A very interesting, though not unexpected, offshoot of the cloak industry was the dressing of dolls in Shaker clothing. Miniature Shaker dresses, cloaks, and bonnets were made from the remnants of those industries and were designed to fit dolls of various sizes. Shakers sold the dolls at gift stores within their communities, on sales trips, and through their published catalogs. In 1893, the Church Family Deaconess noted, "we make three doz miniature cloaks."[12] Examination of existing dolls, originating from Mount Lebanon and Watervliet, New York,

Hancock, Massachusetts, Canterbury, New Hampshire, and Sabbathday Lake, Maine, reveals doll cloaks made from the same fabrics used in the cloak-making industries in those communities. The design of the doll cloaks is clearly related to that of those constructed for women, but without linings, pockets, or the finer details often seen in the hoods.

Another ingenious use of remnants from the cloak industry was the employment of that material for making the skirts of penwipe dolls. Certainly a less well documented activity in Shaker manuscripts, but one visible in photographic images of sales rooms of Shaker gift shops, are penwipe dolls. These were part of the larger "penwiper" category of Victorian fancy goods; the soft folds of the absorbent wool fabric in the doll skirts were used to blot excess ink from fountain pens. They required just a few pieces of fabric, often assembled in alternating colors and utilizing even the smallest remnants from cloak-making. These were combined with feet, arms, torso, and head (with hand-painted features) made of bisque. Penwipe dolls were made and sold well into the twentieth century in most of the communities where cloaks were made.

Two dolls (Wool broadcloth, bisque, and lace, h-2½" diam. 2½". Miller Collection)

There was no momentous closure of cloak making industries at Shaker communities. Declining requests for cloaks and fewer hands to make them led to the demise of the business. Special requests continued to be accepted from time to time, even to the middle of the twentieth century, by sisters at Canterbury and Sabbathday Lake. 🌿

LEFT: Anna Delcheff (1889–left 1928) was born in Bulgaria and joined the Hancock community in 1901. It is believed she modeled this beautiful cloak, made at nearby Mount Lebanon, around 1910. It is said that she wanted to send it to an ill brother in Bulgaria.[13] (Studio photograph mounted on card stock, image size 9" × 6". Courtesy of Hancock Shaker Village.)

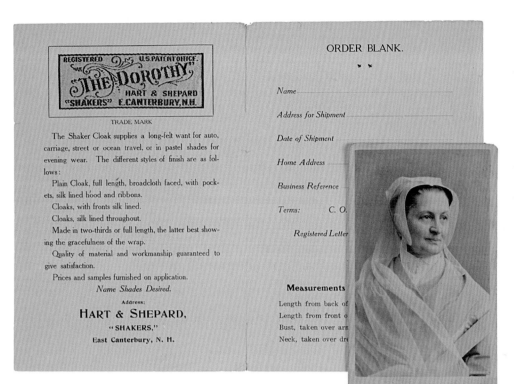

Along with Mount Lebanon, Canterbury was a center for cloak manufacturing from the last decade of the nineteenth century until the early 1940s. As Sharon Koomler indicated in her essay, the question of which community originated the cloak industry is still an open one; while Mount Lebanon sold cloaks earlier, it is unknown whether these were representative of an industry—with standardization, division of labor, and a marketing strategy. What is known is that Mount Lebanon received trademark protection for their design two years before Canterbury received it for "The Dorothy" (named in honor of Eldress Dorothy Durgin, 1825–1898). Illustrated here is the gathered hood for a fawn colored "Dorothy" cloak and a close-up of the silk label affixed inside every one sold. (Wool broadcloth, full length-55". Miller Collection.)

This order blank offers numerous options: "Plain . . . with fronts silk lined . . . silk lined throughout . . . two-thirds or full lengths, the latter showing the gracefulness of the wrap." As with all Shaker-made products, it stipulated: "Quality of material and workmanship guaranteed to give satisfaction." Included on the form are instructions for how and where women were to take measurements. Accompanying this form is an undated photograph of Eldress Dorothy Durgin. (Form: black ink letterpress on stiff white paper [and, verso, photoengravings of modeled cloaks], 5¾" × 8" and *carte de visite*, 4⅛" × 2½". Miller Collection.)

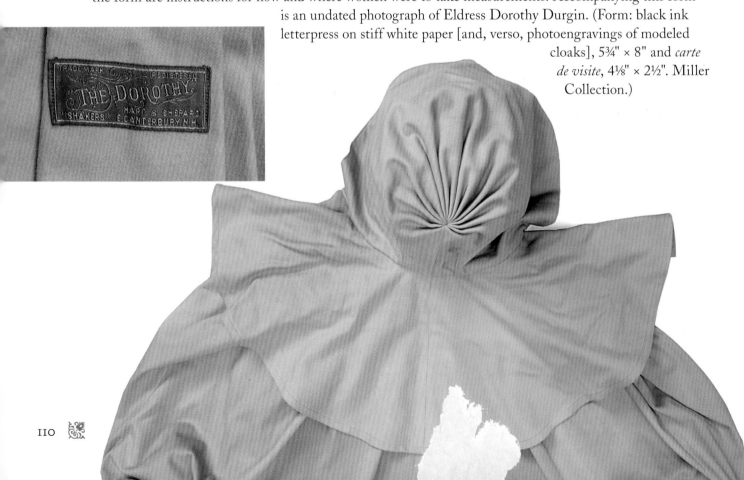

Canterbury's special contribution to this industry was the production of children's cloaks (sometimes referred to, when lacking hoods, as "capes"). These were available for infants in a "6 month size, hood lined" in pink, white, and blue silk. They sold, in ca. 1920, for $5.00—about $54.00 in 2009 dollars.

The illustrated catalog also notes that children's capes were offered with silk lining throughout for an additional three dollars. The example here, in bright "Little Red Riding Hood" red,

Children's Capes

Furnished in the popular shades

☐

INFANTS' CAPES

Made in best quality white broadcloth.

First size and 1 year . . $5.00
(Hood lined with white, pink or blue silk.)

Lined throughout with silk $3.00 extra

has a rayon bow and gathered hood that is lined in rayon; a semi-synthetic fabric first produced in 1891 from regenerated plant fibers—cellulose.

(Cloak: red wool broadcloth and rayon, l- 24" and order form, black ink letterpress on stiff white paper [unfolded size] 4½" × 10½". Miller Collection.)

By 1850 if not earlier, every one of the true industries the Shakers created required a marketing strategy. No matter how highly regarded the products of their lands and hands are today, in their time they had to be promoted. Illustrated here are three formats used by Canterbury for marketing cloaks. Below is a simple billhead from about 1930 that records the sale of a "Dorothy" cloak but also calls attention to "unique gifts and home-made fancy articles"—much more about these in chapter 9. This pre-printed letter [right] that responds to "Your favor with inquiry concerning 'The Dorothy' or Shaker Cloak duly received." It goes on to enumerate options and prices. Sisters Emmeline Hart (1834–1914) and Lucy Shepard (1836–1926) were responsible for developing this industry and their names were used long after their deaths, a common Shaker practice of venerating past Believers. This simple broadside, undated but probably circulated in

Telephone, ⎫ Concord, N. H.
Telegraph, ⎭

HART & SHEPARD
Manufacturers of SHAKER CLOAKS

East Canterbury, N. H.,_____191____

Esteemed Friend:

Your favor with inquiry concerning ''The Dorothy'' or Shaker Cloak duly received. Under separate cover we are sending samples of material. Prices affixed are for the usual style or plain cloak with broadcloth facings and pockets, silk-lined hood and streamers. A desirable finish is given by lining the shoulder cape with silk; cost, $2.00 extra.

An additional charge of $ for Cloaks with silk-lined fronts and $ for Cloaks silk-lined throughout.

Enclosed please find order blank giving general directions and required measurements.

In favoring us with your order, kindly state if we shall ship the Cloak express C. O. D. with privilege of examination, or if you choose to remit by check, the Cloak to be sent parcel post.

Children's Cloaks, ''The Dorothy'' style, furnished in the general shades. Infants' Cloaks in white, pink and blue, a specialty, as follows:

Infants', 6 mo. size, hood lined............	$2.00 and $3.00
Infants', 1 yr. size, hood lined............	3.00 and 4.00
Infants', 6 mo. size, lined throughout	4.00 and 5.00
Infants', 1 yr. size, lined throughout	5.00 and 6.00

Awaiting your valued order, we are

Cordially yours,

Hart & Shepard.
(Shaker Sisters.)

EXHIBIT & SALE
BY THE
SHAKERS
From East Canterbury, N. H.
OF THEIR
Fancy Goods and Shaker Capes

the 1930s, would have been posted at a location away from the community. In the later nineteenth and early twentieth centuries, it was common for brothers and sisters from Canterbury (and Sabbathday Lake) to undertake sales trips to seaside or mountain resorts and fairs throughout New England. There, a variety of garments, fancy goods, and foodstuffs were offered for sale.

(Billhead [below]: black ink letterpress on red and blue ruled white paper, 5¾" × 8½"; letter [above]: black ink letterpress and lithography on white paper, 10½" × 8"; broadside: black ink letterpress on white paper, 12¼" × 9½". Miller Collection.)

PHONE: Canterbury 801

The CANTERBURY SHAKERS
EAST CANTERBURY, N. H.
MANUFACTURERS OF
''*Dorothy*'' *Shaker Capes*
IN SIZES FOR LADIES, MISSES AND INFANTS
UNIQUE GIFTS AND HOME-MADE FANCY ARTICLES

Sold to_____

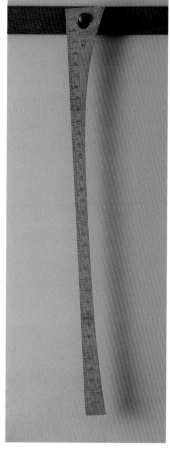

The first sister to be appointed chief cloak maker at Mount Lebanon was Clarissa Jacobs (1833–1905). Illustrated is her three-tiered workbox, with her name label pasted inside, and some of the tools she used. The mallet and chisel were used to make button holes, the awl to puncture the material for sewing buttons, and the spiked wheel for tracing around a paper pattern laid atop a bolt of material (usually French wool broadcloth) to allow for accurate cutting. Sister Emma J Neale (1847–1943) succeeded her in 1899.

(Box: hickory, elm, and poplar, 6" × 10"; tools: various woods and iron, mallet l- 9½". Miller Collection.)

Curved tailoring rules were probably a Shaker innovation originating at Mount Lebanon. Anecdotally, they were made to conform to the curvature of a body (although the numbers conform to the straight, not the curved, edge of the wood.) Brother James X. Smith made this in 1877 for an unknown Shaker, "R.G." The straight tailoring rule [detail above], a full four and a half feet in length, was made and used at Canterbury in their cloak industry.

(Curved rule: maple, 36" × 3⅝"; straight rule: cherry, 54" × 1½"; broadside: black ink letterpress on white card stock, 14¼" × 19½". Miller Collection.)

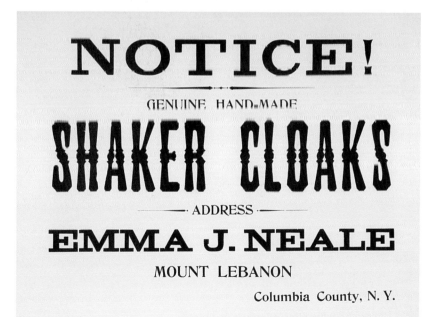

NOTICE!

GENUINE HAND-MADE

SHAKER CLOAKS

— ADDRESS —

EMMA J. NEALE

MOUNT LEBANON

Columbia County, N. Y.

Canterbury initiated another important textile industry in 1886—knitted wool sweaters. They used commercially made machines but produced them in a stitch that has since become known as "Shaker knit." Between 1886 and 1923 when the business was terminated, many thousands of sweaters were sold: 1,489 in 1910 alone. At that time the most expensive examples sold for $7.50 apiece. They were available in four weights, from light to extra heavy, and a limited number of colors. The Shakers based most of the colors on the Ivy League schools to which they marketed them, hence the Dartmouth green and Harvard crimson illustrated here. They also made them in several styles: shawl collar, turtleneck, and v-neck.

(Green: wool and leather, l- 33"; white: wool and mother-of-pearl, l- 28"; red: wool, l- 30". Miller Collection.)

This cardboard box was intended to package sweaters, but garments of the heaviest weight would have been too bulky to fit in it. The sisters at Canterbury recycled this example, for written in pencil across the top is "neckerchiefs and collars." The advertising bi-fold, shown front and back, is dated 1910. Added in ink is "Terms COD or prepayment," indicating that evidently even the Shakers had problems with accounts receivable. The two sweater samples are for # 0 ("Extra Heavy Weight") and # 3 ("Light Weight").

(Box: blue ink letterpress on cardboard, 2¾" × 17¼" × 11"; brochure: 6" × 9⅛"; wool and cardboard samples, approx. 3½" × 2". Miller Collection.)

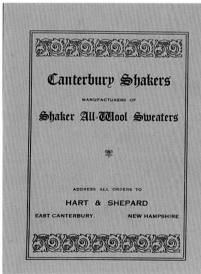

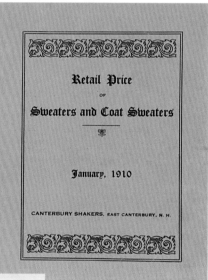

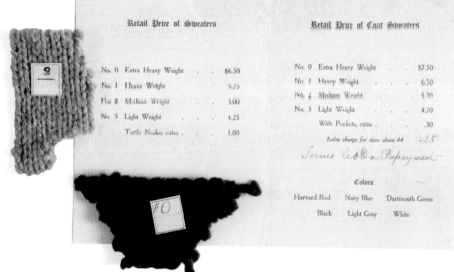

A true innovation thought to have originated at Sabbathday Lake was a process for making fabric wrinkle resistant and water repellent. Beverly Gordon writes in *Shaker Textile Arts*: "They put cotton or wool fabric into a special press with paper that had been treated with zinc chloride, and applied heat and pressure."[14] The bolt of fabric illustrated here is from Canterbury and is composed of very fine blue and red wool fibers, combined to form an overall purplish-colored cloth. (Treated wool: 38" × 12'. Miller Collection.)

In 1884, a few sisters and brothers at Mount Lebanon started a small business making gloves from the fur of raccoons, and spun with silk fibers. One brother was recorded making a trip to Michigan in 1888 to buy "Coon Skins," and that summer three hundred pairs were made. The last reference to the business is 1898. The woven linen label was presumably sewn inside the gloves, though these examples do not have them.

(Gloves: Raccoon fur and silk, l- 9". Courtesy of the Shaker Museum and Library; Label, black ink letterpress on off-white linen, 2" × 4". Miller Collection.)

THE ONLY GENUINE
COON FUR & SILK GLOVES
MADE BY THE **SHAKERS** AT
MOUNT LEBANON.
SAM'L BUDD,
MADISON SQR., N. Y.,
SOLE AGENT FOR THE U. S.

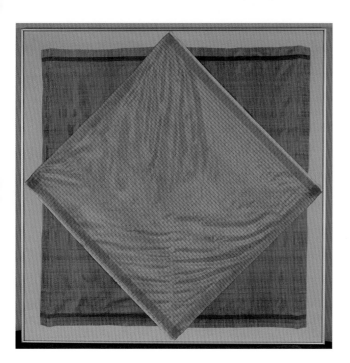

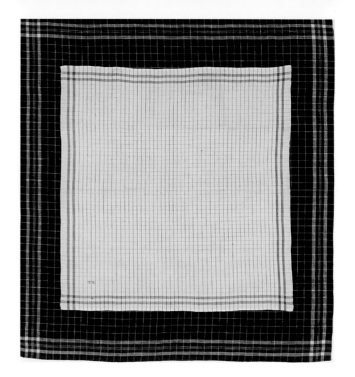

Every Shaker sister had linen and/or silk scarves that she wore for various occasions, from everyday work to Sunday meeting. Although most of the fabric the Shakers used after the middle of the nineteenth century was made in the World, they did make all of their scarves, including weaving the fabrics for them. An entire silk culture industry was developed in the western Shaker communities to meet the needs for scarves and other items. This involved cultivating silkworms and planting mulberry trees to feed them; harvesting their cocoons; unwinding ("reeling") the silk into single, long fibers; and dying and weaving them. It was a labor-intensive endeavor. (Andrews, in *The Community Industries of the Shakers*, wrote that a Brother Abner Bedell of Union Village, Ohio invented a silk reeling machine but no other information about this is known, as it was not patented.)

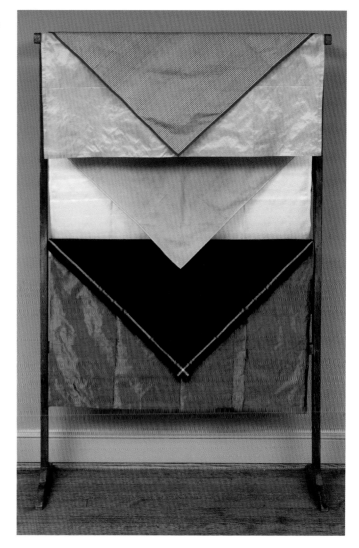

Shakers at most if not all communities wove textiles from home-grown linen, wool, cotton, and silk—often combining two types of fiber in one fabric. This activity began at the time the communities were first organized and continued at some level and in some form into the twentieth century. Illustrated here are a variety of silk and linen scarves that were worn by sisters but not necessarily made by them or even made by their own community—the silk ones worn in the East were made in the West. The tall drying rack on which a number of these are hanging (for display purposes) was almost surely intended for another purpose—to hang damp towels or washrags. The other scarves, two of silk [top left] and two of linen [top right], are other examples of this signature article of Shaker women's attire.

(All textiles: Miller Collection.)

Shakers also wove their own wool blankets. Since the sect numbered almost five thousand members at its peak in the mid-1850s, one can easily imagine how many blankets were needed to see all of them through a winter night. Yet, surprisingly few of these have survived. The three examples above came from New Lebanon and were probably woven there. One is initialed in pink silk cross-stitch "C.D." but otherwise all three are identical.

(Blankets: wool, 78" × 61". Miller Collection.)

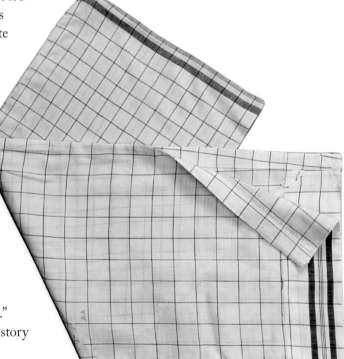

The regular practice of thrift led many sisters to adapt remnants to new purposes. The white with blue remnant or laundry or "rag" bag appears to have been made up from several discarded white cotton scarves with blue trim. The linen "pocket" [left] is something of an anomaly—for Shaker sisters generally had no need to carry small items with them in their daily work. Both textiles have the initials sewn in cross-stitching on them: sister "R S" [left] and "A.A." [right] have not yet been identified; the pocket has a history of coming from the Harvard community.

(Pocket [left]: linen with cotton string, 5½" × 4½" and Bag [right]: cotton, 27¾" × 10½". Miller Collection.)

In addition to their innovative work with fabrics, the Shakers developed a number of sewing accessories, some of which were made for sale and others for their own use. These three pincushions with "disc clamps" were a Canterbury Shaker innovation that they called "screwballs." They are extraordinary examples of woodworking art. Each is made from only two pieces of wood—a long threaded and shaped shaft that includes two wide platforms, one supporting a pincushion and the other forming the upper disk of the clamp. A second turned piece rotates on the threaded shaft to secure the device to a tabletop. There may be no better example of a Shaker brother's skill at the lathe than these humble pieces, yet this work cannot be considered an industry, for no two of the relatively few surviving examples seem to have the same dimensions. (Maple and wool with wood shavings: left to right, 6½" × 2⅝"; 7" × 2¼"; and 10¼" × 5". Miller Collection.)

The two pincushions [right] do seem to have been part of a small-scale business, for they were produced in the two standardized sizes seen here. Making them also required a reasonably high degree of lathe skills, but almost surely "jigs"—devices for controlling and shaping the woodcutting—were used. It is thought that this type of pincushion was part of the industry at Hancock that produced collapsible swifts (see Chapter 12) but no documentation of this has been found. (Maple and wool with wood shavings, 8¾" × 3⅛" and 10½" × 3½". Miller Collection.)

These two spool holders were made at and used by the sisters at Enfield, Connecticut. The taller example also exhibits very fine lathe work and has iron pins that hold 27 exquisitely turned spools, many of which still have their old silk threads attached. It descended through that community's Copley and Lyman families to granddaughter Clarissa Stow, a non-Shaker. The lower example belonged to another member of that family, Sister Sarah Maria Lyman (1833–1918). Each stand was designed to suit a specific need, be it the ability of the spools on the upper disk to be rotated or narrow profile of the other to fit into a confined space. (Left: cherry with iron rods and maple and cherry spools, 8¾" × 6¼" and walnut and iron rods, 1–10". Miller Collection.)

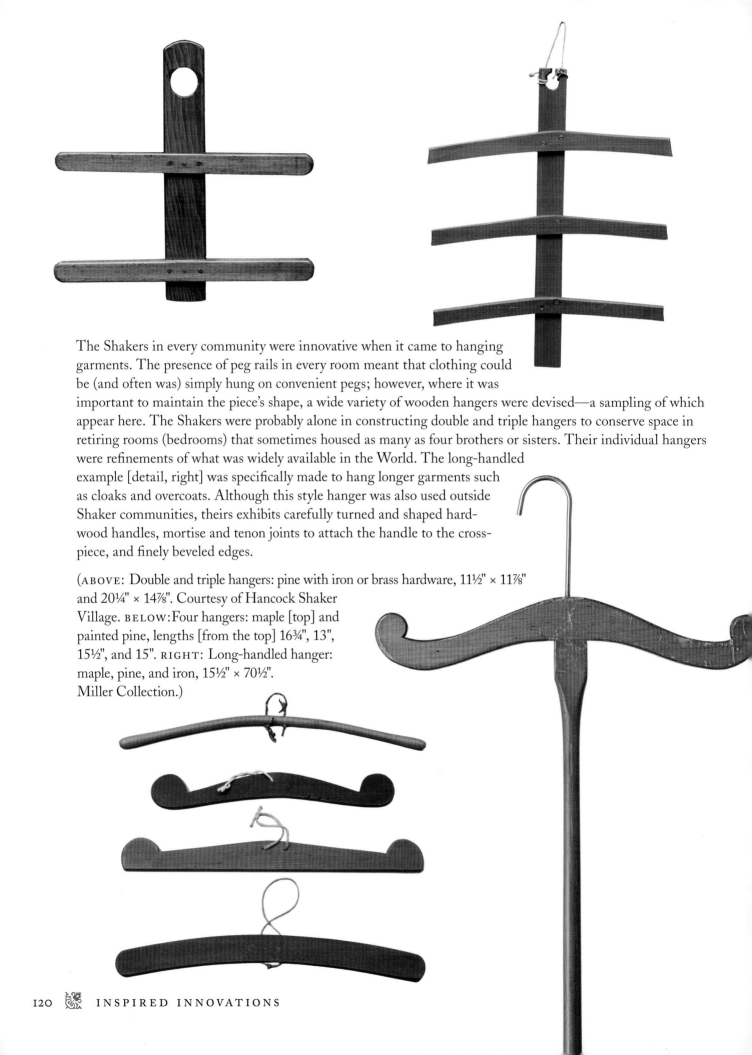

The Shakers in every community were innovative when it came to hanging garments. The presence of peg rails in every room meant that clothing could be (and often was) simply hung on convenient pegs; however, where it was important to maintain the piece's shape, a wide variety of wooden hangers were devised—a sampling of which appear here. The Shakers were probably alone in constructing double and triple hangers to conserve space in retiring rooms (bedrooms) that sometimes housed as many as four brothers or sisters. Their individual hangers were refinements of what was widely available in the World. The long-handled example [detail, right] was specifically made to hang longer garments such as cloaks and overcoats. Although this style hanger was also used outside Shaker communities, theirs exhibits carefully turned and shaped hard-wood handles, mortise and tenon joints to attach the handle to the cross-piece, and finely beveled edges.

(ABOVE: Double and triple hangers: pine with iron or brass hardware, 11½" × 11⅞" and 20¼" × 14⅞". Courtesy of Hancock Shaker Village. BELOW: Four hangers: maple [top] and painted pine, lengths [from the top] 16¾", 13", 15½", and 15". RIGHT: Long-handled hanger: maple, pine, and iron, 15½" × 70½". Miller Collection.)

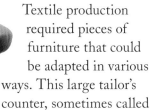

Textile production required pieces of furniture that could be adapted in various ways. This large tailor's counter, sometimes called simply a "counter," is notable for several reasons. It has a large work surface, one that can be increased by raising a hinged leaf on the back. There are also large drawers to accommodate bolts of fabrics and the tools for making them into finished garments. Finally, another Shaker innovation: the presence of drawers facing in another direction so that smaller tools, buttons, or fasteners could be reached while another Shaker was working in the front. Tailoring counters were used in most communities, but their shapes, sizes, and arrangement of working/storage spaces varied greatly. At Canterbury they were very large and usually had shaped bases. At Hancock and Enfield, Connecticut, they were modest in size and usually sat on a base with legs. At New Lebanon and Watervliet, counters tended to rest directly on the floor, as does this example. (Pine with hardwood knobs and iron hardware, 32½" × 86" × 32⅝" [without leaf]. Courtesy of Hancock Shaker Village.)

The exact use for this Shaker tall stool is unknown, though it typifies the sort of seating piece that could have been used in association with the counter. The threaded iron post fits into an iron collar that allows the seat to be raised or lowered. Wear on the maple rungs is a sign of heavy use over the years. The leather seat is a late replacement. (Birch, maple, and pine with iron hardware and leather, 33" × 18". Miller Collection.)

In addition to a high stool, a variety of seating pieces could have been found in a typical Shaker sewing room. Two likely examples are the "revolver" and low-seated "sister's" chair. The former was a Shaker innovation developed at Mount Lebanon in 1860. As Charles Muller and Timothy Rieman tell it in *The Shaker Chair*, forty-eight of these were made in 1863.[15] All seem to have been made solely for community use. A cast metal mechanism, similar to that found in the high stool, allows the seat to move up and down. Several similar forms eventually were made—one style with narrow iron spindles replacing the turned and steam-bent ones—but none was more simply elegant than this style. The chair [below], sometimes called a sister's chair due to its relatively diminutive size and low seat, was an earlier seating type, circa 1840, that will be addressed further in Chapter 12, for its most distinctive feature is the presence of tilter buttons on the bottom of the rear posts.

(RIGHT: Revolver: maple, pine, and cherry with iron hardware, 27" × 15" and LEFT: chair: maple and cotton tapes, 38¼" × 18" × 14". Miller Collection.)

Sewing steps were another necessity in rooms where sewing was done. There was no single size or design for them, but they were all simple affairs. Sisters used them by placing one foot on either of the treads so that they could rest their work against the upper portion of their leg while sewing. This, of course, was done in the World as well. The significant difference is that Shaker craftsmen pared theirs down to the most basic elements—often two vertical slab sides, two treads, and a single back brace. (BELOW: Pine: 8¼" × 10¼" × 8¾". Courtesy of the Art Complex Museum.)

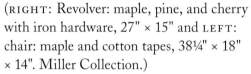

Specialized furniture for sewing tasks became popular items in most of the Shaker communities in the northeast in the second half of the nineteenth century. The brethren made these objects for the sisters and the sisters used them, at times, to sew items for the brethren. The sewing desk [right] is quite typical of the kind made in the Maine and New Hampshire communities and is from either Canterbury or Enfield, New Hampshire, circa 1860. Most of these desks use frame-and-panel construction on legs with a gallery of smaller drawers (and sometimes a cabinet) above a counter top. Below the top is usually a board that can be pulled out for additional working surface, and below that is a series of drawers, often of unequal sizes. The most distinctive feature of many, however, is the arrangement of side-facing drawers that allowed two sisters to work simultaneously.

(RIGHT: Figured maple and pine with fruitwood knobs, 38" × 30½" × 25¾". Courtesy of Hancock Shaker Village.)

Innovation meant improvement through adaptation. That was the case with this sewing table from Enfield, New Hampshire. First there was only a simple birch wood table. Its slender legs with a delicate "ring" turning at the transition from round to square, restrained shaped skirt, and one-board top all indicate that it was made during the "classic" period at Enfield, 1820–1840. Then, to make it more useful for another function, probably sewing, a pine "add-on" was created for the top and a narrow molding was added to keep it in place. This happened some time after 1850. Except for the top surface of the table, the piece retains its original brick red paint, a color often seen on Enfield furniture.

(LEFT: Birch and pine: 40" × 20¼" × 30½". Miller Collection.)

8
Shaker Chairs

Charles R. Muller

"The Shakers were pioneers in the [chair] business, and perhaps the very first to engage in the business after the establishment of the independence of the country. . . . The year 1876 is the centennial year of the first Shaker settlement in this country, and the commencement of our chair business is recorded back to this date." (1876 Shaker chair catalog)

Although chair businesses were active and advertised in Williamsburg, Virginia, as early as 1745 and in Philadelphia and New York shortly thereafter, the Shakers can certainly be credited as one of the longest, most successful and innovative producers of seating furniture.[1] Most Shaker communities produced chairs for their own use or acquired them from a neighboring community. Documents show that chairs were made and sold to the world from Union Village in 1813, Watervliet, New York, in 1814, Harvard in 1828, Alfred in 1834, and Pleasant Hill in 1843.[2]

New Lebanon sold chairs from 1789 to 1942 and was the largest producer of chairs among the Shaker communities, as they transformed what had been the work of single craftsmen into a manufacturing business. Assembly-line efficiency supplanted individual skills, progressive advertising methods replaced word-of-mouth sales, and multiple options took the place of one-size-fits-all. Just as Shakers refined the design of the simple slat-back chair to make it extremely light and durable, they used innovation to make the chair-making process efficient and very profitable.

An early account book records the presence of a chair-making business at New Lebanon as early as the late nineteenth century. An 1814 record refers to the destruction of "a chair makers shop with a large number of unfinished chairs, stock and tools" on August 28 when streams flooded.[3] The trade of the craftsmen there remained relatively small throughout the first half of the nineteenth century with the 1854 inventory accounting for only 120 chairs,[4] but the Census of Manufactures of New York for 1860 and 1870 reported that production had increased to about six hundred.

In 1872, under the leadership of Brother Robert M. Wagan, New Lebanon constructed a new chair factory that employed ten people and was "expected to finish two doz. Chairs per day. . . . Already they have orders for more than they can furnish."[5] Increased production brought standardization. Sizes were no longer described as "small, "sewing chair," or "common" but were designated with a numbering system (0–7), and workmen introduced the concept of using interchangeable parts for chairs of the same size. Converting chair (and stool) making into an industry also brought increased advertising, with eighteen-page catalogues replacing single-sheet broadsides. Distribution increased beyond the community's store and through sales made from wagons brought to resorts. Soon Shaker chairs could be found in stores from Boston to Burlington, Iowa. Advertisements appeared in such publications as Harper's Weekly, and recognition became widespread with the award of a bronze medal

at the 1876 International Exhibition in Philadelphia. Here, a gold transfer decal was utilized for the first time to distinguish these unique Shaker-made chairs from imitations made and sold by the world.

The New Lebanon order book for February 1884 through March 1885 recorded almost three thousand chairs shipped.[6] In five months beginning in December 1894, more than a hundred chairs and three settees were sent to Marshall Field & Co. of Chicago alone. That company later published its own catalog of Shaker chairs.[7] In 1909 the New Lebanon shop wrote a check for the purchase of ten thousand gold transfer trademarks, a clear indication that business was thriving.[8] When the factory burned in 1923, the need for new equipment coupled with a dwindling workforce meant purchasing more material from outside sources and the slow demise of Shaker chair making.[9]

In discussions of the historic Shakers, the words Shaker and chairs are almost synonymous. Thomas Merton wrote, "The peculiar grace of a Shaker chair is due to the fact that it was made by someone capable of believing that an angel might come and sit on it."[10] Sister Mildred Barker of Sabbathday Lake is often quoted as saying, "I don't want to be remembered as a chair." Nonetheless, the large number of chairs needed to furnish the Shakers' own substantial dwellings and the development of an industry to provide needed income brought forth an abundance of chairs and a thriving business.

Chairs are forms of furniture that lend themselves to the use of interchangeable parts and mass production. While other makers much earlier utilized such methods, the Shakers perfected the idea of diversity within standardization. All Shaker communities constructed ladder-back chairs with open seats, usually covered with thin wooden splint, and turned posts. Yet each community had a turning (pommel or finial) at the top of the post whose shape distinguished it from the work of other communities. At New Lebanon, the decorative pommel varied little over the years. Once an observer learns the slight variations, he or she can readily identify a Shaker-made chair, determine where it was made, and estimate the approximate date of manufacture.

The Shaker chair is especially adaptable for production because there are only four basic parts: vertical posts, horizontal stretchers, horizontal slats, and a seat. As noted in the journals of Brother Freegift Wells, the craftsman might turn back posts one day, front posts another, stretchers on the third; and shape slats on the fourth. He would then assemble the parts and add the seating material.

The division of labor, with the brothers producing the frames and the sisters adding the seats, enhanced the efficiency of the industry. While chair factories in the world were paying women to weave cane chair seats, they also found themselves having to deal with wage demands and work stoppages; the Shakers, in contrast, had a ready, compliant workforce in the sisters.[11]

By the 1880s, the Mount Lebanon Shakers had begun to purchase some chair parts from outside firms, assembling them in their facility, and then "seating" them with purchased cotton braids (or tapes). Although it can be argued that these later products were not really the work of Shaker hands and the finer points of their design were compromised, this market strategy was in its own way innovative. The chair factory mass-produced thousands of chairs over seven or eight decades that were essentially alike in the shape of their frames but varied in size, options available, and the details of their component parts.

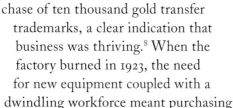

The catalogues offered the chairs in eight different sizes. Additionally, the "Directions for Ordering Chairs" requested that the buyer "State definitely the Arms and rockers. Do you wish both, either, or neither." The buyer should also "State the frame wished, as Mahogany, Ebony, or White (natural) finish." A bar could be added between the posts to hold cushions, and the back could be slatted, cushioned, or fitted with woven tapes. These options provided hundreds of possibilities. Further choices included plush cushions or taped (braided) seats in many different colors. In all, there were more than 100.000 possibilities.[12]

Even with all these choices, the Shakers still filled special requests such as "Seat 1 in. higher than regular" or "The seat to be 20" from the floor or 4" more than the . . . frame old cushion chair."[13] Mount Lebanon accomplished in their chair production what all Shakers achieved in their communities—individualism within uniformity, diversity within homogeny, variation within standardization.

The Shaker originality and adaptation reflected throughout this book can readily be seen in the early rocking chair with wheels added (see Chapter 10). Other examples of improvements are a side chair at Pleasant Hill with "boots" added to the bottoms of the legs to make the seat higher and appropriate for use with a loom; a Union Village dining chair with added wheels for accommodating the handicapped; a simple armless rocker with a drawer beneath for holding sewing implements; and an example from New Lebanon with front posts as tall as the back ones, and stretchers between them at the top, probably for holding blankets to keep drafts off an invalid.

The use of taped or braided seats also reflects Shaker innovation. Like their contemporaries, Shakers used splint or rush for seating in their early chairs. Splint is listed on a 1850s broadside, along with tape at half the price, but does not appear in catalogues after 1870.[14] The sisters at Watervliet were weaving woolen tapes as early as 1814, and Brother Henry DeWitt made "Little spools for to weave tape with."[15] As production grew, tapes were purchased from outside sources. Whereas the world generally used cane, the Shakers preferred seats of colorful wool and later cotton for their own chairs and those for sale to the world. They lent added color to otherwise rather plain furnishings.

Perhaps the most notable example of Shaker ingenuity in chairs is the "button join tilt." Brother Freegift Wells at Watervliet, New York, wrote on September 27, 1819, that he started "to trim off and ball the chairs."[16] The next month he "finished off balling the new chairs." On January 20, 1836, Brother Benjamin Lyon in New Lebanon noted it was "a day to doe chores doe some in the shop at making buttens to put in the bottom of chares poasts (or nubs) to keep from maring the floor."[17] The New Lebanon 1850s price list referred to above included a charge of twenty-five cents for the addition of button joint tilts on ordered chairs.

Correspondence between the leaders of Harvard and Enfield, Connecticut, in 1853 discusses the design of new chairs to be ordered from a company in the world. One letter includes the paragraph: "As to Balls in the back posts, I have heard nothing particular said, but suppose Believers generally will want them as they prevent maring the floor etc. But most likely, we shall have that part to do our selves. But the hind posts will have to be turned suitable for the purposes."[18] It is apparent that ball joint tilts were common on Shaker chairs.

On March 2, 1852, Brother George O. Donnell of New Lebanon received Patent No. 8771 for "Chair Feet," "a new and improved mode of preventing the wear and tear of carpets and the marring of floors, caused by the corners of the back posts of chairs."[19] Whereas previous ball joint tilts were wooden balls inserted into rounded out hollows in back posts and secured with leather thongs, his patent utilized brass ferrules and balls. Today, there are only a few surviving examples of the brass devices and a few made with pewter, but millions of contemporary extruded aluminum institutional chairs utilize this Shaker invention.

An exhibition organized by the Danish Foreign Ministry for the celebration of the 1976 American Bicentennial was entitled "An American Inspiration: Danish Modern and Shaker Design." It recognized the influence of Shaker-inspired design and the use of mass-produced parts in the making of Danish furniture. As the Shakers and their production were declining in the 1920s, their chairs were being discovered anew in a distant land and shaping a new movement in unornamented, elegant, functional furnishings.

For more than 150 years, the Shakers produced seating furniture that was simple, yet refined. Pared down to the minimum, the chairs are strong and serviceable. They add color and design to an otherwise plain room. They inspired Danish Modern, and left a lasting imprint on our society in reproductions and in classroom furnishings. Shaker chairs bear witness to days long ago, a time of simple, honest craftsmanship, while fitting comfortably into our contemporary world.

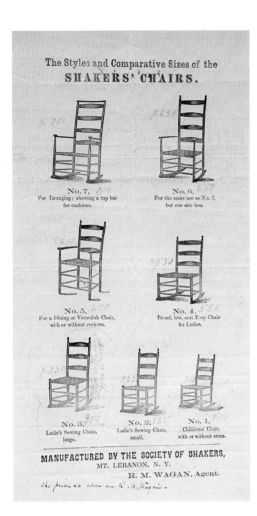

Once chair making at New Lebanon was transformed into a full-blown industry, a number of changes took place, many of them discussed in the introductory essay to this chapter. The images and captions below will illuminate and expand upon the points raised therein.

The hallmark of an industry is standardization. Beginning in about 1867, when this two-sided broadside (or technically, "broadsheet") was printed, chairs made for sale at the South Family of New Lebanon were assigned numbers. This document is the earliest printed evidence of organizing chairs by size and numbering them from # 1, the smallest to # 7, the largest. Handwritten by Elder Robert Wagan, who was in charge of the business, are the prices: they range from $3.00 to $ 7.00. In the early 1870s even smaller straight (without rockers) and rocking chairs were added. They were designated # 0.

(Black ink letterpress and manuscript on white paper, 10" × 5¼". Miller Collection.)

This is a nearly pristine example of a chair made in the 1870s, probably before the use of decals [see following page]. It has the number "6" impressed into the back of the top slat and its original Shaker-woven woolen tapes seating. The rear posts are topped by well-formed acorn-shaped finials. The front posts are far more delicately turned and the "mushroom cap" handholds smaller than one finds on chairs manufactured after about 1880. The general form, though, never changed.

(Maple and wool with dark stain and varnish, 36" × 22" × 19". Miller Collection.)

At about the time of the 1876 Centennial Exhibition in Philadelphia, the Shakers added a gold color decal either to the back of slats or to the inside of rockers on every one of their chairs in order to distinguish them from non-Shaker made look-alikes. This detail of a full sheet of fifty-five decals shows them reversed.

(Gold ink letterpress on clear substance on white paper, each approx. 1½" × 2", full sheet 10" × 24". Miller Collection.)

Once the industry had a new, dedicated factory in 1872, the chairs were marketed aggressively. Beginning in 1874 and continuing for about seven years, a series of chair catalogs was printed, eight different editions, with color variations. This group is representative of their usual exterior appearances with an interior view from one [below] where the # 2 and # 4 chairs are not shown. Some catalogs are illustrated with a card from the time of the 1876 fair [right] "advising" potential customers that "If you want the genuine Shaker Chairs, send your orders to R. M. Wagan, Mount Lebanon."

The Shakers' Slat Back Chairs, with Arms and Rockers.
WORSTED LACE SEATS.
Showing a Comparison of Sizes.

No. 0	No. 1	No. 3	No. 5	No. 6	No. 7
$3.50	$4.00	$5.00	$7.00	$8.00	$8.50

The Shakers' Slat Back Chairs, with Rockers.
WORSTED LACE SEATS.
Showing a Comparison of Sizes.

No. 0	No. 1	No. 3	No. 4	No. 6	No. 7
$3.25	$3.50	$4.50	$7.00	$7.50	$8.00

(Catalogs: black ink letterpress and metal engraving on white and variously color papers, approx. 5" × 3"; card: black ink letterpress on tan card stock, 3" × 5½". Miller Collection.)

Variations on the basic form of a "production" chair were almost limitless. Illustrated here are a # 0 with rockers, arms and taped back; # 1 with rockers, arms, and slat back; # 5 straight chair with arms and a rail intended for suspending a cushion; and an unusual piece, a high chair that was available by special order. Although all of the chairs illustrated have arms and taped seats, no arms and rush seats (made from reeds) offered still more options. There were also choices in finishes, from light (natural) to dark (mahogany), and in the colors of tapes.

(# 0, # 1, and high chair: maple with wool or cotton tapes, 23½" × 12¾" × 10"; 28⅞" × 14⅞" × 17"; 35½" × 17⅛" × 16½". Courtesy of Hancock Shaker Village and # 5 [left]: maple with cotton tapes, 36" × 22" × 19". Miller Collection.)

Along with the production of chairs
from New Lebanon's South Family was
the production of footstools. These apparently were first offered for sale in the early 1870s and
appear in all of the chair catalogs. The advertisement above is from
the catalog illustrated on the first page of this chapter. It shows an upholstered
example of the low stool and lists its cost as $2.75. Illustrated nearby is a rare surviving example of this same
type. Other chair catalogs illustrate this kind of stool without a cushion—it sold for $1.00 (and many examples
of it may be found today). The 1876 *Centennial Illustrated Catalogue,* issued to correspond with the extensive display of Shaker production chairs at the fair in Philadelphia, has this to say about these stools: "This pattern for
foot bench has superceded all others which we have ever made, and we have adopted it as a specialty."

(Image from p. 13 of a chair catalog listed in Richmond's *Bibliography of Shaker Literature* as #239. Image size
2½" × 3". Miller Collection. Stool: maple with cotton velvet and stuffing, 7" × 12" × 12". Courtesy of the Shaker
Museum and Library.)

Thousands of stools fashioned in this other style were also made, in several heights and at a later date. These
were never advertised in the chair catalogs that ended their run in the early 1880s. The lower stools are rectangular and the taller ones square. All were covered with tapes
of either fine wool, as in these examples (which are original),
or cotton. The Shakers also wrapped a gold transfer decal
around one leg of every stool; the same kind of decal was used
for chairs. It was their guarantee of authenticity.

(Maple with wool, 9¼" × 12⅞" × 10" and 16¼" × 14" × 14"
Miller Collection.)

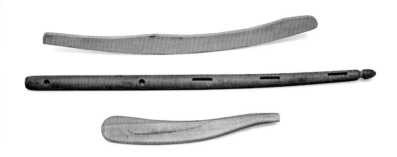

Despite the fact production chairs were a very profitable business for about seventy-five years, there were ups and downs. Manufacturing virtually stopped in the early years of the twentieth century as manpower at Mount Lebanon dwindled. In 1900, there were only thirty-five male members in all of the families there and 40 percent were younger than sixteen or older than sixty. The only way for production to continue—as it indeed did until about 1940—was for the Shakers to buy component parts from the World and assemble and finish them. They also depended increasingly on the labor of sisters. This # 7 rocking chair is an example of a chair made up from parts bought from the World: illustrated also are its major components—rocker, post, and arm. Stretchers were simple dowel stock that was also bought from outside sources. These piles of chair parts [below] made outside Mount Lebanon are now in the attic of the dwelling house at Hancock Shaker Village.

(Chair: maple and cotton tapes, 40" × 22" × 17". BELOW: piles of chair pieces: various dimensions. Courtesy of Hancock Shaker Village. ABOVE: Three chair elements: maple, dimensions unrecorded. Courtesy of the Shaker Museum and Library)

This chair-taping device might easily have been placed in the chapter on Shaker inventions. It is an ingenious device that held the back of a chair rigidly with a screw-activated clamp. This was mounted on a pivoting device that allowed the chair to be tilted at any angle or even inverted; the result was faster and more efficient "bottoming" (a Shaker expression) of chairs.

(RIGHT: Chair-taper: Unknown hardwood(s) and iron, 14⅜" × 25½" [without handle] × 15½". Courtesy of Hancock Shaker Village.)

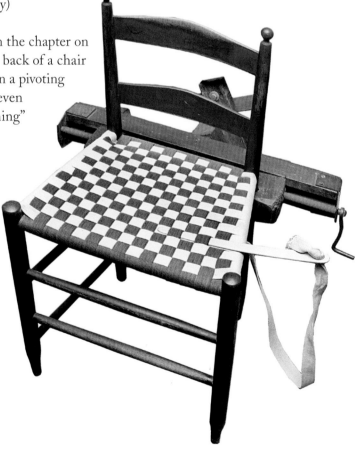

Every business endeavor required paper ephemera to label, keep track of sales and shipments, instruct in the use of, and advertise the product, and the chair industry was no different. Illustrated below is a large letterhead, useful for almost any purpose that required a letter but also a ready reminder of chairs for sale. It was printed for use in the 1880s. Elder Robert M. Wagan (1833–1883) oversaw the establishment of the chair enterprise at the South Family after the leadership at Mount Lebanon split this group off from the Second Family. As we see throughout this book, a beloved brother's (but curiously, not sister's) name was frequently associated with a business long after his death. In this case, Wagan's name was synonymous with production chairs until the last chair was made in about 1941.

(BELOW: Letterhead [detail]: black ink letterpress on red and blue ruled white paper, full size 14" × 8¾". Miller Collection.)

These three billheads are dated, from top to bottom, 190 _ , 1914, and 1940. This latest one shows that two chairs—a # 6 and a # 3—were sold for $15.00 and $11.00 respectively, along with a stool (with a rush seat). It is signed by Sister Lillian Barlow (1876–1942), the last Shaker to actually make and repair chairs.

(RIGHT: Billheads: black ink letterpress [and manuscript ink] on off-white paper, 8½" × 5½". Miller Collection.)

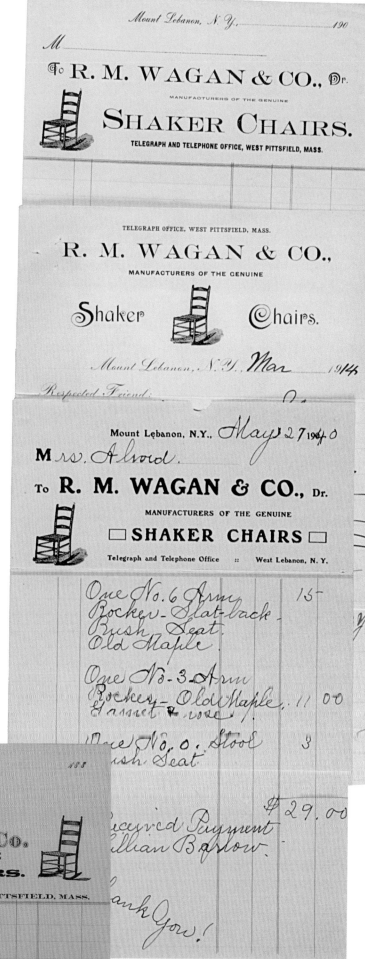

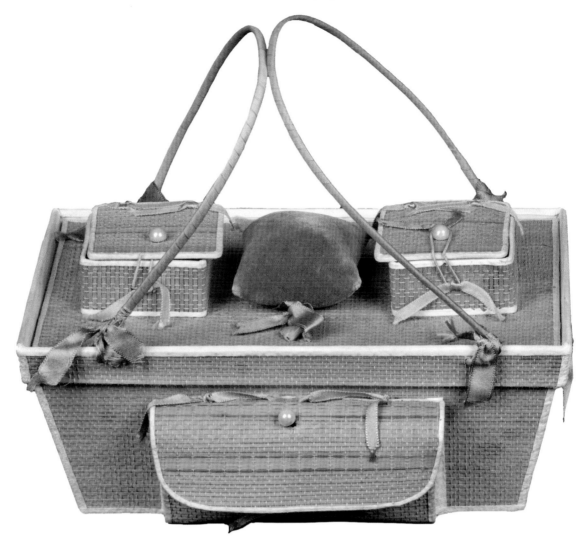

ABOVE: Work casket from Mount Lebanon: woven poplar, silk, kid leather, velvet, wax, emery powder, and pearl buttons, 8¼" × 8½" × 6". Private Collection

BELOW: Photograph on card stock (of Canterbury gift store, ca. 1910), 3½" × 5¼". Courtesy of Canterbury Shaker Village.

9
Fancy Goods
Poplarware

RICHARD DABROWSKI

ONE OF THE MOST INTERESTING aspects of the work produced by Shaker hands in the years following the Civil War is the development of the "fancy goods trade." After the war, Shaker communities were affected not only by a decline in the financial success of the brothers' industries but also by a dramatic decline in the brethren's membership. The sisters responded by commercializing some of their skills, particularly in textiles, and inventing a new product line they called "fancy work" or "fancy goods;" chiefly the manufacture of decorative boxes made from woven poplar wood that is called poplarware.

The concept of weaving with plant fiber was actually well known to the Shaker sisters in many communities, where they made bonnets of imported Cuban palm leaf and, later, native-grown straw for their own use, for sale to other Shaker communities, and for sale to "the world." Andrews reported that it was an "important Shaker industry at New Lebanon and other societies from the late 1820's."[1] In addition to bonnets, a journal kept by the deaconesses at the Church Family in New Lebanon from 1839 to 1870 reveals that during the years 1840–49 the Shaker sisters there were also fashioning other products of palm leaf—fans, salvers, cup mats, table mats, and most curious, "draw boxes" (drawer boxes), an example of which is illustrated [right]. The weaving

was done not by hand but on large looms. White and Taylor credited Brother Abner Bedell, active in the Union Village, Ohio, community in the 1830s, with the invention of a "large loom for weaving Shaker palm leaf."[2] However, as Andrews stated, "the effect of the Civil War on the bonnet industry was instantaneous." As the war progressed, the Union blockade of Southern ports became increasingly more effective for it prevented the importation of Cuban palm leaf.

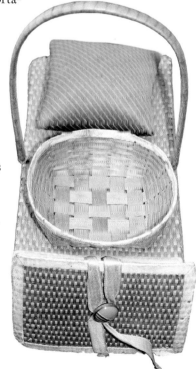

In response to the shortage of Cuban palm leaf, the sisters at the Church Family in New Lebanon switched to weaving poplar wood. Poplar (*Liriodendron tulipifera*), also known as the American tulip tree, tulip poplar, or yellow poplar, was of interest to the Shakers for several reasons. It is abundant throughout the Eastern United States, the sapwood is creamy white and straight grained with a comparatively

Sisters Edith (Eunice) Clark (1891-1957), left and Ida Crook (1886-1965), right attend to a customer at the Church Family Office gift store at Canterbury in about 1930. Courtesy of Hamilton College, Burke Library, Clinton, NY.

uniform texture, and most importantly, it is very flexible and easy to work with.

Sister Elsie McCool (1900–1993), in an article for *The Shaker Quarterly* in 1961, described the process that the Sabbathday Lake, Maine, Shakers used for transforming poplar wood into cloth.[3] As she recalled, the preparation of the poplar wood required the combined efforts of the entire community. The brothers carefully selected the trees, which had to be from moist land and of the appropriate diameter, and harvested them in the coldest days of the winter. At the sawmill, they removed the bark, cut, quartered and squared the logs, and produced "sticks" or blocks approximately 2" × 2" × 20". From this point on, it was very important to keep the wood frozen at all times, often by covering the blocks with water and stacking them out-of-doors to freeze because frozen poplar wood was found to be much easier to mill and process. After an inspection for imperfections, they shaved the blocks or planed them along their length into very thin strips, 2" wide x 20" long, which tended to curl, quite like a raw carrot's curl when shaved. At this point in the process, the sisters took over. The still-frozen shavings were straightened, stacked into large baskets, taken to the ironing room in the Sisters' Shop—where an enormous cast iron stove provided the heat—and placed on "purpose-built" racks to dry. Next, the dried shavings were passed through a shredder that "gauged" them (as the Shakers called it) into very thin strips, $\frac{1}{16}$" wide by 20" long.

The looms for weaving the poplar wood were warped with 216 threads of No. 30 cotton sewing thread, and the thin wood strips were each drawn through the warp threads with specially designed tongs fitted with sandpaper to prevent slipping. A weaver's shuttle with fine threads was used to change the pattern somewhat and to make the poplar cloth stronger and easier to cut. Young girls in the community were required to weave at least one yard of poplar before they went to school each day. Once twelve yards of poplar was woven on the loom, about ten yards were cut off and pasted to a plain white paper on the "wrong side" to prevent raveling. White cotton cloth was then pasted onto the paper and ironed thoroughly until dry. With that, the poplar cloth was finished and ready for cutting.[4]

The earliest documentation of the new poplarware industry in the Church Family at New Lebanon are journal entries by Brother Daniel Crosman (1810–1885) for the month of December 1862. Although he spent most of his working days at his usual trade of making oval boxes, and a few days trimming apple trees in the orchard, he noted that for three days, "I work at popple."[5] The close connection between the work of Crosman, an oval box maker, and the Shaker sisters, who were poplarware makers, can be seen in the oval "work stands"—elaborate "drawer boxes" suspended from an oval platform with a tiny, finely-woven black ash basket and square velvet pincushion attached to the top surface. The wide variety of work stand shapes seen in early stereopticon views of Shaker gift shops indicates that these were among the first poplarware products to be developed and sold commercially by the Church Family. Work stands were followed soon after by an assortment of lidded "ladies work boxes" that included needle books, pincushions, and hard waxes (these were the days before mercerized thread). Lidded poplarware boxes from New Lebanon were always fabricated on bodies of clear pine, about ⅛" thick, to which poplar cloth was affixed on the outside with embossed, glossy white paper on the inside.

In 1869, Sabbathday Lake Elder Otis Sawyer (1820–1883) visited New Lebanon and returned home with an understanding of how to produce poplarware. Both villages in Maine, Sabbathday Lake and nearby Alfred, immediately began to weave poplar cloth and to produce poplarware in very large quantities. Gordon cites a Sabbathday Lake journal reference from April 2, 1878: "The sisters christen their new Loom for weaving Popple Webbing for sale work by putting on a web of one hundred yards warp."[6] By any standard, a hundred yards is a huge amount of poplar cloth. The Maine communities, particularly Sabbathday Lake, became the heart of the poplarware trade and produced the greatest bulk of products sold, between 2,500 and 5,000 pieces annually until 1965, when the work ceased. Early poplarware from Alfred, unlike poplarware at Sabbathday Lake, was made on bodies of thin pine similar to that used at New Lebanon. Sabbathday Lake attached their poplar cloth to cardboard that was reinforced by flexible wire hidden inside the top edge of the pieces.

Wetherbee suggests that the New Lebanon Shakers supplied the Canterbury, New Hampshire, Shakers with baskets and poplarware products for resale in their gift shop, and an invoice from 1874 does appear to support that idea.[7] The Canterbury Shakers began to produce their own

poplarware in the early 1890s, using poplar cloth woven at Alfred, an arrangement that continued until 1923 when Canterbury obtained its own loom with the arrival of Sister Flora Appleton (1881–1961) from the Enfield, New Hampshire, community. Eldress Bertha Lindsay (1897–1990) was the last head of the poplarware industry at Canterbury until it closed in 1958. Poplarware made there is almost identical technically to Sabbathday Lake's and the later work at Alfred; a flexible copper wire around the edges helps to hold the shape of the boxes.

Poplarware was also produced at the Shaker communities in Enfield, New Hampshire; North Family, New Lebanon, New York; and Hancock, Massachusetts, but in relatively small quantities. None of these sites added any major technical innovations to the process and at none of them was poplarware production a significant part of their economy. Yet, the weaving *patterns* at each were sufficiently different that a discerning eye can make positive communal attributions based solely on these patterns. ❦

Mount Lebanon, N. Y., August 2th 1874

Friend Sister Mary W. Pitcher

Bought of Sarah A. Lewis & Co.,

DEALERS IN

Baskets, Fans, Spool Tables, Cushions, and a variety of Fancy Articles.

STORE OPPOSITE THE CHURCH.

1	Work stand at 2,00, 1, at 2.50			2	50
2	Oval shape at 3,00, 1, at 2.00			5	00
1	Heart shape 1.30			1	30
3	Square turned 1.00 each			3	00
3	Covered spoon baskets at 3.00			3	00
3	Spoon with back 1.58			1	58
3	Spoon with Ears 1.50			1	50
3	Round Box baskets 2.75			2	75
3	Summer shape 2.10			2	10
4	Fish shape 4.25			4	25
6	Cat head shape at 35¢ each			2	10
6	Mullen heads shape at 25¢ each			1	50
				33	15
	Less 12½%			4	15
				29	00
1	Pendant 3.75			3	75
				32	75

Toward the end of the nineteenth century, the economy of the Shaker communities everywhere was threatened or faltering. Few able-bodied men were available to carry on the traditional duties of the collective farms. Moreover, few young men were joining, and even fewer of them were staying. The industries that successfully saw the Shakers through most of the nineteenth century—garden seeds, medicinal herbs and preparations, wooden wares, and even chairs made for sale—were overwhelmed by competition from far larger counterparts in the World. The few communities that were able to succeed in the twentieth century did so as a result of the roles that Shaker women played. They assumed greater responsibility for leadership and accounted for nearly all of the earned income in their respective societies. Their main economic engine was fancy goods. These took a variety of forms, poplarware being the major one, but there were others as well. In most instances fancy goods were items made for women in the World to use in sewing crafts.

These two small round pincushions are a late innovation in the poplarware trade. Several villages made them, using a base of woven poplar cloth wrapped around a cardboard disk and topped with velvet-covered "stuffing." The lavender-colored one was made at Canterbury—its bottom is covered in what appears to be a remnant of wallpaper. The other comes from their sister New Hampshire community and is stamped in ink on the bottom, "From the Shakers / Enfield, N.H." Many thousands of these were made from the 1920s to the 1940s. (Woven poplar, paper, velvet, and silk, 1¼" × 1⅞" and 1½" × 1⅞". Miller Collection.)

This woven length of poplar cloth is eleven inches wide. It was made at Mount Lebanon on a cotton-warped loom in the last quarter of the nineteenth century and does not yet have its paper lining. The boxes made at this community used forms made of poplar or pine as a base: the one illustrated here was the proper size for the finished piece also shown. (Cloth: poplar and cotton, 11" × 108" and finished box: woven poplar, silk, and kid leather, 2" × 4¼" × 4¼". Private Collection.)

This octagonal box made at Canterbury is shown with some of the components that went into making it. Each community that made poplarware had a distinctive pattern for the weave, and when examined closely, this weave differs from that shown on the previous page. At Canterbury, rather than a solid box form, only a wooden base (upper right) was used and the poplar cloth wrapped around it. The device below the box was used to mold melted beeswax with a short length of silk ribbon was left to set in the center of it. The upper portion pivots in the center, allowing the hardened wax to be easily removed. At the right are small bags of emery powder shaped like strawberries, and above them are green felt "hulls" that reinforce the fruit like illusion. Not shown here but present on almost all poplarware pieces is the fine white kid leather used to line their edges to prevent wear. (Box: woven poplar, silk, kid leather, felt, wax, and emery powder. 2½" × 7¼" × 4¾". Private collection.)

These two punches were used for different purposes in Mount Lebanon's fancy goods industry. The punch on the right played an integral role in poplarware and sewing carrier production.

Both types of goods used needle books made with woven poplar covers and felt leaves. This sharp punch, made from heavy wood and very sharp steel, was used to stamp out those shapes. (Hickory and steel: 7". Courtesy of the Shaker Museum and Library.)

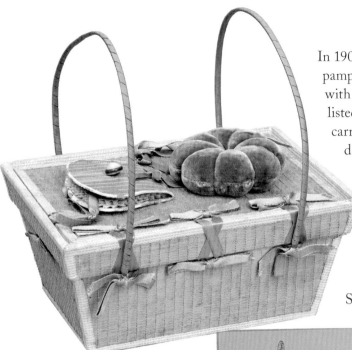

In 1908 the Shakers at Mount Lebanon issued this sixteen-page pamphlet, *Products of Intelligence and Diligence.* It was illustrated with numerous drawings of fancy goods available for sale and listed their prices. These items included sun bonnets, sewing carriers, and dressed dolls—10" and 15" high. Shown here are drawings of several styles of poplarware boxes from pages 8 and 9, along with several surviving examples. (Black ink lithography on off-white paper, 7" × 4⅝". Miller Collection.)

The catalog drawing [upper left] shows an "Oblong work box, $1.75" and the piece [left] is the same type, in "mint" condition. (Woven poplar with silk, velvet, felt, and kid leather: 5½" × 6¼" × 4½". Courtesy of the Shaker Museum and Library.)

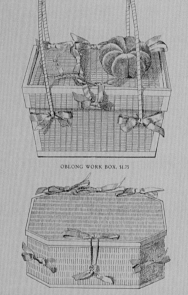

OBLONG WORK BOX, $1.75

OCTAGON WORK BOX, $1.90

SILK-LINED WORK BOX, $2.50

SQUARE WORK BOX, $1.00

Similarly, the drawing on the lower right is of a "Square work box, $1.00." The illustration is a surviving example in perfect condition. Both of these pieces have delicate handles wrapped with rye or oat straw, and it is remarkable that they have remained intact for about one hundred years.

(Woven poplar with silk, velvet, felt, and kid leather: 5¼" × 4¼" × 4¼". Private Collection.)

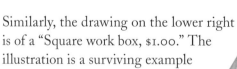

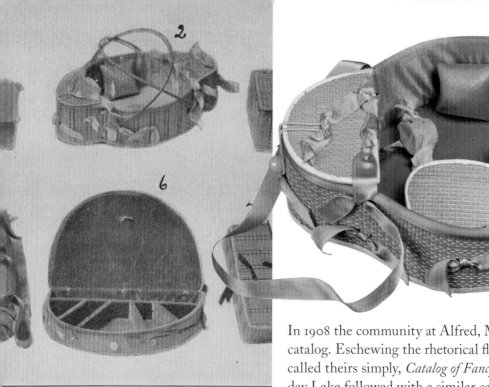

PLATE I.

In 1908 the community at Alfred, Maine also issued an illustrated catalog. Eschewing the rhetorical flourish of Mount Lebanon, they called theirs simply, *Catalog of Fancy Goods.* Two years later, Sabbathday Lake followed with a similar catalog with the same title. Both formats were horizontal rather than vertical, and both used photoengraved renderings rather than line drawings. Plate 1 from the former, shown above left, has images of eight offerings crowded together. The two largest pieces bear a closer look. (Black ink letterpress and photoengraving on off-white paper with tan covers, 5⅜" × 7⅝". Miller Collection.)

This gorgeous piece with bright pink silk was called a "Bifold" because of the lidded compartments at each end. It was offered in two sizes: this 7½" model that sold for $1.85 and a 10" one that cost $2.35. Its description reads, "These are satin lined, furnished with emery-ball, wax-ball, needle-book and cushion." (The present example lacks the wax.) Note that the words silk and satin were often used interchangeably in 1910, and still are in 2009, but that silk is a fabric, satin is a type of weave (usually *used* for silk). (Woven poplar with silk, felt, and kid leather: 2" [without handles] × 7½" × 5½". Private Collection.)

This half moon shaped box is called a "Ladies' Jewelry Case" in both Maine catalogs. It sold for $2.00 at Alfred (or the equivalent of $45.00 in 2009), and $1.75 at Sabbathday Lake, where it was made. It is lined in deep red velvet with matching silk ribbons. On the bottom of their work, Sabbathday Lake used a round, inked stamp designed by Brother Delmer Wilson in 1903 and first used to mark his sewing carriers. (Woven poplar, velvet, silk and kid leather, 1¾" × 8¼" × 5½". Miller Collection.)

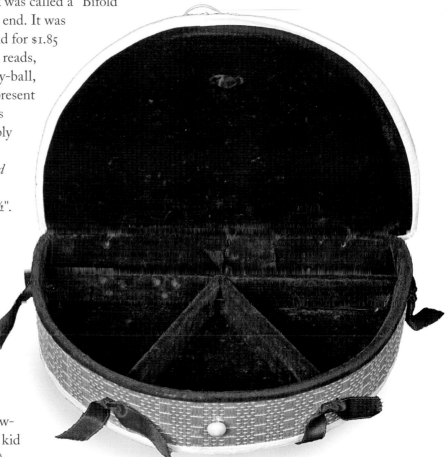

The most common forms to be produced at Sabbathday Lake, generally between 1920 and 1940, were the square and the octagon. An example of the latter using "baby blue" silk shows the usual four sewing accessories (which never varied over time or from one community to another)—pincushion, wax, emery bag, and needle case. Both pieces are stamped on the bottom: "Sabbathday Lake Shakers / Maine / SC." The initials stood for Shaker community. (Woven poplar, silk, wax, emery cloth, and felt. 2¾" × 6⅛" × 5⅝" and 2¼" × 6½" × 6½". Miller Collection.)

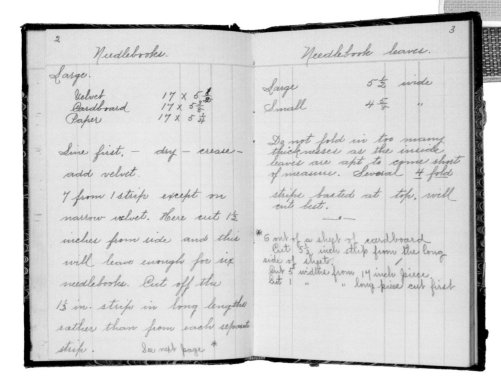

Eldress Bertha Lindsey (1897–1990) was the last sister to hold that position at Canterbury. From 1944 to 1958 she was in charge of the poplarware industry. At some point she recorded the processes for the manufacture of these pieces so that unlike that community's heritage of basket making (see chapter 5), this knowledge would not be lost. Her notebook is opened here to pages 2 and 3, "Needlebooks" and "Needle-book leaves." She is methodical in her descriptions and includes details of sizes and steps needed. (Black manuscript ink on red and blue lined white papers with stiff board covers, 7⅞" × 5¼". Private Collection.)

According to Stephen Paterwic, this rare stereoview of the fancy goods sales room at Mount Lebanon was taken as early as the 1870s. He believes the sister on the left is Sarah Ann Lewis (1813–1877) and the sister on the right is Florinda Sears (1825–1901). The card is the first of a series: "Photographs of Shaker Village / Mt. Lebanon" taken by A. J. Alden of Pittsfield, Massachusetts. (Photographs on green card stock, 3⅞" × 7". Private Collection.)

This work stand is a complex piece. The base is an oval pine disk, similar to a header used in making oval boxes, to which four turned maple feet are attached. On the underside is a drawer made of cardboard, and on top are a basket woven from fine ash splint, a half-round poplarware and silk basket, a cushion, and six iron spindles. All of the surfaces are covered with woven poplar cloth trimmed with straw braiding. Apparently few pieces in this style were made, as very few remain. (Pine, maple, ash, woven poplar, velvet, silk, straw, and iron, 4½" × 8½" × 6". Private Collection.)

The piece on the right is called a handkerchief box in the 1908 Mount Lebanon catalog, and it sold for $2.50. Though it appears rectangular in this photograph, it is actually square, and its interior is lined with quilted white silk. It sits atop the exact type of wooden "carcass" that it would have been constructed upon. The view is of the back, showing how the lid was retained with three silk ribbons. This was the largest-sized square poplarware box made anywhere. (Woven poplar, silk, and paper trim, 2½" × 7¼" × 7¼". Private Collection.)

Heart-shaped poplarware pieces were made at Canterbury in the 1930s and 1940s, but this is a much earlier—and more rare—example. It was made at Mount Lebanon around the turn of the twentieth century. Next to it is the solid wood mold around which it was formed. In this case the poplar cloth was glued to cardboard, allowing it to be bent. Applied blue paper around the top emphasizes its heart shape. (Woven poplar, paper, and velvet, 3" × 6½" × 6½" and pine, 2" × 5¾" × 5¾". Courtesy of the Shaker Museum and Library.)

After mastering their great innovation of making woven poplar cloth, some Shakers seemed to feel that there was no limit to the ways in which it could be applied. The flattish piece on the left is composed of two disks of woven poplar cloth with several strands of darker sweet grass added for contrast. They enclose a spool of silk ribbon. This piece came from Alfred but does not appear in their sales catalog. (Woven poplar, sweet grass, and silk, 1" × 3¾". Private Collection.)

Also coming from Alfred, and made in enough quantity to be advertised in their *Catalog*, is this cylindrical "work box." The interior is lined with deep lavender-colored silk and has a pincushion at each end. The construction is unusual in that it consists of a single kid-trimmed, woven poplar "roll" with two round disks of woven poplar sewn around three-quarters of each end, thus forming the cylinder. These sold for $1.00 in 1908. (Woven poplar, silk, and kid leather, 4¾" × 2⅝". Private Collection.)

The piece at the lower right was made at Mount Lebanon and is called a "Pin Box." Inside is a cardboard cube that is filled with glass-headed straight pins. It too was not a standard form made for sale. There is a blue and white glass button on the front that would have been used with an elastic band (now missing) to hold the lid closed. (Woven poplar, and kid leather, 2¼" × 2¼" × 2". Private Collection.)

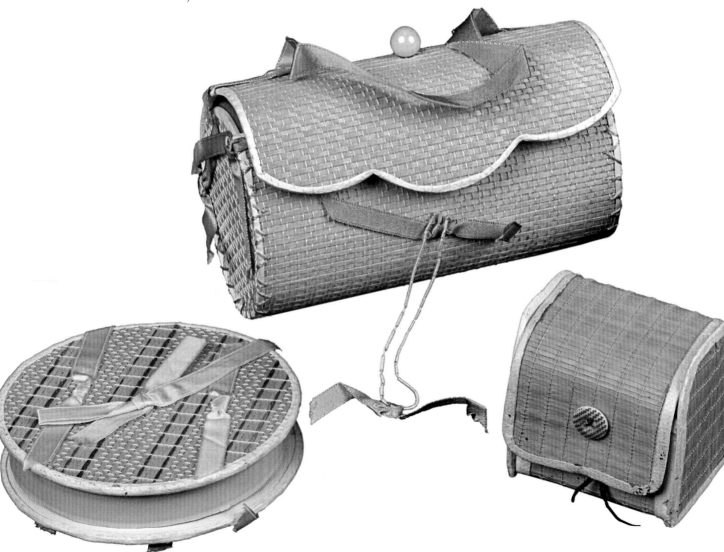

Pincushions in a wide array of shapes and configurations were popular sales items in the years before and after 1900. These two scallop shell examples were made at Sabbathday Lake in the 1880s. The shells were harvested from the Maine shore, thus no two are alike. The cushions also varied a bit; in this case the example on the left has a covering of buff-colored brocaded silk, the other is russet cotton velvet. By the time their first catalog was issued in 1910, this style of pincushion was no longer being made.

(Shell with silk and velvet, 1⅜" × 1¾" and 1¾" × 2⅞". Miller Collection.)

An offshoot of poplarware production at Alfred was this large style of cushion called "Toilet Cushions" (with reference to their use to hold hair pins and such). They were offered in their 1908 catalog in three sizes, this being the smallest and selling for sixty cents. In place of woven poplar cloth the base is surrounded by "rickrack"—narrow strips of poplar woven as braiding. The technique has been connected, anecdotally, to Native Americans living in Maine. The piece rests on a base of pine or poplar that has three short, conical-shaped brass feet.

(Braided poplar, velvet, brass, and silk, 2" × 4". Miller Collection.)

SPOOL STAND, $1.75

A very popular and long-lived style of sewing accessory was the combination of cushion, spool holder, wax, emery, and needle holder or "needle safe." Many examples survive today. They were made at Alfred, Canterbury, Hancock, Mount Lebanon, and Sabbathday Lake. It is usually not possible to identify their community of origin but with these two examples there are distinctive clues. The pink-topped one has a needle book with velvet covers. Since Hancock did not have a poplarware tradition, it is safe to assume that this spool stand was made there. (The Shaker-made spools illustrated with it are only for demonstration purposes—these stands did not come outfitted with spools.) (Maple, velvet, wax, emery powder, felt and iron, 5" × 6". Miller Collection.)

The cream-colored one is shorter and narrower; it fits perfectly into a box that was apparently made for it at Canterbury. The box is something of an enigma; only this community packaged their poplarware in cardboard boxes similar to but smaller than this example. This, however, is the only known box of its size. If it was a planned packaging arrangement for spool stands, is it possible that the plan never took hold? (Maple, velvet, wax, emery powder, felt and iron, 4¾" × 5⅝" and Box: blue ink letterpress on white paper on cardboard, 6" × 5¼" × 5¼". Miller Collection.)

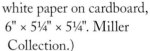

Manufactured by the
Canterbury
Shakers
EAST CANTERBURY,
NEW HAMPSHIRE

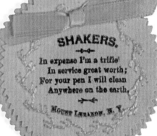

In their *Products of Intelligence*, the Mount Lebanon Shakers called these four pieces "Chamois eye-glass cleaner[s]." They do, indeed, appear on close inspection to be made from soft and supple animal skins. The community used the round punch shown here to stamp out saw tooth–edged disks and stamped each with a message in ink, embroidered them with silk thread, and tied them in stacks of three with silk ribbons. The cute "messages" are similar to this: "Don't call an optician / To look at your eyes; / Till you wipe from your glasses / The speck of a fly." All in all it seems like a great deal of labor went into an item that, in 1908, sold for only twenty-five cents. (Chamois cloth and silk, 2¾". Miller Collection. Punch: maple and steel, 6¼". Courtesy of the Shaker Museum and Library.)

In her essay for chapter 7, Sharon Koomler explained how these fancy goods dolls were an offshoot of the cloak-making industry at Mount Lebanon. They were also advertised for sale in the 1908 catalog as, "Hand painted chamois pen wiper[s]" and sold for seventy-five cents. In fact, while their bisque heads were painted by hand, the voluminous folds of their skirts were made from wool broadcloth, not animal skins (chamois). Each doll also had a full collar of decorative lace, making them collectable playthings as much as functional pieces. This may explain why the examples the editor has seen are not stained with ink. (Wool, bisque, silk, and lace, 2¼" × 2½". Miller Collection.)

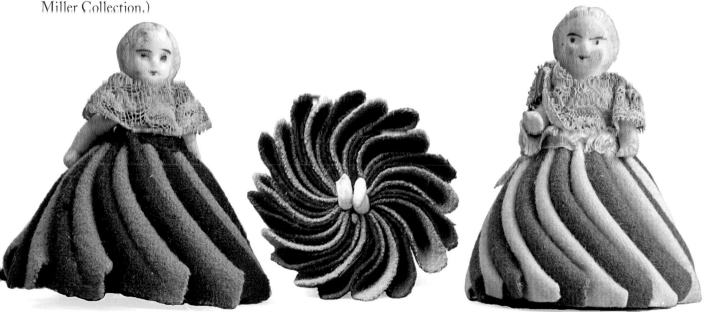

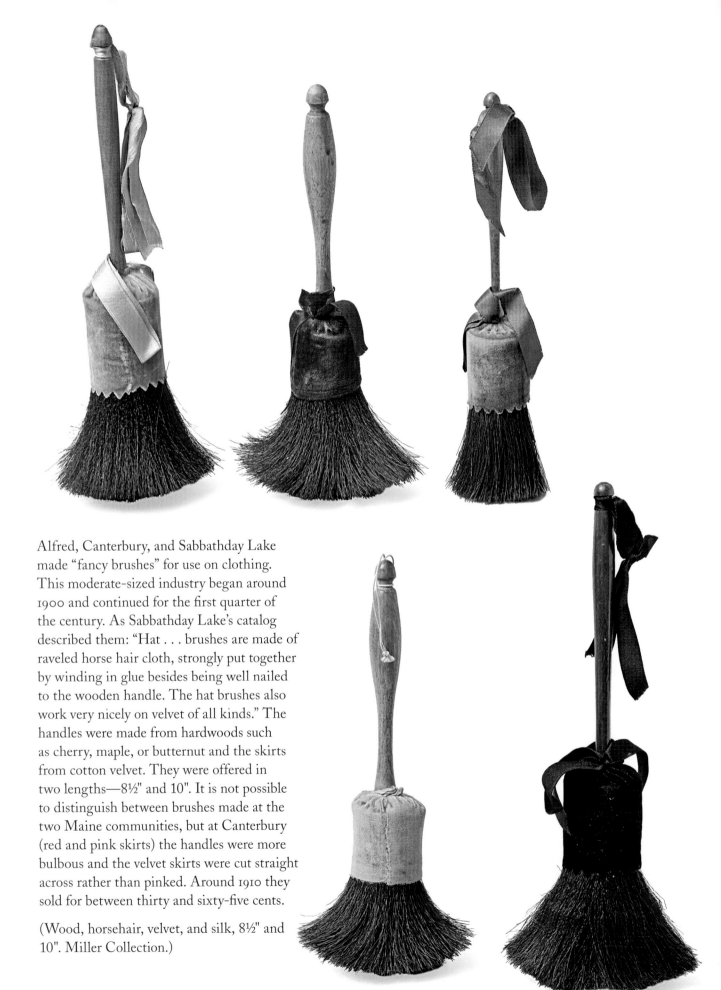

Alfred, Canterbury, and Sabbathday Lake
made "fancy brushes" for use on clothing.
This moderate-sized industry began around
1900 and continued for the first quarter of
the century. As Sabbathday Lake's catalog
described them: "Hat . . . brushes are made of
raveled horse hair cloth, strongly put together
by winding in glue besides being well nailed
to the wooden handle. The hat brushes also
work very nicely on velvet of all kinds." The
handles were made from hardwoods such
as cherry, maple, or butternut and the skirts
from cotton velvet. They were offered in
two lengths—8½" and 10". It is not possible
to distinguish between brushes made at the
two Maine communities, but at Canterbury
(red and pink skirts) the handles were more
bulbous and the velvet skirts were cut straight
across rather than pinked. Around 1910 they
sold for between thirty and sixty-five cents.

(Wood, horsehair, velvet, and silk, 8½" and
10". Miller Collection.)

10
Health and Sanitation

M. Stephen Miller

AN UNIDENTIFIED PHYSICIAN had the following to say about the Shakers in 1853: "Their village health is proverbial. They seem scarcely liable to the prevailing maladies in their vicinity; and in respect to this general immunity from disease, and the consequent length of days, clearly exhibit the advantages of habitual cleanliness, temperance, simplicity of diet, pure air, and an approving conscience."[1] It is worth examining this statement in some detail for it contains a large draught of useful information (as well as a small dose of opinion). The unidentified village referred to was most likely New Lebanon, New York, the first fully organized Shaker community and the model, or "the Lead," that in 1853 the other seventeen Societies were expected to follow.

A good deal can be said about each of the topics the writer touched upon, but the meaning of "an approving conscience" will have to be left to the reader. It is important to remember that this statement was written several years before Louis Pasteur elaborated his landmark germ theory in 1857–58 that forever altered the ways in which health would be understood and health care would be practiced. The term "immunity *from* disease" would today be called immunity *to* disease, for we have since learned that exposure to a foreign protein, such as a germ (in an immune-competent individual), mobilizes a defense against that protein. Therefore, healthy individuals are capable of developing immunity to diseases.

Throughout the nineteenth century, visitors consistently commented on the Shakers' "length of days"—their long lives. Reporter Charles Nordhoff toured fifteen of the seventeen Shaker communities extant in 1875 (Tyringham, Massachusetts, closed that year, the first to do so). Among his observations at each village was Shaker longevity. He began his journey at Alfred, Maine: "Only a week before . . . died at the Church Family Lucy Langdon Newell, aged ninety-eight. She was born on the 4th of July, 1776."[2] "At New Gloucester [Maine—now called Sabbathday Lake], also, the people are long-lived, some having died at the age of eighty-six; and many living beyond seventy." His reports continued in this vein as he traveled from the most northeastern to the most southwestern communities. While most of the nineteenth-century reports were anecdotal, there are some statistical data that reinforce this notion. Andrews substantiated many visitors' impressions; he looked at the average age at death, by the decade, at Enfield, New Hampshire, and Harvard, Massachusetts, from about 1790 to about 1890.[3] There was a clear trend toward longer lives at both communities with the last period showing members living until their early seventies to early eighties. (Any data that look at average life spans, on the contrary, are unreliable since the rate of infant mortality in Shaker villages was all but non-existent.)

"Habitual cleanliness, temperance, simplicity of diet, pure air"—each will be examined in this chapter or in those dealing with foods (diet and temperance) and inventions (pure air). At present, let it be said that each played a vital role in the regulated pattern of life that was established at a very early date in

149

every Shaker society. Regulation—a clearly established set of rules that all members could and would adhere to—was absolutely necessary in order for families of a hundred or more to function as a coherent group. For the Shakers, this meant ". . . work, rest, and worship were carefully balanced. Appetites were fully nourished by a healthful, varied diet based on the freshest possible ingredients. Some pipe smoking and the modest consumption of alcoholic beverages (for 'good digestion') were tolerated, if not overtly encouraged. In addition, Believers' rooms were well ventilated; periodic bathing was provided for and personal hygiene encouraged; clothing and bed linens were laundered regularly; work assignments were rotated to prevent stress, boredom, or carelessness; and safe working environments were a priority."[4] It should also be stated that while each of these areas benefited from various forms of Shaker innovation, one must be cautious about making casual or general statements about *any* aspect of a sect that stretched across 940 linear miles, from Sabbathday Lake to South Union, Kentucky, and encompassed 223 years of existence to date. To expect any semblance of uniformity among an estimated total of 16,000 people who were once Believers, over such an expanse of space and time, is folly, yet there were general principles of health and sanitation that played out in the lives of all who lived the Shaker life.

Visitors to the various Shaker communities frequently wrote about their cleanliness, neatness, and order. These terms are not synonymous. Putting cleanliness aside for the moment, neatness can be summed-up in a phrase: "A place for everything and everything in its place." It was a matter of practical necessity in a community of hundreds where domestic, agricultural, and craft activities were integral parts of everyday life. The means for conducting all of these had to be well organized; the alternative would have been chaos. There were other practical reasons for neatness as well. The paint on buildings was maintained in order to protect the underlying wood from decay, trimming fruit-bearing vines encouraged more abundant production, clearly delineated spaces for brethren and sisters—separate sides in dining rooms and meeting rooms, separate doors and staircases—all helped to reinforce the separation of the sexes.

Order has several differing meanings in Shaker life.[5] Living in a Shaker community meant nothing less than establishing a living kingdom of heaven here on earth. For Believers, their villages were a reflection of the world "beyond." The clear rules, "chain of command" in leadership, the commitment to the Shaker way of life, insured all member's roles in their village's hierarchy and the proper path to heaven. Metaphors of the "straightness" in Shaker life included the way that buildings and paths in villages were laid out in a grid pattern and the ways furniture was designed to reflect strict recto-linearity. It can be said that the simplified, logical, symmetrical, and tightly patterned arrangement of everything in their lives, from social organization to the doors and drawers in furniture pieces, reflects a commitment to order.[6]

"I went into one of the buildings inhabited by ladies, and was shewn (also) the sleeping-room of men; throughout was apparent the greatest attention to neatness and convenience, without any ornament. . . . great importance is attached to cleanliness; this luxury they appear to enjoy in a truly enviable degree."[7] This visitor to New Lebanon in 1820 clearly had a favorable impression of the visit. Another world's person who visited the nearby Watervliet, New York, community at that time had this to say: "The walls were bare, the tables and chairs extremely plain, but everything looked so spotless it seemed as if the walls and even the floor had been varnished."[8] Many years before the elaboration of germ theory, the Shakers instinctively understood the connection between cleanliness and good health, probably to a greater degree than their rural neighbors or even urbanites. The profusion of cleaning devices depicted in the pages ahead will serve as testimony to that understanding.

To be fair, there are contemporaneous reports that contradict the notion of unusual good health among Shakers. "But the appearance of the women was melancholy and unnatural; I say unnatural, because it required to be accounted for. They had all the advantages of exercise and labour in the open air, good food, and good clothing; they were not overworked, for they are not required to work more than they please; and yet there was something so pallid, so unearthly in their complexions, that it gave you the idea that they had been taken from their coffins for a few hours after their decease. . . . the men, on the contrary were ruddy, strong, and vigorous."[9] And finally, this: "What is the cause that so many pale faces, so many sunken eyes, so many parched lips, are invariably seen among them? What is the cause that they become old men and women, before they arrive at the age of manhood?"[10]

Yes, there were troubles in paradise, and the Shakers, as always, approached those challenges as opportunities. In 1821, the New Lebanon community created an Order of Physicians and Nurses, acknowledging: "As the natural body is prone to sickness and disease, it is proper that there should be suitable persons appointed to attend to the duties in administering to those in need."[11] The other communities were expected to follow this initiative and many did. The variety of pharmaceuticals and mechanical devices that the Shakers used for their sick, and sent to the World—inventions, improvements, adaptations, and refinements—are described in the chapter ahead, as well as in "Medicinal Herbs and Preparations." 🌿

The Shakers' care of the sick and infirm is documented in disparate sources, and this chapter looks at some the devices they developed to enhance this care. This bed was made and used in New Lebanon. The casters permitted it to be easily moved. Of greater importance was a Shaker-invented mechanism that allowed the head or foot of the bed to be raised or lowered as needed. The bed was constructed with upper and lower frames. An eccentric-shaped cam on the head- and footboard in the upper case rests against the horizontal frame of the lower. As its handle was rotated, the cam forced the head or foot portion of the bed to be elevated. The process was reversed to lower them. (Maple and pine with iron hardware, 72" × 36". Courtesy of Hancock Shaker Village.)

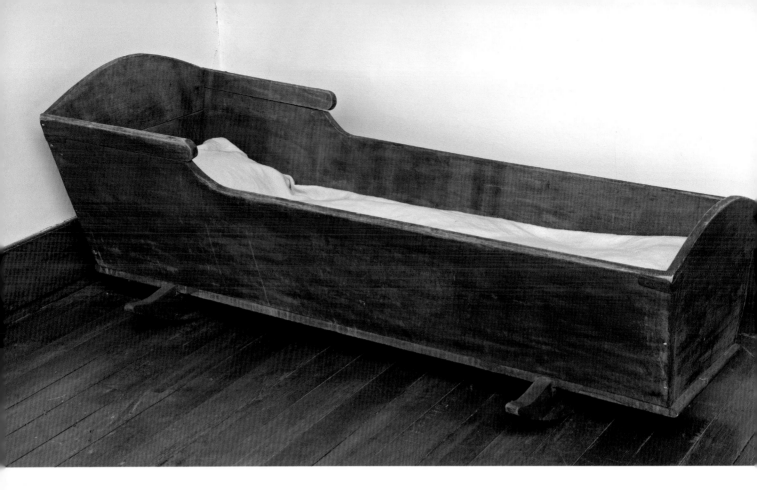

Adult cradles were used at several Shaker villages. They provided a comfortable but confined space for the most debilitated of patients to rest and be soothed by rocking. It is now thought that these cradles were used to comfort the terminally ill in their final days.

(Pine with iron hardware, 24" × 24" × 66½". Courtesy of Hancock Shaker Village.)

These two packages of "straws" came directly from the infirmary building at Canterbury in the 1950s. In 1849 the Shakers there converted an older building into a dedicated infirmary with rooms on the first floor for treating medical and dental patients as well as compounding and storing medicines. The second floor was used to house the sick in standard beds in separate rooms. A kitchen to prepare food only for infirmary patients was located in the basement. These bundles of straws, adapted from local marshland reeds, would have been used for patients who found it difficult to drink from cups and glasses. A paper label on the tin reads, "Straws for taking Iron."

(Reed with tin and cardboard, lengths 7" to 9". Miller Collection.)

This vibrant blue standing cupboard was used in the infirmary at Sabbathday Lake. In 1981, Brother Theodore E. Johnson of that community wrote: "Indeed for many years it was used as a medicine cupboard in the tiny infirmary of the Girl's Shop. When I first encountered it the cupboard was redolent of the variety of medicines that had been stored in it for so long." (Note: It *still* is.) "You can perhaps notice some of the stains which medicines have made against its mustard [color] interior."

(Pine with iron hardware, 54¾" × 31" × 9¾". Miller Collection.)

The small tabletop cupboard is made from cherry wood; the top and bottom are each a single slab with moldings formed by a molding plane rather than "applied" as was usually the case with worldly cabinetry. We do not know in which Shaker community it was made or used. Inside is a wide variety of pharmaceuticals from different Shaker villages. They are representative of the kinds of small containers that held medicines of their own making.

(Cherry with brass and iron hardware, 24" × 17¼" × 7¼". Miller Collection.)

This photograph, published in *Life* magazine on March 21, 1949, shows Eldress Marguerite Frost (1892–1971) in the Canterbury infirmary surrounded by bottles of medicines the Shakers put up there. Many of these same bottles may be found in this group [below], photographed recently.

(BELOW: Glass and paper, heights: from 3½" to 11¾". Miller Collection.)

The ability of convalescents and invalids to move about certainly received attention from the medical and nursing staffs at Shaker villages, and they came up with some refined and innovative approaches to it. The pair of crutches was made at Canterbury and is distinguished by the addition of padding at the top to make them more comfortable to use. Otherwise, they did not differ from what was commonly available.

(Ash, velvet, stuffing, leather, and brass. l- 44½". Courtesy of Canterbury Shaker Village.)

Also from Canterbury, the walking cane is notable for the refined detailing of its top—a "squashed" ball with a well-defined collar. This piece was turned on a lathe, on which it is very difficult to achieve smooth contours and fine details, for these thin lengths of wood have a tendency to "whip" as they are turned.

(Hickory, l- 37". Miller Collection.)

The four-legged cane and three-sided walker may be from New Lebanon. The cane is a very sturdy affair, able to support a heavy individual. The triple-cross bracing is secured with iron bolts. The walker is more delicate and would have been used for steadying a patient's balance rather than for supporting his or her full weight.

(Cane: maple and pine with iron hardware, 30" × 6" × 5⅞". Courtesy of Hancock Shaker Village. Walker: maple, 32½" × 17½" × 23". Courtesy of the Shaker Museum and Library.)

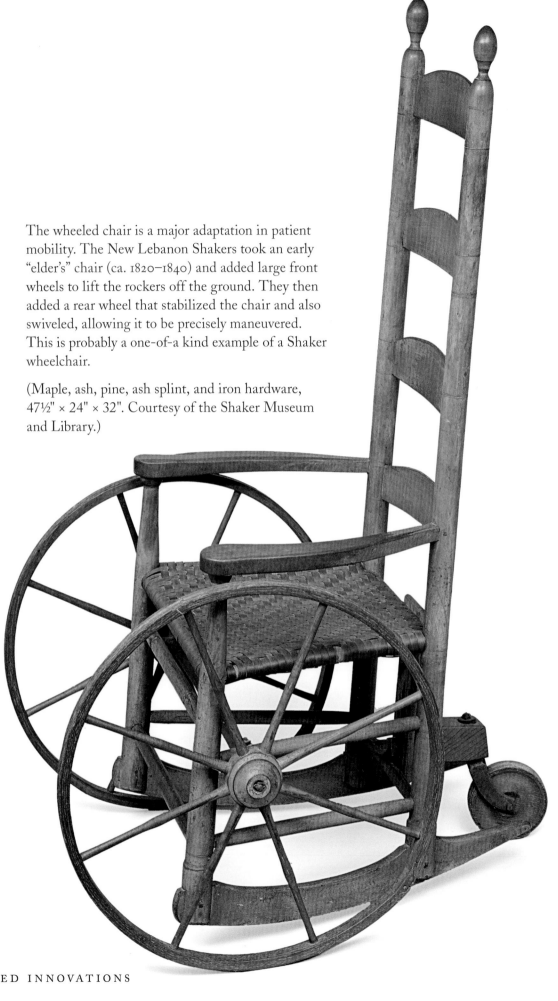

The wheeled chair is a major adaptation in patient mobility. The New Lebanon Shakers took an early "elder's" chair (ca. 1820–1840) and added large front wheels to lift the rockers off the ground. They then added a rear wheel that stabilized the chair and also swiveled, allowing it to be precisely maneuvered. This is probably a one-of-a kind example of a Shaker wheelchair.

(Maple, ash, pine, ash splint, and iron hardware, 47½" × 24" × 32". Courtesy of the Shaker Museum and Library.)

It is possible that the Shakers were first to develop a means of manufacturing medicines in pill form with the use of these types of devices. The all-wooden pill maker is the earlier example of this form, and nothing is known about it other than a history of association with the Shakers. The wood and brass example was acquired by Ted and Faith Andrews at Mount Lebanon in the 1930s or 1940s. Although this indicates that the community used it, it does not prove that they either invented or even made it. The device worked as follows: a long, narrow roll of medicinal material in paste form was formed and laid across the grooves in the "table." The top crosspiece slid over this material, creating parallel "tubes" that were then pushed to the edge of the table. A sharp knife drawn across the projecting tubes cut round pills that fell into the collecting tray below the table.

(All-wood: pine and butternut, 4¾" × 16" × 15¾". Wood and metal: walnut, cherry, and brass, 1⅞" × 18" × 16½". Courtesy of Hancock Shaker Village.)

Beginning in 1827, the Shakers used an electrostatic machine at New Lebanon to treat a host of ailments, especially rheumatism.[12] Years later a journal noted: "Elder Sister remains feeble but it relieved some of her cough by vapor bath and electricity." A few days later, "Elder Sister . . . is not much better, we keep her in and continue shocking her."[13] Electricity was created by turning a cylinder of glass against a piece of silk or leather. It was then conducted through ball-tipped metal wires acting as electrodes. The balls were placed against a patient's skin. Although the Shakers did not create this technology, it is interesting to see what they did with it. This platform, for example, is elevated (thus insulated) on four short glass feet made from the necks of bottles. The glass cylinder is a cut-down glass jug, and the low-backed chair is a basic Shaker dining room chair.

(Platform and device: pine, glass, iron, cork, amber, and silk, 5⅛" × 26¾" × 21⅞". Chair: maple with cotton tapes, 25¾" × 18½" × 15¾". Courtesy of the Shaker Museum and Library.)

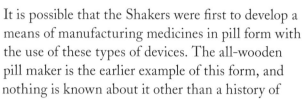

"The Shaker doctrine as regards hygiene is simple, and includes . . . good ventilation. The latter is a constant study. Slats are placed in every window . . . small holes along the base-board in all the halls aid this end. In the gathering rooms are round openings from out-doors."[14] A transom or ventilator was built over all of the doors in dwellings. It is not clear where the use of transoms began, but the Shakers valued a constant influx of fresh air in all of their rooms, and they were probably the first to incorporate ventilators systematically. Sister Jennie Wells told a visiting twentieth-century reporter: "'First of all I want you to notice that transom.' The transom, which was open, was a wooden panel fixed on a vertical pivot. 'Most of our rooms have them,' she said. 'They're much more sensible than ordinary transoms, of course, because they create a real draft." The Shaker-made examples—one glass and one wood—use a central pivot for horizontal movement while the "ordinary transoms" that Sister Wells referred to used a pane of glass that only tilted vertically resulting in an opening toward the ceiling that did not allow as much air to circulate. Both examples come from the dwelling house at the North Family, New Lebanon.

(Glass: pine, glass, and iron hardware, 5" × 31½" × 7½".
Wood: pine, maple, and iron hardware, 5¾" × 38½" × 7".
Courtesy of Hancock Shaker Village.)

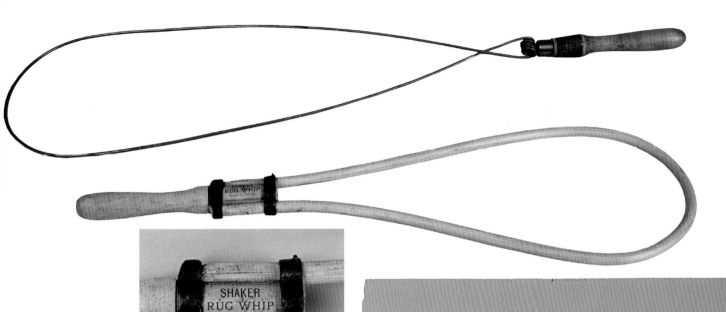

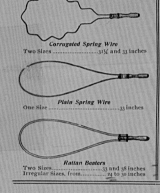

The "Shaker Rug Whip" was not a Shaker invention; their role was refining it. A non-Shaker named Charles Comstock patented one style—a softwood handle with steam-bent cane ("rattan")—in 1898, and assigned the manufacturing rights to the North Family at Mount Lebanon. There, under the direction of Brother Levi Shaw (1819–1908), the community made whips between 1898 and the first years of the twentieth century. It is no surprise that the Shakers were willing to take on a product line that could make a home in the World more sanitary while simultaneously turning a profit for the community. Two styles of rug whips are shown here—one made of cane (the patented model) and one with a hardwood handle and heavy coiled wire. It is not known if this latter form originated with the Shakers. (Soft and hardwoods with spring wire and iron or brass fasteners: [top] l- 31"and [bottom] l- 24". Miller Collection.)

As with every other industry, advertising was an important component. The rare surviving broadside illustrated here depicts a third style of carpet beater, one with "corrugated" wire. By now, Elder Daniel Offord (1843–1911) was in charge of the business. "They combine lightness, simplicity and strength of construction," the advertisement announced, ". . . rattan beaters are the best and cheapest in the market. . . . Wire beaters will neither break or come loose." (Black ink letterpress and wood engravings on pale pink paper, 9½" × 6". Miller Collection.)

NORTH FAMILY SHAKERS
MOUNT LEBANON, NEW YORK,
MANUFACTURERS OF
Shaker Carpet and Rug Beaters

Corrugated Spring Wire
Two Sizes......................31¼ and 33 inches

Plain Spring Wire
One Size.....................................33 inches

Rattan Beaters
Two Sizes...............................33 and 38 inches
Irregular Sizes, from..............24 to 30 inches

If a Carpet Sweeper Why not a

CARPET BEATER ?

Shaker Carpet and Rug Beaters are Indispensable to every Household. Why? Because they combine lightness, simplicity and strength of construction.

Our Rattan Beaters are the best and cheapest in the market for the above reasons. A child can handle them. The 38 inch size, above illustrated, is intended more for carpets, and the 33 inch size for rugs. They should go together. With a patent iron ferrule joining the cane to the handle they are reduced to the simplest principles of construction and utility. *Try them and prove their selling qualities.*

The coppered spring wire loop beater also illustrated, length 33 in. contains the same principles of construction to be found in the rattan beaters, namely: lightness, simplicity and strength with cheapness added.

The coppered spring corrugated wire beater at the head of the illustration has the additional feature of distributing a blow over a broader surface, and removes the possible objection of injuring the fabric of article beaten. It is also beautiful in formation. Hung up for sale this beater is sure to attract attention, especially where a number are displayed together. These wire beaters will neither break or come loose.

Order any of the Shaker Carpet and Rug Beaters and you will find them good selling articles.

WRITE FOR SAMPLE AND PRICES.
NORTH FAMILY SHAKERS, Mount Lebanon, New York.
DANIEL OFFORD, Agent.

The Shakers are widely credited with developing the flat broom and, to date, no evidence has surfaced to contradict that claim. Brother Theodore Bates (1762–1846) of Watervliet invented a vise—no doubt similar to the Shaker-made one illustrated here—that flattened the bristles of the traditional round broom so they could be stitched across with sturdy twine, resulting in a flat broom. This shape was much more efficient and soon became the standard for the World. Nearly every Shaker community was involved in broom production, with large tracts of land for growing broomcorn and large-scale turning mills for making handles. At Canterbury, for example, brooms were made from 1847 to 1890, and in the peak production year of 1860 the community produced 36,000. This example was made at Mount Lebanon and was the *last one* ever made at any Shaker community—November 1911.

(Broom: maple, broomcorn, wire, and cotton thread, l- 55½". Miller Collection. Vise: pine and iron, 41½" × 11¼" × 23". Courtesy of Hancock Shaker Village.)

Whiskbrooms may have evolved from broom technology, since, after all, they are miniature brooms. The Shakers made brushes by the hundreds of thousands and at nearly every community as well. With brooms, only Mount Lebanon affixed a paper label and very few examples survive. Identifying Shaker-made brushes is an even greater challenge, for setting aside "fancy" brushes, discussed in chapter 9, the Shakers left virtually no information about their design, manufacture, or sale. They were never advertised as fancy brushes were, and they were not labeled. Still, certain clues can be found: for example, the turnings on the handle in the example pictured [above] resemble those on other small craft pieces from Canterbury. (Two brushes: [left] maple, broom-corn, wire, and cotton thread, l- 10½" and [above] cherry and horsehair, l- 14¼". Miller Collection.)

There are also instances of "air-tight" provenances, pieces collected from the Shakers themselves like the three oblong brushes that match brushes collected at Mount Lebanon by Ted and Faith Andrews. In addition, the middle example has the initials of Trustee David Meacham Sr. (1743–1826) stamped into one end. "D.M." was used at New Lebanon as a sign of respect for their first trustee and as a subtle guarantee of quality for more than fifty years after his death. (Top and bottom: maple and bristle, l- 8¾" and 12½"; center: walnut and bristle, l- 5½". Miller Collection.)

The manufacture of dustpans at several communities may have been a cottage industry. At Canterbury, these were made with elegantly turned wood handles, usually with several scribe marks at the height of contour—a restrained form of decoration—and a knob at the end where a hanging string or thong could be attached. New Lebanon's dustpans used only soldered, tin-plated iron—always with an attached wire ring for hanging. All Shaker-made dustpans have one feature not seen on worldly examples. A heavy round wire runs along the top edge around which the back and side flanges are bent in order to maintain the piece's rigidity. (Birch and tin-plated iron, l- 14⅝"; tin-plated iron, 10½" and 9¾". Miller Collection.)

RIGHT: This image is titled "Rebecca & girls at Syrup Shop making dusters." Sister Rebecca Hathaway (1872-1958) is pictured with six younger sisters at Canterbury in this 1910-1915 post card image. (Photograph on card stock, 3½" × 5¼". Courtesy of Canterbury Shaker Village)

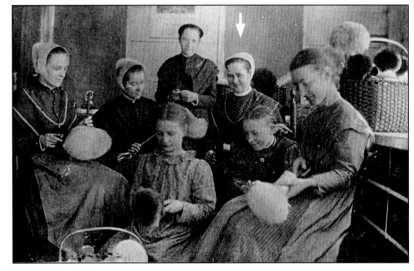

Canterbury (and probably Mount Lebanon) made dusters by the tens of thousands. The Shakers turned handles from maple wood, coated them with a thick layer of orange-tinted varnish, and attached dyed wool to the thicker end. The duster on the right was made at Canterbury, a fact recorded on the tag on the unfinished one.

(Maple and wool, l- 15½", 12¾", 16½". Miller Collection.)

This dish mop is a rare survivor. Although it is constructed with similar materials (with cotton rag substituted for wool) and in a similar manner to dusters, this was not part of an industry. The Shakers had to wash large numbers of dishes, eating utensils, and cookware three times daily, and items such as this would have undoubtedly been a big help.

(Maple and cotton, l- 10½". Courtesy of the Shaker Heritage Society.)

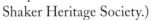

Throughout every Shaker village, furniture was continually moved and reconfigured for new functions. This plain table with a separate "add-on" top typifies an adaptation that could have been used in an infirmary setting although there is no history that it was. The arrangement combines two basic needs: a working surface and a storage space. The design of the table is "generic" Shaker, and its community of origin unknown. The case of drawers, however, was made and used at Enfield, Connecticut. A close-up view shows the construction of the case's interior structure—dovetailed joinery. It is difficult to imagine anyone but Shakers going to this extreme length in the construction of what was a simple, everyday storage piece. (It is also difficult to visualize a cherry tree large enough to yield a two foot wide tabletop.)

(Table: birch and cherry, 28¼" × 38¼" × 24" and Add-on: cherry and pine with brass pulls, 8¼" × 38¾" × 8¾". Miller Collection.)

Ultimately, when considering matters of health and sanitation, one must take toileting functions into account. The Shakers, like the World, used outhouses for almost all of the nineteenth century. There were, however, special cases: the aged and sick—and perhaps at times the Ministry—who had alternative arrangements called commodes (or close-stools). These took many forms, but most used innovations that entirely separated them from examples in the World. This "barrel" form is the simplest type to enclose a chamber pot. It is small and lightweight enough to be carried by its handle from a room and taken outside for disposal with its pot still inside. Its community of origin is unknown.

(Pine with red stain, 14" [without handle] x 14". Courtesy of The Art Complex Museum.)

This commode, made at Canterbury (with their typical shaped skirts) is more properly a close-stool. One had to open the lid and then open the door in order to sit down. The chamber pot was located in the lower compartment. Closed, this appeared to be just another piece of room furniture.

(Pine with red paint, 28¾" × 25" × 17½". Courtesy of the Art Complex Museum.)

Another furniture form, though with its purpose not as well hidden as the previous example, probably comes from Hancock or New Lebanon. It may have been used in an infirmary; the addition of arms could have helped to support a weakened patient. Overall it is a clever adaptation of a conventional seating form to an entirely new function.

(Birch, ash, cherry, and pine with iron hardware, 32¾" × 20" × 16⅜". Courtesy of Hancock Shaker Village.)

The final form to be considered was made by New Lebanon Brother James X. Smith (1806–1888). The basic form is Windsor style, a form that was popular fifty or more years before this piece was made. Its most innovative aspect is a lever device [near the bottom right] that raises and lowers the wooden crosspiece, thus raising and lowering a metal chamber pot placed on top. A wooden wedge attached to a leather thong (now missing) kept the lever and the pot in an "up" position. Smith was a member of the Church Family for

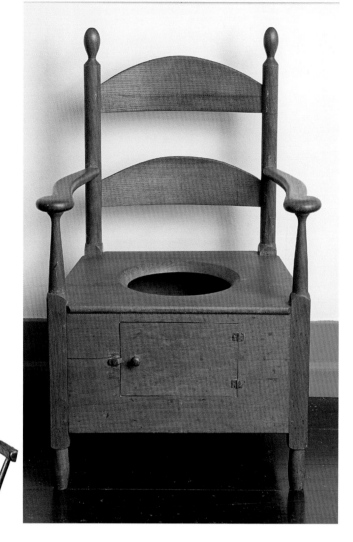

the last thirty years of his life and this piece was probably made for the Ministry there, who were the leaders for the entire movement.

(Chair: cherry, maple, ash, poplar, and pine, 24¾" × 21" × 15¾"; pail: tin-plated iron, 14" × 11½". Miller Collection.)

11
Retiring Rooms

M. STEPHEN MILLER

A SHAKER RETIRING ROOM is nothing more than a bedroom or, more accurately, a dormitory room. Each communal dwelling house was divided into zones of activity. There was space for food preparation (in kitchens, where it was done on an industrial scale) and storage (in ample cellars); space for food consumption (dining rooms—one for the family's Ministry and one for regular members who sat on separate sides of the same room); space for worship (a family meeting room); vast spaces for the storage of out-of-season bedding and clothing (the attic); and space for sleeping. It is the latter that is the subject of this chapter.

Retiring rooms were initially shared by from two to four brothers, or sisters, and while always gender-specific, they were often located on the same floor—separated only by a wide hallway. Among the widely scattered Shaker villages, the furnishings of retiring rooms seem to have been quite consistent throughout the nineteenth century. By the beginning of the twentieth, more individual decorative touches appeared. These had been forbidden earlier but with the diminished number of members, and with the predominance of sisters over brothers, pictures were hung on walls, patterned linoleum was laid on floors, and relatively fancy, non-Shaker made furniture was sometimes used. All of these can be found in photographs from that era.

Perhaps the first thing that present-day visitors to restored Shaker village sites notice is the sparseness of the Shaker retiring rooms. This impression should not be judged by the photographs in the early

books that appeared about the sect. Those images were staged, often by historian Edward Deming Andrews, his wife Faith, and photographer William F. Winter Jr.[1] While these rooms *were* sparely furnished when Shakers inhabited them, they were neither cold nor drab.

These spaces were intended primarily for sleep and not for work. The Shakers went to bed by nine and rose up as early as four o'clock in summer and as late as five-thirty in winter.[2] Shaker beds were at first made to accommodate two brothers or sisters. During the first decades of their communal life, so many converts were joining that their carpenters had a difficult time keeping up with furnishing retiring rooms. The sharing of beds was not an uncommon practice in the World, so having two or more members of the same sex in one bed must not have seemed out of the ordinary. After the middle of the nineteenth century, when their numbers began to decline, some beds were narrowed in order to accommodate just one person. What is probably unique to Shaker beds is the presence of casters at the bottom of the four posts. These allowed the beds to be rolled to the side so that sisters—who did all of the housekeeping in the dwelling houses—might sweep under

FACING PAGE: This large built-in cupboard over drawers, located in Room 20 of the dwelling house at Hancock Shaker Village, is typical of the large storage units found in retiring rooms throughout the Shaker East. The case (frame) retains its original chrome yellow painted finish while the butternut drawer fronts are covered in old, now crusty, varnish. (94¼" × 39½ ". Courtesy of Hancock Shaker Village.)

them. This is one more example of adapting a simple, readily available mechanical device to serve their ever-present concern for health and sanitation. Simple straw mattresses were supported either by a rope structure or, later, by slats.

Another prominent feature in all retiring rooms is the presence of built-in case pieces for storage. These were generally made with frames, drawer sides, and bottoms of pine and drawer fronts of a hardwood. A single threaded hardwood knob was placed in the side of cupboard doors and one or two in drawers. The arrangement of doors (when present) and drawers varied greatly as, presumably, they adapted to the specific needs of the first occupants or met the patterns established by the different communities. When doors are present, they are typically placed above drawers but examples exist of the reverse and also of doors at the top and the bottom of cases. Sometimes, there were even cutout portions in their bottoms that were covered with an iron grate where heat registers would otherwise be blocked.

It was common for the soft- and hardwood components of built-ins to be stained or painted or varnished for the protection of the wood surfaces, and often this was done using contrasting colors or finishes. Shaker retiring rooms were colorful. It would not have been unusual to have walked into one in the mid-nineteenth century and found beds painted green, chairs and tables painted a deep red, built-ins ocher, and/or varnished, and walls, floors, baseboards, and peg rails a bright yellow. Colorful braided or rag rugs were sometimes placed on floors and multi-color woven wall sheets hung from peg rails. All of these elements would have made Shakers' retiring rooms cheerful and bright, particularly during the dark, cold winter months.

Candlestands, or light stands, were found in all retiring rooms and served to hold candles in some sort of a sconce, as well as perhaps a member's eyeglasses, prayer book, or false teeth. The design of these was quite similar, varying mainly in the details of construction. Tops were almost always round and they all had three legs. The latter were either "snake"-shaped (a double ogee) or "spider"-shaped (a single convex-concave arch). The turned shafts were free from any carvings, and if any "rings" or "urn shapes" were incorporated, they were far simpler than those found on worldly pieces. In place of simple round stands, small, four-legged stands with or without drawers were also frequently deployed for the same purposes.

Every room had one or more chairs on which the occupant could sit while reading, mending, or in quiet contemplation. They varied greatly in form, but they either had arms or, more likely, were armless and frequently had rockers. This was about the only place in a Shaker village where a sister or brother could actually relax—if there was time!

Some rooms, depending upon the specific community and the time period, had some sort of washstand and towel rack. The forms of both were so varied that it is sometimes difficult to tell them apart from examples made and used in the World. The matter of refinement comes into play here; for it is clear that the Shakers were not unique in their use of well-seasoned woods, fine construction techniques, and simplified designs. A great deal of simple, well-made furniture was produced in the World. Still, there are often small "signature" features found in Shaker-made pieces that make them readily attributable; for example, the tapered drawer sides of case pieces made at Hancock and Enfield, Connecticut, that were the work of Elder Grove Wright and Brother Abner Allen. While the reason for this unique construction technique is unknown, its presence is limited to work found only at these two communities.

Finally, the presence of a wood stove (initially designed by the Shakers), with its accompanying accoutrements, was nearly ubiquitous across the Shaker world. (When heat registers were placed in the walls, ceilings, or floors of dwelling houses built in the second half of the nineteenth century, stoves were no longer needed.) The Shakers almost surely did not invent these cast-iron devices, but the designs of the wood patterns they made and sent for casting outside their communities were so refined that the stoves are instantly recognizable. At New Lebanon and the nearby villages, the forms are very spare and recto-linear. At Canterbury, in contrast, the fire boxes either had chamfered or scalloped top edges, and the side panels often had a raised "tomb stone" pattern. Along with stoves were iron tools, tongs and shovels, as well as a round box for wood shavings. A rectangular box or leather-lined basket, with handle, was used to hold kindling and split logs. In parts of dwellings where larger groups congregated, such as the meeting room or dining room, an extra long pipe connected the stoves to flues in the walls, allowing more heat to be radiated into the room along its length.

It should be noted here that most of the above refers to the work found in the eastern Shaker villages. More variations in design existed in the Shaker West. Yet even there, the furnishings found in Shaker retiring rooms were quite distinct from their Ohio and Kentucky neighbors. 🌿

Shaker beds (or, as they were often called, bedsteads) came in many styles, but the basic format was always similar to the two examples illustrated. All were simple affairs: a horizontal frame attached to four short legs with mortise-and-tenon joints (with heavy dowels or iron bolts), a headboard, and a lower footboard. A tick-covered mattress filled with feathers or straw was supported either by wooden slats laid widthwise on the frame or by a rope lattice threaded through the frame and tightened with a "key." These were the essentials of Shaker-made beds and were not very different from those of their country neighbors.

What distinguished Shaker beds from the others were two features: the refinement of the parts and the presence of wheels on the legs. Typically the legs of Shaker beds incorporated flat portions, where the rails joined them, and round portions above and below. At their finest, the square-to-round transitions were elegantly done with either broad "lamb's tongue" bevels at the corners or a broad chamfer all around the collar, top and bottom. Wheels fashioned from hardwoods—usually rock maple—were

mounted in cast-iron swivel casters that either screwed directly into the bottom of the bed's legs or had collars that fit over the ends of them. Wheels allowed sisters, whose chore it was to clean their own as well as brethrens' retiring rooms, to easily move the beds so they could reach under them. (Maple and pine with cast iron, 24½" × 65⅝" × 31⅞" and 25¼" × 79¼" × 32½". Courtesy of Hancock Shaker Village.)

Almost all retiring rooms had stands that were often similar to these round-topped examples that are commonly called candle or light stands. The section dealing with "Furniture in Retiring Rooms," in the *Millennial Laws* of 1845 stipulated: "One table, one or two stands."[3] In making candle stands, Shaker craftsmen avoided the fancy turnings and/or carving always found on worldly pieces. Their shafts were sometimes straight, sometimes slightly bulged. Legs were either cabriole style (seen here) or arched ("spider leg"). In either case the legs have large dovetails that fit into slots at the base of the shaft and were usually covered by a round iron plate with three short flanges, each with a screw that secured the legs and kept them from spreading and loosening.

(Above: cherry with butternut top, 26⅜" × 17½" and left: all cherry, 25" × 15". Miller Collection.)

This square stand is representative of many slightly different styles that shared a common form: four usually round legs with a square (or nearly so) top, and skirts often holding a drawer or two. This stand, from Alfred or Sabbathday Lake, combines highly figured maple legs with mahogany—the latter being a very unusual wood choice for Shakers since it was an import. They may have acquired it from the nearby port city of Portland, where mahogany was used as ships' ballast.

(Maple and mahogany, 28⅞" × 19⅛" × 18⅝". Miller Collection.)

The use of freestanding chests for clothing storage in retiring rooms, in addition to built-ins, changed over time and varied from community to community. This example comes from New Hampshire, where blanket chests were in use after 1860 or so. There is a clear history of use and ownership by Sister Myra Green (1835–1942), who resided first at Enfield, New Hampshire, and, after 1918, at Canterbury. The blue paint exactly matches the color on the woodwork on the first floor of the Meeting House at Canterbury, painted in 1878, lending weight to the argument that the chest was also made there at that time. Although some early non-Shaker sources claimed that the Shakers did not use locks because they were not needed, even a casual look at Shaker furniture—including most examples in this book—will show that this clearly was not true. The studio photograph of Sister Green was taken in Lebanon, New Hampshire, when she was about fifty-three years old.

(Pine with cherry knobs and brass and bone fittings, 26¾" × 41" × 21½". Photograph [image size] 5½" × 3⅞". Miller Collection.)

This cupboard over drawers represents another style of freestanding furniture used in retiring rooms to store garments. An almost endless number of variations in doors and drawers exist in both built-in and stand alone storage pieces. This one comes from New Lebanon and was made before the middle of the nineteenth century. The drawer configuration has "reverse graduation"—they are larger at the top and smaller at the bottom—a somewhat unusual but by no means unique arrangement. Inside the cupboard portion are two spaces of unequal size formed by a full-size shelf. The slightly projecting divider below the door is a common feature of casework made at New Lebanon.

(Pine with hardwood knobs and iron hardware, 56½" × 27½" × 17½". Miller Collection.)

In order for members to reach the upper portions of tall storage pieces, Shaker brothers constructed sets of steps in several similar styles. These usually had three treads and were called "three steppers." This elegant set was made at Canterbury and combines restrained elements of curvilinear shapes (the lower edges of the sides and the back of the top step) within rigid rectilinear form. Many "two-steppers," such as the one illustrated in Chapter 7, were actually *sewing* steps, not climbing steps.

(Butternut and cherry, 23¼" × 17½" × 19½". Miller Collection.)

Some, but certainly not all, retiring rooms had facilities for washing. In general, common washrooms were used, for there was very little space for washing and drying in retiring rooms. Where they did exist, they were of three basic designs: these two plus a simple cabinet style similar to the exterior of the Canterbury closed stool found in chapter 10. The one on the left is not much different from a non-Shaker type: four square tapered legs with a backsplash, a shelf with a circular cut-out for a washbowl, and a lower shelf for a water pitcher. The differences are in the details. Shakers dovetailed the corners of this backsplash and secured the shelf beneath it by cutting it into the legs. At some later date, they added a drawer with finely dovetailed sides and a threaded hardwood knob. By contrast, the rare large washstand from New Lebanon is an example of the most accomplished Shaker cabinet making, a frame and panel case connected to square-to-round tapered legs, surmounted by a dovetailed, overhanging gallery. The door permitted the washbowl and pitcher to be stored out of sight. The overall proportions of this simple, functional piece confirm its status as a minor masterpiece. (Left: maple with pine and unknown hardwood knob, 34½" × 17¼" × 15½". Miller Collection and above: cherry and pine, 30½" × 35¾" × 17¼". Courtesy of Hancock Shaker Village.)

Wherever there was a washstand, there had to be a rack for hanging damp towels. The standing rack with a "box top" and "shoe" feet was one form; more commonly they had two, three, or four horizontal bars without the box. Rack sizes varied with the number of people (and towels) they served. The box was a Shaker refinement that accommodated extra towels without taking up more space. The towels shown here belonged to Sister Sophia Copley (1846–1898) of Enfield, Connecticut. All the tenons (square projections) have wedges in their open mortise joints—a more sophisticated but less common means of securing these than the use of pegs. The hanging rack is a very rare form. The Andrewses bought this one from the Shakers at Mount Lebanon, probably in the 1930s. It is one more example of how useful their ubiquitous peg rails were.

(Standing rack: cherry, 32½" × 35¼" × 12¼". Miller Collection and Hanging rack: cherry with iron hardware, 16½" × 24⅝" × 4⅛". Courtesy of Hancock Shaker Village.)

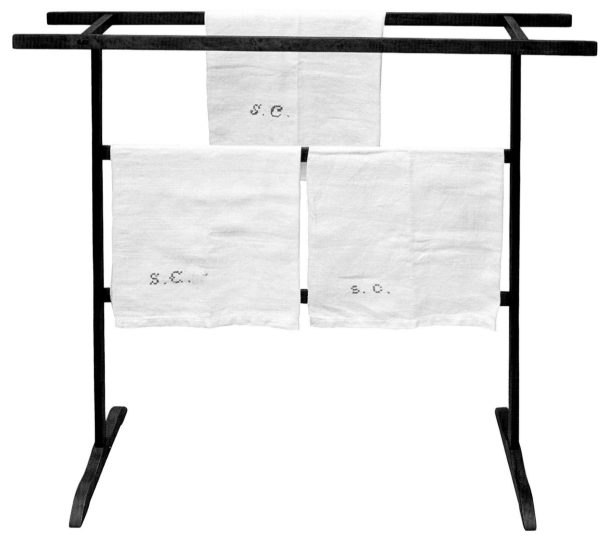

Although we are sure that every retiring room had one or more chairs, the type and number was not consistent. The often quoted, but not always obeyed 1845 *Millennial Laws* stated: "One rocking chair in a room is sufficient, except where the aged reside."[4] Even after Shaker interiors began to be photographed late in the nineteenth century, retiring rooms were seldom included. The images that survive from other rooms—usually where textile work was accomplished—show a mixture of Shaker and non-Shaker made chairs, with and without arms or rockers. Since armed rockers took up more space, these two examples represent what *might* have been found in a typical room at Enfield, New Hampshire, before about 1860. Relatively few of their bulkier, armed rockers are known to have come from there. These two armless types are compact and lightweight, but quite sturdy. At other villages, production chairs made at Mount Lebanon were used frequently, as is evident in period photographs.

These two rocking chairs may appear identical at a quick glance since both were made at Enfield, New Hampshire, between 1820 and 1840 and share many characteristics. In fact, most of the chairs made at this community during this period are generally similar, the main differences being the thinness or thickness of the front and rear posts and, to some extent, precise dimensions. All have three arched slats and "candle flame" finials; most have seat rails that are drilled with a series of holes to accommodate woven cane seats. These two examples differ mainly in their finishes and the heights of their seats: 17 inches at the front edge on the left and original red paint; 18¼ inches on the right with reddish-brown stain.

(Birch and cane, 39¾" × 18" × 20½" and 41" × 18¼" × 20½". Miller Collection.)

With time, more living space was allotted to individuals as many communities continued to expand existing living quarters or build new ones.[5] As late as 1883–84 Sabbathday Lake built a new dwelling house, one that is still in use. Yet, at about the time the number of rooms was growing, the number of Believers was declining. The net result was that brothers and sisters had more space in their rooms—space that could well have been taken up by a table such as this. Made at Enfield, New Hampshire, it exhibits elements that are considered to be "classic" for the 1820–1840 period at this community: the use of all birch wood; narrow, very slightly tapered round legs; plain skirts; flat-faced drawer with narrow beading around its edges; and a broad overhanging top with "breadboard" ends. (This was a means of preventing the top from warping by the application of a strip of wood to each end, with the grain running counter to the grain of the single-board top.) As with so much of the furniture from here, it is covered in a coat of brick-red paint. (Birch with pine drawer parts, 26½" × 28¼" × 23". Miller Collection.)

Sitting atop this table is a lift-top writing desk made at Canterbury. Before the last half of the nineteenth century, Shakers who did not hold positions of authority, or were not recording information of some sort, were discouraged from writing, which was regarded as an unnecessary display of individuality or even vanity, a distraction. In the latter part of that century though, a variety of writing desks were made for the use of rank-and-file members. Most desks were smaller and of lighter weight than this one, and generally of pine; whereas this one is made primarily of butternut. It would not have been uncommon to see a desk similar to this in a late nineteenth-century retiring room. More often than not, desks were outfitted with a lock set for privacy. (Butternut and pine with brass hardware and bone escutcheon, 6½" × 23" × 19¼". Miller Collection.)

More will be said about the Shakers' involvement with box stoves in the following chapter for they were a significant and innovative means for heating most of their spaces. Nearly all, if not all, retiring rooms in dwelling houses built in the eastern communities before about 1860 used this basic type of stove for warmth. In order not to singe wooden floors, slabs of stone or tin-clad planks of wood were placed under the feet. A shavings box for starting the fire (see chapter 4) was always close by as was a chip box (or full-sized, lidded wood box). Chip boxes generally held kindling and small logs rather than chips.

(Stove, without reproduction stovepipe: cast and forged iron, 20" × 35" x 13¾". Miller Collection.)

The box on the left is more typical of the functional pieces used for this purpose. The bottom and all of the corners are reinforced with brackets of strap iron; this made the lightweight piece very sturdy. The dovetailed corners, high arching hoop handle, and bright yellow paint of the box on the right went beyond mere function; it is an example of Shaker elegance and would have brightened any room.

(Left: pine and ash with metal hardware, 17¼" × 18" × 11⅝" and Right: pine with hardwood handle, 15" × 20" × 10⅜". Courtesy of the Art Complex Museum.)

12
The Shakers and the Invention of the Circular Saw
A Circular Argument

CHRISTIAN GOODWILLIE

PERHAPS THE GREATEST of all Shaker inventions was the circular saw, developed by Sister Tabitha Babbitt at Harvard, Massachusetts, in 1813—or so myriad sources would have us believe. In fact, it is unlikely that the Shakers invented the circular saw, despite numerous Shaker and non-Shaker printed claims. This brief examination of the history of the circular saw cannot hope to be definitive, but an examination of primary source materials relating to the question reveals that if the Shakers were not the very first to use the circular saw, they were certainly early proponents.

Since the late Middle Ages, carpenters had used waterpower to drive saw mills with reciprocating blades. As large logs, or "deals," were slowly moved forward along a horizontal surface or "carriage," a blade or series of blades worked up and down, cutting them into smaller pieces. Until relatively late in the eighteenth century, split and hewn timbers were considered superior for building because the wood was separated along its natural grain, thus retaining maximum tensile strength through the wood fibers.

Although split and hewn timbers may have been misshapen, they were generally considered stronger than sawn timbers whose grain had been disrupted by cutting.

As with many other important inventions in history, the circumstances surrounding the development of the circular saw are unclear. There are many early references, so it is almost impossible to establish primacy for any given example. For sawyers, carpenters, and joiners the advantage of the circular saw was immediately clear: the rotary blade allowed for continuous cutting at a very high rate of speed. The combined motions of the advancing wood and rapidly spinning blade made processing materials faster, more accurate, and more efficient.

The radius of early circular saw blades was relatively small and allowed only for the cutting of what carpenters of the late eighteenth and early nineteenth centuries called "small stuff" i.e.,

FACING PAGE: This stove was called a "super-heater" because the presence of an upper firebox forced the heated air through this second chamber and radiated much more heat into a room.

clapboards, lath, and sash. These smaller circular saws were commonly referred to as "buz" or "buzz saws." Herein lies a key point in the argument over whether the Shakers invented the circular saw. Though it is certain that they did not invent the smaller "buzz saw," could they have developed the larger circular saw used in mills to process large timber?

The first documented patent in an English-speaking country that refers to them reads: "saws, which are a circular figure" for cutting wood (as well as metal, stone, and ivory). It was granted to Samuel Miller in Southampton, England, in 1777.[1] Smaller, circular metal blades had been used in surgical instruments for many years prior to this date. Other than a series of vague references in secondary works on the history of saw technology, there is a dearth of primary source material about circular saws through the rest of the eighteenth century. Part of "An Oration" delivered by a "citizen of the United States" on July 11, 1800, reads, ". . . we have learned the use of the saw mill from the Hollenders: if the Russians should further instruct us in its improvement, by the application of the circular saw, without a retrograde motion."[2] This passage mirrors claims often found in a variety of secondary sources that the Russians and Dutch both influenced the development of the circular saw in England. Further research in primary source materials in those countries may yield much valuable information.

An early book on the history of saws cites the following British uses of circular saws, though without documentation: "In 1804 a man named Trotter secured a patent on a circular saw, and Sir Samuel Bentham (who later invented a circular saw made in segments) made a circular saw for the British Admiralty prior to 1800. Historians credit T. Brunel with first bringing circular saws into important service. He employed them for cutting ship's blocks—an application adopted by the British Admiralty Board in 1804 for the Portsmouth Yard. Brunel patented a veneer-saw in 1805, marking another advance."[3]

So, where do the Shakers fit into all of this? Intriguingly, the next contemporary reference located is an advertisement, originally published in the *Pittsfield [Mass.] Sun* and reprinted in the *United States' Gazette for the Country* for December 8, 1813.

We the subscribers, having been threatened with prosecution by certain purchasers of patent rights, for making and using of certain kinds of machinery, which are of our own invention, and have been in use among us for many years prior to all patent dates, we take this opportunity, in order to prevent all further imposition upon ourselves and the publick, to publish the following useful machines viz. Circular Saws, of all sizes, from 19 to 21 ½ inches in diameter, fine or coarse, suitable for splitting of lath, grooving of boards, or any other use, to move by water, and or foot, and have been in use for 20 years. Likewise, a saw for the purpose of sawing, a circle, such as Half Bushel, Tub, and Pail Bottoms, and Fellies of Wheels of any description, and has been in use 15 years."

From the People Called Shakers, Nov. 1, 1813.[4]

This startling claim, that the Shakers had been using large diameter circular saws since at least 1793, is unsubstantiated by any other contemporary source and would give them priority over any other known American developer or user. The Shakers' had to establish their rights for the use of such a saw without the purchase of a patent right because the sale of such patent rights for circular saws first occurred sometime around 1815.[5]

Brother Isaac Newton Youngs of New Lebanon, New York, published his monumental history of the Shakers, *A Concise View of the Church of God,* in 1856. This remarkable work comprehensively treats every aspect of Shaker life, including many industries. In the section on "Carpenter & Joiner Work" he states: "After the year 1813 there were some important improvements, particularly the buz saw was introduced, for straightening & slitting stuff."[6] Strangely, Youngs makes no mention of a circular saw in the sections on building, coopering, blacksmithing, or anywhere else in his manuscript. In terms of chronology, he seems to indicate that the circular saw was not introduced, at least at New Lebanon, before 1813. This omission is significant in light of Youngs' careful attention to accuracy and detail in noting the appearance of other new technologies among the Believers. The date conflicts with the newspaper advertisement cited above, as well as with other Shaker claims which will be examined later.

The mid-1810s seem to have been a time of ferment regarding circular saw technology in the United States and England. An undocumented reference in a 1916 book states: "The first circular saw in this country is supposed to have been produced by Benjamin Cummins, about 1814, at Bentonsville, N. Y.—his facilities consisting solely of the ordinary tools and equipment of a blacksmith's shop."[7] George Smart of London patented a bench-mounted circular saw in 1815. An engraving of this saw was first published in Philadelphia in 1816.[8] A newspaper article from Baltimore dated July 21, 1817, trumpets a saw "four feet, or upwards, in diameter" used for cutting mahogany veneers.[9] This manifestation of the circular saw was patented by Adam Stewart and powered by a steam engine. An October 10, 1817, advertisement in the *Dedham [Mass.] Gazette* announced that a "Circular Saw will in a few weeks be in operation for sawing Veneers."[10] Other newspaper notices of the period demonstrate the quick spread of Stewart's patented mill, as well as the use of circular saws based on Stewart, and the Frenchman Brunot (possibly the Brunel cited above?), in New England and the mid-Atlantic states. According to an early history, "Circular saws for manufacturing lumber [are] supposed to have originated in a patent granted March 16, 1820 to Robert Eastman and J. Jaquith of Brunswick. Me."[11] Advertisements for Robert Eastman's "Rotary Sawing Machine" began appearing in New England newspapers in 1821, and a full description and an illustration of it were published in the *American Journal of Science* in 1822.[12]

The Shakers reenter the picture at this point through an article published widely in American newspapers in 1821. Originally published in the *Ballston [N.Y.] Farmer*, it read:

> Mechanics. *Useful discovery*— The circular saw, as far as I know, is a recent invention, and certainly a very useful one. The shakers, at their village in Watervleit, near Albany, have this invention in very excellent use and great perfection. In a saw mill there, they have a set of machinery on this principle, erected at a very trifling expense, which, for cutting stuff for a

window sash, grooving a floor plank, gaging clapboards, &c. with one man and a boy to attend it, will perform the labor of thirty men.

> But I saw a new and novel machine in operation in this house, so full of ingenious machinery, which deserves a place among the most useful discoveries in mechanics of the present day. It is a circular buzz of thin soft sheet iron, six inches in diameter, which cuts the hardest steel almost with the ease of tallow. The buzz is well secured by cottrels on an axis turned by a band, and moves with inconceivable velocity, and the engine is so constructed as to secure in a proper position and bring into contact whatever you wish to cut. A steel saw-mill saw-plate was placed in the machine, having the old teeth all taken off, and in four minutes it cut, with perfect accuracy eleven teeth—or half cut—for, in order to finish the cutting, the saw must be turned in the machine, so as to come work-wise for cutting the other half. With a machine of this kind in perfect order, I should say that the old teeth might be all cut from an old saw-mill saw, by a perfectly straight line, and a new set of teeth cut, gaged perfectly, in less than an hour. The cutting is done so accurately, that very little filing is necessary to complete the dressing of the saw for business. I saw it in operation in July, 1817, and immediately sent a description of it to the publishers of the Cyclopedia, but I do not know whether it has been published.—The Shakers consider the discovery too useful to be monopolized by a patent, and consented to my giving it publicity as public property. Like most others, this discovery was by accident. A piece of sheet tin nearly round, was put into the lathe, and a file applied to the edge, in order to dress it down to a perfect circle. The file had no effect upon the tin, but the tin cut the file, as, in other matters, it sometimes happens that the biter gets bitten. Learning this fact, an ingenious young Shaker, Freegift Wells, tried the experiment, succeeded, and constructed the machine which I saw. I applied to it pieces of old files, and it cut them in two almost as quick as a candle could have been cut with hot iron.[13]

This article describes a circular saw for cutting metal, apparently developed by the Shakers, but interestingly describes it as being used for cutting new teeth for a traditional straight-blade reciprocating saw. So, were the Shakers using large diameter saw blades for milling timber by 1820? The answer by the account in this article seems to be no.

Circular saws were in widespread use by the early 1820s, so tracking their development further is not germane to this article. Yet, what of the repeated Shaker claims to have invented the circular saw? A manuscript history of the Enfield, New Hampshire, Shaker community written in 1858 states that "The first 'wheel' or 'circular saw' used here, was a slab saw, made with spokes and a rim of steel. This was first used, in the mill about 1803."[14] If this claim could be verified, it would certainly put the Shakers at the forefront of circular saw use in the United States.

The *Transactions of the New York State Agricultural Society* for 1870 records the gift of "a circular saw 12½ inches in diameter, said to have been forged in 1792, by Benjamin Bruce, of New Lebanon, N.Y." This saw was donated by Brother George Wicker-sham and is still in the collection of the New York State Museum. However, the date attributed to it by Br. Wickersham cannot be proven independently.[15] The Shakers themselves published news of the gift in *The Shaker* for January 1876, with the claim that "the first buzz, or circular saw ever made, was manufactured at Mt. Lebanon Shakers, and the original deposited in the Museum of the State,"[16] thereby asserting that it was they who had actually invented the circular saw. They reiterated that claim in *The Shaker* for August 1877.

Watervliet Brother D. A. Buckingham stated, "The first *circular saw* ever made was invented by the Lebanon Shakers, and may be seen to-day in the 'State Geological Department,' at Albany, N.Y."[17] The 1878 history of Columbia County, New York, stated: "It is generally believed that the buzz-saw was here invented, by a Shaker named Amos Bishop. This saw is now preserved in the State cabinet at Albany."[18] Here, attribution for the invention has shifted from Benjamin Bruce to Amos Bishop.

What of Sister Tabitha Babbitt of Harvard, Massachusetts? The case for her did not appear for another two decades, in the *Manifesto* of February 1899.

> One day while watching the men sawing wood, she noted that one half the motion was lost and she conceived the idea of the circular saw. She made a tin disk, and notching it around the edge, slipped it on the spindle of her spinning wheel, tried it on a piece of a shingle and found that her idea was a practical one, and from this crude beginning came the circular saw of to-day. Sister Tabitha's first saw was made in sections and fastened to a board. A Lebanon Shaker later conceived the idea of making the saw out of a single piece of metal.[19]

Sarah (Tabitha) Babbitt was born at Hardwick, Massachusetts, on December 10, 1779. She was admitted to the Harvard Shaker community on August 12, 1793—the same year Benjamin Bruce or Amos Bishop are supposed to have invented the circular saw at New Lebanon. The information about her invention was first published in the *Boston Sunday Globe* for October 30, 1898, as part of an article on Harvard Eldress Eliza Babbitt. Obviously, the Harvard Shakers supplied the information, but since Tabitha Babbitt had died in 1853, it could not be verified. The case for Babbitt as inventor was re-told by Anna White and Leila S. Taylor in their history, *Shakerism: Its Meaning and Message*, which basically repeated the story from *The Manifesto*.[20] This reference has somehow found its way into countless later works on the Shakers, their inventions, and the history of technology in general.

Where does all of this leave us? It is safe to say that the Shakers did not invent the circular saw, but they do appear to have been among its earliest users, and may have created new forms and uses for it. Too often, proven Shaker innovation is marginalized in favor of unsubstantiated claims for Shaker invention. This is a disservice to a group whose more than two hundred years of success in this country is a tribute to their ability to alter, adapt, and improve almost every technology they encountered. 🌿

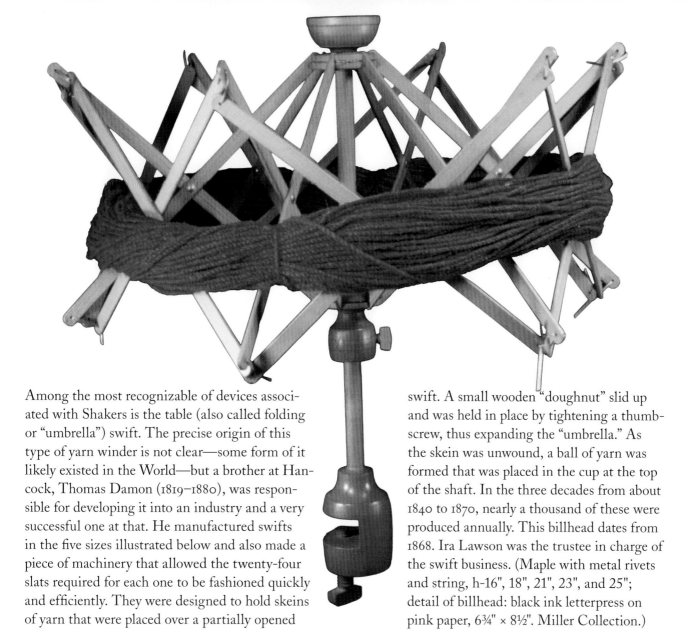

Among the most recognizable of devices associated with Shakers is the table (also called folding or "umbrella") swift. The precise origin of this type of yarn winder is not clear—some form of it likely existed in the World—but a brother at Hancock, Thomas Damon (1819–1880), was responsible for developing it into an industry and a very successful one at that. He manufactured swifts in the five sizes illustrated below and also made a piece of machinery that allowed the twenty-four slats required for each one to be fashioned quickly and efficiently. They were designed to hold skeins of yarn that were placed over a partially opened swift. A small wooden "doughnut" slid up and was held in place by tightening a thumbscrew, thus expanding the "umbrella." As the skein was unwound, a ball of yarn was formed that was placed in the cup at the top of the shaft. In the three decades from about 1840 to 1870, nearly a thousand of these were produced annually. This billhead dates from 1868. Ira Lawson was the trustee in charge of the swift business. (Maple with metal rivets and string, h-16", 18", 21", 23", and 25"; detail of billhead: black ink letterpress on pink paper, 6¾" × 8½". Miller Collection.)

Elder Elijah Myrick (1824–1890) patented a cast-iron chimney cap (U.S. Patent No. 90,380) in 1869. In the Letters Patent he states: "It is well known that the upper courses of brick in commonly constructed chimneys are liable to become loose by the actions of weather upon the mortar. . . . To overcome this difficulty cast-iron caps, made of one piece, have been used to some extent; but the objection . . . has been found in getting caps to fit the various sizes and forms of chimneys. . . . My invention consists in constructing cast-iron or metal chimney caps in sections or divisions, in such manner that the same patterns be used, and the castings therefrom will answer for all the various-sized chimneys."

His design incorporated scalloped flanges of differing heights that stabilized the pieces laterally and a system for connecting the small sections of cast iron with a short pin at the end of one to engage a hole in its neighbor. Some of these caps are still in place on former Shaker buildings at the Harvard community. The corner piece is embossed: "E. Myrick's—Patent—May 25 1869" along with the name of the sales agent, J. D. Otterson and the place of manufacture, Nashua, New Hampshire. (Cast iron: corner piece, 3" × 8¼" × 9". Private Collection.)

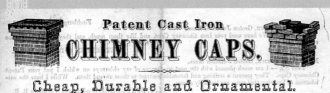

This rare, possibly unique, surviving broadside (detail shown) reads, in part: "This invention was brought to public notice only a few months last season, and received unqualified approval of our intelligent mechanics, masons and builders." Although it only received patent protection in May 1869, testimonials date from June of that year. The last of these is dated February 1870. (Black ink letterpress on off-white paper, [full size] 10¼" × 7½". Courtesy of Hancock Shaker Village.)

E. MYRICK.
Chimney Cap.

UNITED STATES PATENT OFFICE.

No. 90,380.

Patented May 25, 1869.

ELIJAH MYRICK, OF HARVARD, MASSACHUSETTS.

CHIMNEY-CAP.

Specification forming part of Letters Patent No. **90,380,** dated May 25, 1869.

To all whom it may concern:

Be it known that I, ELIJAH MYRICK, of Harvard, in the county of Worcester and State of Massachusetts, have invented a new and useful Improvement in Chimney-Caps; and I do hereby declare that the following is a full and exact description thereof, reference being had to the accompanying drawings, and to the letters of reference marked thereon.

It is well known that the upper courses of brick in commonly-constructed chimneys are liable to become loose by the action of the weather upon the mortar, and the top bricks are liable to get out of place and be blown off by the wind. To overcome this difficulty cast-iron caps, made of one piece, have been used to some extent; but the objection to the extensive use of these caps is found in getting a proper fit, and the difficulty of placing them on chimneys with commonly-con...

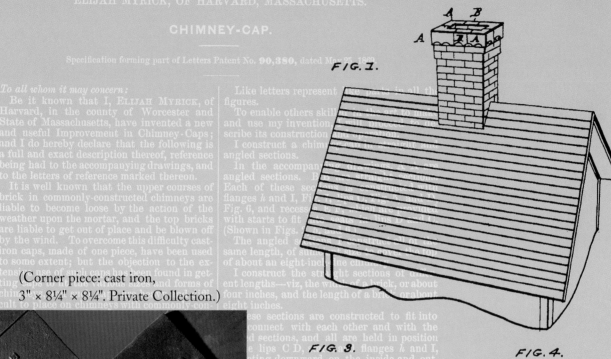

FIG. 1.

Like letters represent like parts in all the figures.

To enable others skilled in the art to make and use my invention, I will proceed to describe its construction and operation.

I construct a chimney-cap in straight and angled sections.

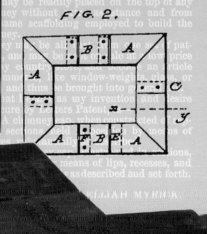

FIG. 2.

FIG. 3.

FIG. 4.

FIG. 5.

FIG. 6.

FIG. 7.

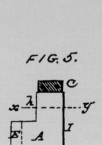

the cap. Fig. 5 is a top view of an angle-section, showing the method of connecting it with the next section. Fig. 6 is a top view of a straight section, showing the method of connecting it with the next section. Fig. 7 is a cross-sectional view through the line of Figs. 2 and 5, showing the seat for the cap and the outer and inner flanges of the cap that hold the cap in place when placed in position on the top of a chimney.

ELIJAH MYRICK.

(Corner piece: cast iron,
3" × 8¼" × 8¼". Private Collection.)

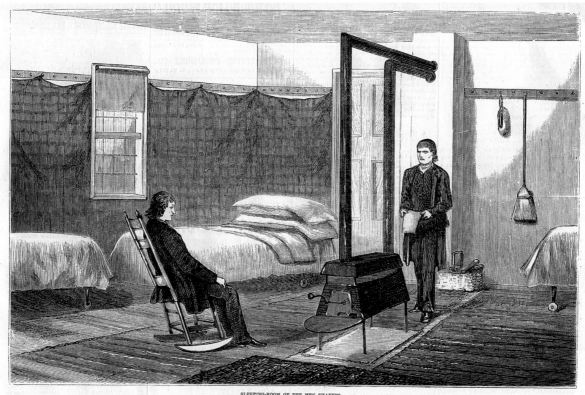

SLEEPING-ROOM OF THE MEN SHAKERS.
THE SHAKERS OF LEBANON, NEW YORK.—Sketched by J. Becker.

The precise origin of the Shakers' version of a box stove is unknown, but early in the nineteenth century, box stoves were found throughout the eastern communities. The "exploded" view of component parts (with the legs not visible) shows how these devices were a model of simplicity: their few parts were held together mainly by the force of gravity (plus simple hinges for the door and air vent). Brethren cut and carved wood patterns for the portions of the stove that were cast, usually in the World—the base, firebox(es), and doors. Shaker blacksmiths forged the other elements such as legs and latches. The example illustrated here was called a "super-heater" because the presence of an upper firebox forced the heated air through this second chamber and radiated much more heat into a room. Sometimes an extended length of stovepipe was used to connect the stoves to a vent in the walls, adding more surface area to diffuse heat. (Cast and forged iron, 24" × 11¾" × 29". Courtesy of the Shaker Museum and Library and Illustration: *Frank Leslie's Illustrated Newspaper*, September 6, 1873. Courtesy of Hancock Shaker Village.)

Almost every interior wall in a Shaker village—rooms, hallways, shops, closets, and attics—was lined with a strip of peg rail (or pegboard). Turning individual pegs must have been a time-consuming job; even more labor intensive would have been the process of making threads in the end of each. Although some pegs were friction-fit into bored holes, most were threaded. These two innovative devices made at New Lebanon addressed this challenge. In both cases, a peg was clamped into place and turned against a blade. The shorter one was a hand-held device, the longer one was mechanical. Here, the top of the box with its fixed blade was gradually advanced while the user slowly cranked the handle. Turning threads in the boards was much simpler; only a drill press and threaded bit—or tap—was required.

(The common clothespin is frequently pointed to by the popular press as a Shaker invention. There is not a shred of evidence to support this contention. Shakers sometimes referred to their strips of peg rails as "clothes pins" since they hung a variety of garments from them and this seems to be the source of the confusion. It should also be noted that they did not "invent" peg rails either, but rather refined them.)

(ABOVE: cherry and hickory with iron hardware, 7¾" × 7" × 29". Courtesy of the Shaker Museum and Library and BELOW: maple with iron hardware, 13¾" × 4⅝". Courtesy of Hancock Shaker Village.)

Near the top of almost every Shaker enthusiast's list of significant innovations is the invention and further development of a tilting mechanism for the back posts of chairs—already discussed to some extent in Chapter 8. These took two basic forms—wood and metal. The wooden one gained popularity with Shakers in the 1830s and reached its apogee of refinement at Enfield, New Hampshire, at about that time. This side chair displays many of the refinements discussed with reference to rocking chairs in the previous chapter but here there are tilter buttons—half-rounded balls set into hollowed sockets at the bottom of each rear post. Close-up views show the ball with its knotted leather thong and, several inches higher, the end of the thong secured in place with a tiny tack. This mechanism not only prevented marring of floors, it prevented wear and even splitting of the post bottoms. (Birch and cane with original red paint, 41" × 18½" × 13½". Miller Collection.)

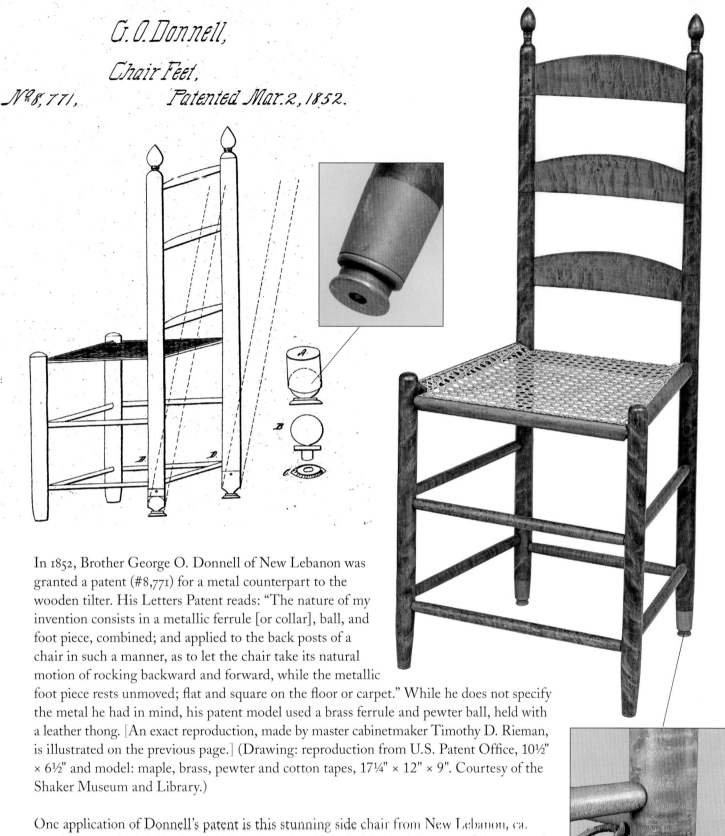

G. O. Donnell,
Chair Feet,
Nº 8,771.   Patented Mar. 2, 1852.

In 1852, Brother George O. Donnell of New Lebanon was granted a patent (#8,771) for a metal counterpart to the wooden tilter. His Letters Patent reads: "The nature of my invention consists in a metallic ferrule [or collar], ball, and foot piece, combined; and applied to the back posts of a chair in such a manner, as to let the chair take its natural motion of rocking backward and forward, while the metallic foot piece rests unmoved; flat and square on the floor or carpet." While he does not specify the metal he had in mind, his patent model used a brass ferrule and pewter ball, held with a leather thong. [An exact reproduction, made by master cabinetmaker Timothy D. Rieman, is illustrated on the previous page.] (Drawing: reproduction from U.S. Patent Office, 10½" × 6½" and model: maple, brass, pewter and cotton tapes, 17¼" × 12" × 9". Courtesy of the Shaker Museum and Library.)

One application of Donnell's patent is this stunning side chair from New Lebanon, ca. 1855. The wood is highly figured birch (posts) and maple (slats) with a coat of clear varnish. The sense of lightness is enhanced by the use of woven cane for the seat and gently arched slats that graduate and flatten from bottom to top, the same features that visually "lift" the Enfield chair [previous page]. The close-up [above] shows that the entire tilter mechanism here is pewter. (Birch, maple, woven cane, and pewter, 42" × 18½" × 14". Courtesy of the Shaker Museum and Library.)

One of only a handful of inventions to be patented by the western Shakers was a sash balance. Brother Sanford J. Russell, who sometimes resided at South Union, Kentucky, sometimes at Union Village, Ohio (and sometimes in the World), advertised that he received a patent for his invention in 1872. What he actually did gain patent protection for that year (#129,367) was an *improved cord clamp* designed to be used with the sash balance. Illustrated on page 193 is a reproduction of the "improved" device, made from an old Shaker window sash but using new parts. Master craftsman John Munro constructed it for the exhibit. A length of cord attached to the lower sash was looped through a single, centrally located pulley fastened to the top frame of the window. The cord was pulled to raise this sash (and its own weight lowered it). The patented cord clamp consisted of opposing toothed cams that gripped the cord, preventing the window from sliding shut. The whole purpose of the system was to overcome the use of side cords and counterweights (which, paradoxically, seem to have been more convenient *and* hidden from sight). Perhaps that is why Brother Russell's invention did not succeed.

Shaker Sash Balance,

PATENTED BY S. J. RUSSELL, JULY 16, 1872, IMPROVED AND PERFECTED WITH CORD-HOLDER ATTACHMENT, FEB'Y 1, 1875.

A long felt want now fully supplied.

For years many our leading mechanics and others interested in the subject have been endeavoring to perfect a device to supercede the cumbrous and expensive sash-weights for the easy adjustment of windows, cheap, durable, easy in operation, and combining economy with utility. We are now fully prepared to supply this great want, having perfected a Sash Balance, combining the three great requisites, to-wit:

SIMPLICITY, ECONOMY, and DURABILITY.

We furthermore claim, and can fully establish, that our device is so utterly simple in its workings, in the impossibility of its getting out of order, the advantage it possesses over the unsightly catches and locks in an ornamental point of view, settng aside the cheapness of our Balance, that no intelligent housekeeper will fail to possess it as soon as its advantages are thoroughly understood.

OUR SASH BALANCE HAS THE UNQUALIFIED APPROVAL OF ALL BUILDERS, HOUSE CARPENTERS, ETC.

To further simplify the matter, we claim for the SHAKER BALANCE the following undoubted advantages over all other devices: 1st. The readiness with which it can be attached to any window, large or small, without the slightest cost. 2nd. The ease with which it can be operated. 3rd. Its great durability. 4th. The window is more securely locked in any position. 5th. Its perfect ventilation. 6th. It obviates the necessity of curtains or other hangings, as it is of itself highly ornamental. 7th. The advantage in a pecuniary light over every other device of the kind ever offered to the public. THE SAVING IN COST IS IMMENSE.

INSTRUCTIONS FOR OPERATING THE BALANCE.

Balanged sash when closed top and bottom: by raising the lower sash, the top one will come down that much, giving the most perfect ventilation possible; this convenience supercedes anything extant.

To operate each sash seperately, when the upper one is closed at the top: Throw up the lower one and with the left hand under it, pull it against the front strips, thus it is easily held there, and with the right hand, pull the cord to the right, and down so as to raise the top sash up a little, this releases the grip of the eccentrics, and while you hold the cord to the right you have full command of either sash, and can place them in any desired position; now bring the cord to the center and the eccentrics resume their grip firmly.

When the lower sash is thrown up so as to double the upper one, with the left hand under both sash and the right hand at the cord, both are easily thrown up to their highest point, leaving all the ventilation or opening below.

To raise the lower sash easily, leaving the top one closed: Throw it up as high as you wish, holding it there with the left hand, and with the right by the cord, pull the top one up again. In repairing the sash with the balance, take off the butterfly-cord-holder on the top sash and both are free. This butterfly-cord-holder is an improvement and of malleable iron, will bear hammering on to the cord and screwing tight; put the open end down at the lower edge of the upper rail of the sash.

We append the following, descriptive of the above cut, from the Scientific American, without comment:

THE SHAKER SASH BALANCE.

Our illustration represents a very simple and ingenious device, which does away with the usual cords and pulleys on windows, by making one sash balance the other. It is cheap, readily applied, and will afford all the ventilation side weights do.

A cord (Fig. 1.) is firmly attached to the lower edge of upper rail (as exhibited in cut) with a single screw, by means of a metalic button, placed end downward, inside of which the end is coiled, and is then passed over a pulley, adjusted, as represented, in the upper part of the window frame, placed at a sufficient distance from the upper sash, to enable the cord to work freely, yet near enough to guide the sash into its proper place, obviating the necessity of parting strips in old buildings, where there are none usually. A short piece at the bottom is all that is necessary to steady the lower sash. The end of the cord extends down through the apparatus A, which is shown in detail in Fig 2, forms the essential portion of the device. It consists simply in two eccentrics (B), secured in a suitably ornamental metal case, and fastened to the upper part of the lower case. It needs no explanation to show that one sash counterpoises the other, so that by a touch of the finger they may be raised or lowered to a given distance. If, however, it may be desired to move but one, and that the top sash, the operation is easily accomplished by drawing the cord to the right or left, which releives the grip of the eccentrics. On straightening the cord, the latter immediately resume their clasp and hold the sash in any position. To raise the lower sash it is only necessary to hold the cord firmly and lift the sash with the hand, then it will remain as placed.

If you are building, the SHAKER SASH BALANCE will prove a great saving, both in cost and labor. If you have old windows permanently closed by broken springs, disordered box frames of old-fashioned construction, the "SHAKER BALANCE" will provide the means of opening and closing at pleasure, securing perfect ventilation.

GOOD AGENTS WANTED, for further particulars, samples, etc. address,

S. J. RUSSELL,

So Union, Logan Co., Ky.

(Broadside: black ink letterpress and wood engraving on off-white paper, 21" × 12". Collection of the United Society of Shakers, Sabbathday Lake, Maine)

(Window sash with frame, pine, glass, and brass, 44" × 34¾". Courtesy of John Munro and Hancock Shaker Village.)

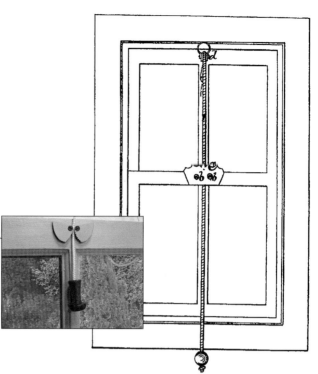

(Detail from Letters Patent, dated July 16, 1872; "Improvement in Cord-Clamps." Copy: Miller Collection.)

This cast brass clamp cover is a rare surviving example. (Brass, 1½" × 3¾". Private Collection.)

SHAKER'S
WINDOW SASH LOCK.

A new device for securing ventilation.

SIMPLE AND EASILY MANIPULATED, ADJUSTABLE TO ALL WINDOW SASH, SAFELY HOLDING EITHER AT ANY POINT, WITHOUT MARRING PAINT OR VARNISH.

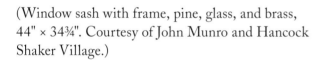

It consists of a clamp bar let loosely into the left side of the window frame, having two small lever eccentrics attached thereto by a screw or rivet, at the center where the each comes together. The strip which holds the sash in place is let on the eccentrics, the lever or points only being visible. If a parting strip is used it should be cut off at the bar, so that the top may be used at pleasure.

By pressing on the points the position of the eccentrics is changed so as to press against the lower sash, causing the catch on the end of the bar to pull against the top sash, thus locking them so tight that it is impossible to move either without opening the points.

Also, the eccentrics, if desired, may be put on the left face of each sash frame, in which case they will perfectly lock and tighten the sash and destroy all shaking and rattling by winds or otherwise. In this case the eccentrics are visible. The strip must be sawed off from the lower eccentric upwards, the thickness of the eccentrics, so that it will work against the under frame. When the sash is too loose to be tightened by the eccentric, tack two bits or a strip on the right-hand edge.

In short, it is the simplest, safest and best sash lock in existence, and needs only to be seen to be appreciated. Sample sent by mail for twenty-five cents.

South Union, Logan Co., Ky.   S. J. RUSSELL.

In about 1877 Brother Russell (if, indeed, he was a Shaker at this time) came up with another invention that was advertised heavily in *The Shaker Manifesto* the following year. This was a window sash lock. It was attached to a window sash and when the swiveling cams were apart it did not make contact with the frame. Users wishing to secure a window— open or closed—pinched the levers, forcing the cams against the frame and preventing someone from moving the window from the outside. Russell never received patent protection for this invention and no more is known of it, nor are there any known surviving examples.

(LEFT: Black ink letterpress and engraving on pale green paper, [detail] 7" × 7". Courtesy of Hamilton College Library Digital Collections.)

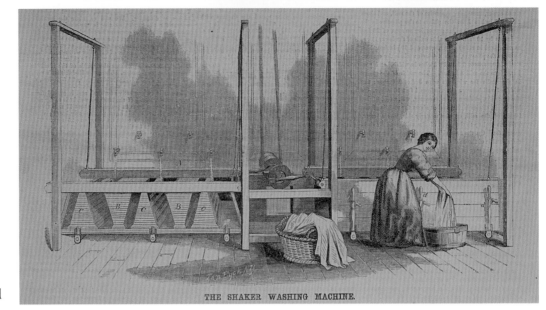

THE SHAKER WASHING MACHINE.

The Canterbury Shakers were justly proud of the washing machine that they consistently advertised as "improved." In fact, Brother David Parker (1807–1867) improved an earlier model of machine devised at New Lebanon and received patent protection for it in 1858. The "machine" actually consisted of two large boxes, three and one-half feet wide, with floors sloping down to a central drain that were outfitted with agitating paddles. Steam power, conveyed through a system of belts and pulleys, was used to move the paddles, and water was supplied (and drained) through a series of pipes with valves. These laundering machines were designed for use in large institutions—hotels, schools, and hospitals—not homes.

The cut-away drawing on the front page of the March 10, 1860, issue of *Scientific American* [above] shows the earlier version of this invention. The large red-painted model [below] has long levers along the sides to manually squeeze the paddles together after the wash water is drained, thus extracting excess water from clothing and bedding. This model won a medal at the 1876 Centennial Exhibition in Philadelphia.

(Black ink letterpress and wood engraving on tan paper, 13¼" × 9½". Miller Collection and Model: mixed woods and metal with red paint, 14" × 36" × 4½". Courtesy of Hancock Shaker Village.)

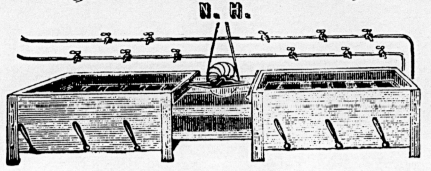

IMPROVED SHAKER WASHING MACHINE,
BUILT AT SHAKER VILLAGE,
N. H.

PATENTED July 23, 1877.

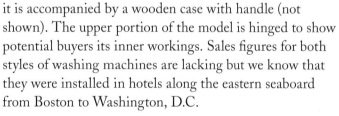

Under the direction of Brother James S. Kaime (1820–1894), further improvements were made, eliminating the cumbersome overhead frame, and this model was awarded a U.S. Patent in 1877. This small working model was probably a salesman's sample; it is accompanied by a wooden case with handle (not shown). The upper portion of the model is hinged to show potential buyers its inner workings. Sales figures for both styles of washing machines are lacking but we know that they were installed in hotels along the eastern seaboard from Boston to Washington, D.C.

(TOP: Black ink letterpress and wood or metal engravings on light blue paper [detail], full page size 9½" × 6". Courtesy of Hamilton College Library Digital Collections; LEFT: Model: unknown woods and metal, 3½" × 12" × 3¼". Courtesy of Canterbury Shaker Village; ABOVE: Medal: recto and verso, bronze, 3". Courtesy of Canterbury Shaker Village.)

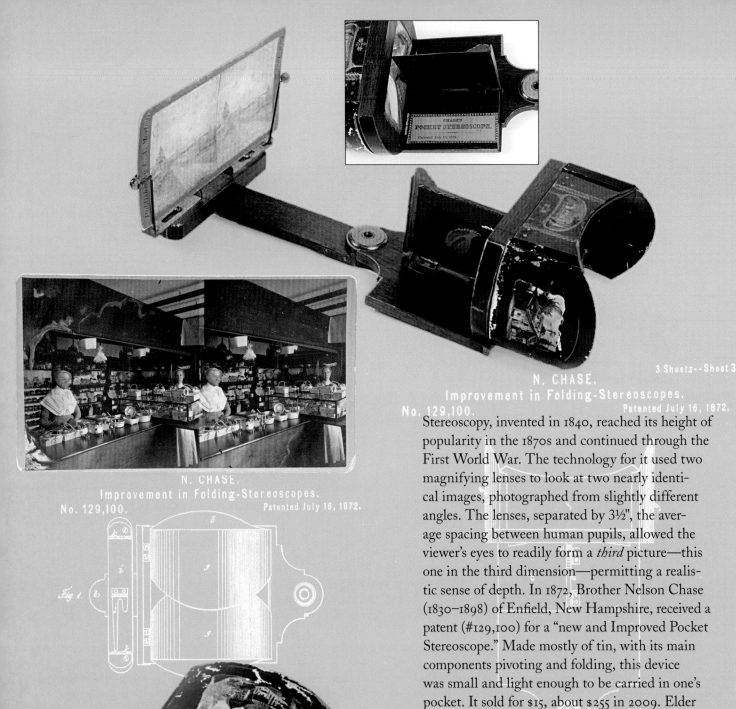

N. CHASE.
Improvement in Folding-Stereoscopes.
No. 129,100.
Patented July 16, 1872.

3 Sheets--Sheet 3.

N. CHASE.
Improvement in Folding-Stereoscopes.
No. 129,100.
Patented July 16, 1872.

Stereoscopy, invented in 1840, reached its height of popularity in the 1870s and continued through the First World War. The technology for it used two magnifying lenses to look at two nearly identical images, photographed from slightly different angles. The lenses, separated by 3½", the average spacing between human pupils, allowed the viewer's eyes to readily form a *third* picture—this one in the third dimension—permitting a realistic sense of depth. In 1872, Brother Nelson Chase (1830–1898) of Enfield, New Hampshire, received a patent (#129,100) for a "new and Improved Pocket Stereoscope." Made mostly of tin, with its main components pivoting and folding, this device was small and light enough to be carried in one's pocket. It sold for $15, about $255 in 2009. Elder Henry Blinn of Canterbury had this to say in 1873 of his efforts to sell them: "Its neatness, compactness, and general appearance was highly commended by all, but the price was thought to exceed propriety . . . [even] with 20 per ct. off at wholesale or by the doz." This may be the finest surviving example, with its label intact.

(Tin and unknown wood, 7" × 5¼" × 2" [folded], 13" × 5⅜" × 2¾" [open]. Courtesy of Hamilton College Special Collections and Stereocard, 3⅞" × 7". Private Collection.)

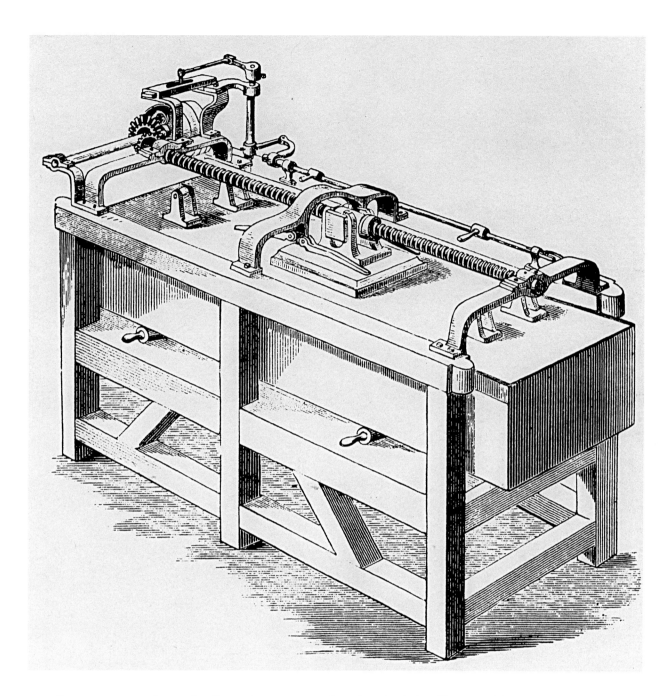

Between 1878 and 1884 the Canterbury community advertised this "Improved Shaker Mangle" in *The Shaker Manifesto*. Mangles were devices designed either to extract water from laundry as a wringer or to press fabrics using heated rollers. This seemingly was designed for the former, with a top connected to a mechanism that lowered it and squeezed the contents inside the box. No drain is evident, though, and the purpose for the rollers is unclear. Perhaps it performed *both* functions. The copy that sometimes accompanied the advertising does not clarify its use: "This mangle is very heavy and strongly built; runs smoothly, and performs excellent work and is easily kept in repair. Even to laundries already supplied with steam cylindrical mangles, this machine is a very necessary addition." It was never patented, and no sales figures for it are known to have survived.

(Black ink letterpress and wood or metal engravings on light blue paper, full page size 9½" × 6". Courtesy of Hamilton College Library Digital Collections.)

This jigsaw is an example of Shakers' clever adaptation in the realm of innovation. The wood or metal cut of a commercial sewing machine [below], manufactured by Grover and Baker, appeared in the 1878 issue of *The Shaker Manifesto*. (Most of the advertisements in this Shaker-published monthly were from the World.) The Shakers at some point took a similar sewing machine, mounted it on a wooden platform, added a wood frame and table, and inserted a fine saw blade where a sewing needle once was. The community of origin for this piece is not known.

(BELOW: Illustration: black ink letterpress and wood or metal engraving, [detail] 3⅛" × 3⅛". Courtesy of Hamilton College Library Digital Collections and LEFT: Saw: ash, pine, cherry, rubber, and iron, 53" × 42" × 21½". Courtesy of the Shaker Museum and Library.)

A GENUINE
Grover & Baker
SEWING MACHINE.

This engraving exactly represents the machine with the box cover off.

$65 FOR $15.

AN
UNEQUALED PREMIUM.

13
Innovations in Music and Song

Carol Medlicott

Music has always played a defining role in Shaker life. The primary distinguishing feature of Shaker worship—divinely inspired bodily movements and dancing—was a "gift" accompanied by singing. Many early observations of the Shakers focus upon Believers' distinctive singing. Perhaps not surprising for a sect based on dissent from established churches, the Shakers for the most part rejected the music and hymnody of surrounding traditional Christian congregations. Instead, they drew on the creativity of their own members to infuse their evolving culture with music. A vast number of Shaker music manuscripts survive, pointing to the importance of this category of their creative output.

Shakers' musical innovations stand in sharp contrast to those of other religious sects. Although Shakers were marvelously inventive in devising their own system of musical notation, that is not the most significant aspect of their musical innovation. Notation mattered to them to the extent that it served the higher goal of facilitating the production and sharing of music throughout the community. A far more profound innovation lay in how they democratized music production among the rank-and-file of members. Shakers permitted music to grow organically from within each community. In contrast, other religious denominations of the nineteenth century removed music production from practitioners' hands and redirected it to distant, institutionalized boards and publishing houses. For the Shakers, the process of producing music was deeply embedded in the everyday lives of all individuals, in all communities, east and west. Every Believer possessed equal potential for experiencing a musical "gift" that could be integrated into the ever-growing repository of music. For a sect in whom rigid leadership hierarchies helped to impose "Gospel Order," music production was remarkably free of hierarchical control. Musical gifts could issue from the humblest Believer to those holding the higher offices of Elder/Eldress or Father/Mother. They came from women and men, teenaged to elderly, white and black, mixed-race, and recent immigrants. And during many periods of Shaker history, songs poured forth spontaneously in seemingly endless quantities, sometimes in the very midst of worship, yet such music was meticulously written down for posterity.

Along with democratization, another remarkable innovation was the application of music to the challenges of geographic separation. Shakers have been the most geographically diffused communal society in American history. Creating and maintaining gospel union resided at the core of Shaker identity, but accomplishing that across a span of a thousand miles was daunting indeed. Yet, because music was democratized and organic, it could be applied more flexibly and prescriptively to a range of social occasions. Manuscripts reveal songs carefully produced by the hundreds to mark specific holidays, visits, funerals, and other cultural milestones. Songs could also act as custodians of Shakers' intimate friendships. Far more mobile than Shakers themselves, songs were regularly transmitted in correspondence, carried by visitors, and given as gifts, in addition to being bound into printed collections. While one Shaker in Kentucky might have little available opportunity to feel in "union" with another in New Hampshire, shared songs allowed Shakers to communicate with distant strangers in a common language.

The Shakers' music-infused physical worship was itself an innovation; and as they further defined their collective identity, more innovations followed. Shaker music became a distinct enterprise, intriguing and recognizable to outsiders, cohesive yet flexible to Believers. Although one finds creativity and adaptability in virtually every dimension of Shaker music, let us consider three categories of innovation: genre, production, and technique.

Innovation in Musical Genres

Shakers did not just create prodigious quantities of music, they also engineered a range of entirely separate musical genres. These evolved, as Shakerism itself evolved, from very simple beginnings to more complex stages. Shaker worship might employ many genres simultaneously, often in the same meeting.

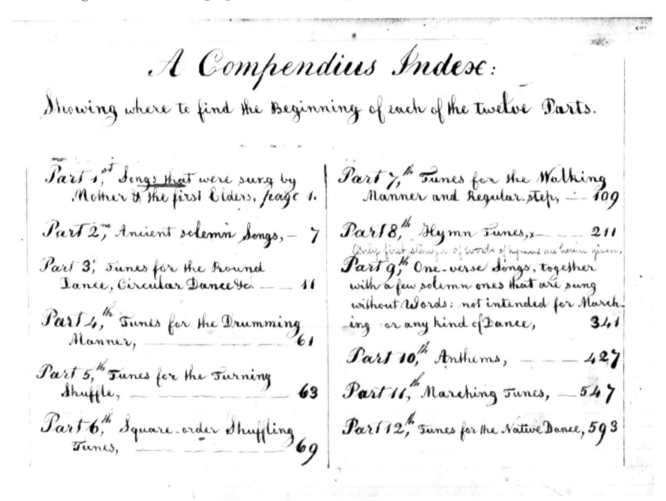

Figure 1. Index page from Russel Haskell's 1845 "A Record of Spiritual Songs," a comprehensive mid-nineteenth century compilation of Shaker music. (Courtesy of the Library of Congress, Music Division.)

Some of the older genres never fell entirely out of use but continued to be used alongside much newer ones. The "Compendious Index" from Russel Haskell's comprehensive 1845 Enfield, Connecticut, music compilation accurately reflects the range of Shaker musical genres at mid-century (Figure 1).[1]

For the first generation of Shakers in America, music consisted mostly of wordless improvised melodies, to which they fitted vocalized syllables or "vocables" (such as "lo-lo" or "vum-vum").[2] This sort of non-verbal singing freed the worshippers both for dancing and for the experience of spiritual extremes, unencumbered by complex lyrics. The use of such tunes to accompany dance continued unabated right through to the late 1870s in some Shaker communities.[3] At least in the early period, the tunes adapted to dancing bore enough superficial resemblance to popular tunes of the Early Republic that detractors declared that Shakers worshipped to the bawdy strains of "Yankee Doodle" and "Black Joke."[4]

In his 1845 compendium, Russel Haskell writes of the earliest period that, "for a short season the young converts were led to sing, some of the time, such as they had been accustomed to sing before they believed."[5] A range of innovations soon ensued. The use of hymns with lyrics seems to be a common enough feature of American sacred music. But for the Shakers, hymn lyrics were an innovation that emerged as the first flush of northeastern expansion gave way to more systematic and wide-ranging missionary work. As a proselytizing tool, lyrics could help convey Shaker gospel themes. Also, the wordless songs alone could lead to spiritual excesses among young Believers that were difficult to reign in. During the early western expansion, worship with young converts could easily get out of hand. Hymns could convey Shaker doctrine and history to people who had never seen Shakers before, while at the same time encouraging orderly deportment among exuberant converts. Several Shaker leaders involved in codifying doctrine also happened to be capable poets, and this contributed to a thriving hymn enterprise (Figure 2).

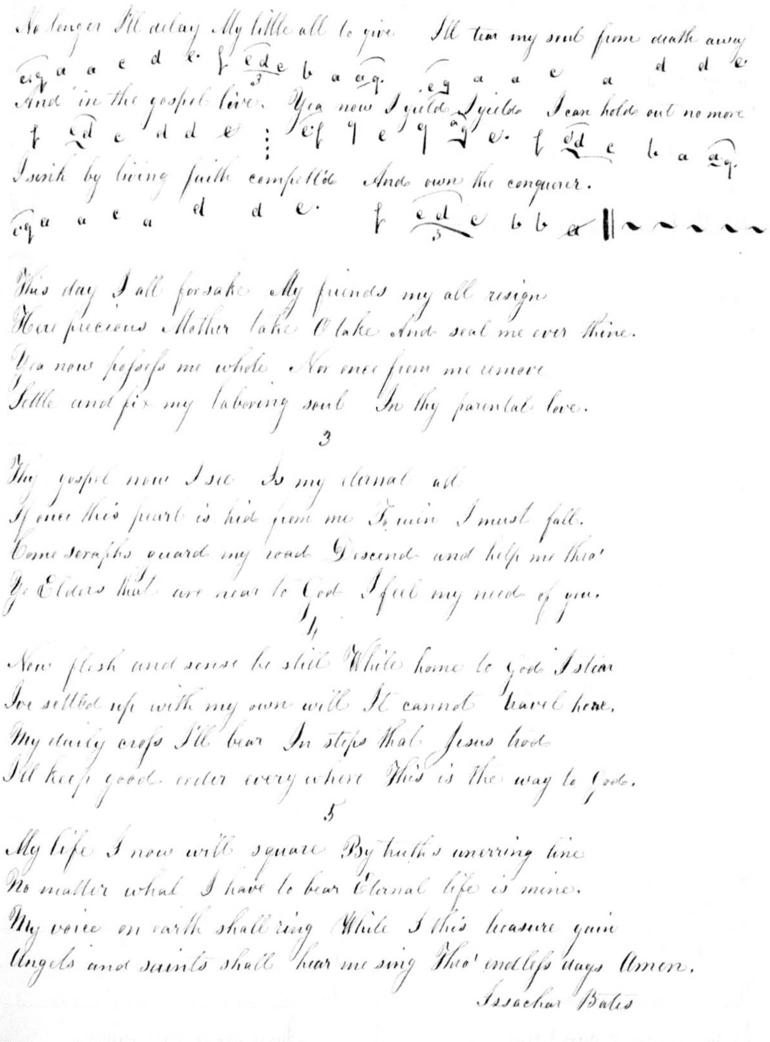

Figure 2. This page from the massive manuscript hymnal compiled by Paulina Bryant of Pleasant Hill, Kentucky, shows one among the multitude of hymns written by early western missionary Issachar Bates. (Courtesy of the Shaker Collection, Library of Congress, Manuscript Division.)

Other innovations followed. Anthems first emerged among Eastern Shakers sometime in the early 1810s. Anthems consisted of lengthy prose texts set to continuous meandering melodies (Figure 3). They offered inspired and scripture-based exhortations, reminding us that Shaker worship consisted of listening as well as "laboring" (dancing).[6] Common anthem motifs include the use of "spirit language" phrases and the spelling out of key words in sung phrase. Still other genres of music emerged as adaptations to the physical dimension of Shaker worship. Wordless songs were divided into different categories corresponding to particular styles of dance. Musically, these categories differed by time signature,

Figure 3. This page from an anthem compilation shows the end of one 1825 Ohio anthem and the beginning of another from the same period. (Courtesy of the Western Reserve Historical Society.)

with 2/4 time intended for "marches" and 6/8 time for "shuffles" (Figure 4). The category of "laboring" songs might include a short rhymed text, also meant to accompany dance. Other short songs, such as Haskell's category of "One-verse Standing songs," were adapted to rest breaks during the dancing.

Obedience, order, and union were all highly valued qualities in Shaker life, and one musical innovation that seemed to underscore them was unison singing. That development occurred gradually. Close examination of some music manuscripts produced by Western Shakers in the 1830s reveals surprisingly extensive experimentation with harmonized hymns and wordless songs in specific communities, associated with specific Shakers.[7] And Shaker musician D. A. Buckingham experienced "gifts" of harmony in the form of clumsily harmonized anthems in the 1840s.[8] Yet it was not until the 1870s, when some of the Shakers' own unique musical innovations began to be laid aside, that vocal harmonies became a regular feature of Shaker singing. Around 1900, Shaker musician Henry

Figure 4. This page from a tune-book by Giles Avery illustrates dance tunes in letteral notation on a five-line staff in two different genres. The tune-book contains more than four hundred wordless dance tunes, most of which are attributed to individuals or specific villages. (Courtesy of the Shaker Collection, Library of Congress, Manuscript Division.)

Blinn wrote of the integration at Canterbury and other Eastern sites of professional choral instruction and the incursion of singing styles similar to those found in mainstream Protestant churches.[9]

Innovation in Music Production

For about a century, Shakers produced music in an organic, dynamic, and profoundly democratized process. Even as the United Society itself became more hierarchical and rule-bound, this evolving organizational structure did nothing to mute the creative energy of music production. Despite the universal deference to Mount Lebanon, location of the Central Ministry, songs from "the Mount" carried no greater potency than songs from any other location. Since songs were regarded as spiritual "gifts," any member of any community might contribute by composing one. Hundreds of surviving music manuscripts contain careful attributions to communities and to families within communities. While not all songs carry geographic attribution, the staggering number that do suggest that these attributions permitted the Shakers to unite with distant brethren and sisters whom they would never meet. Manuscript hymnals could serve as musical atlases, affording the individual Believer virtual mobility around the far-flung Shaker landscape.

Even collections of songs printed and distributed by the Ministry were not intended to stanch the continual outpouring of additional music, as the Gospel "increased." In its earliest printed hymnal, the Ministry clarified its intent that not only did musical gifts lie in Believers' hands, the collective embrace of an ever-changing assortment of music should serve as the basis of unity:

> It is not expected that the people of God will ever be confined, in their mode of worship, to any particular set of hymns, or any other regular system of words—for words are but the signs of our ideas, and of course, must vary as the ideas increase with the increasing work of God. . . . All that his people have to do is to keep in the increasing work of God, and unite with whatever changes that increase may lead to. . . . No gift or order of God can be binding on

Believers for a longer term of time than it can be profitable to their travel in the gospel.[10]

Several of the rules contained in the Millennial Laws, intended by the Ministry to establish norms of daily conduct, pertain to the production of music, both directly and indirectly.[11] For example, the injunction that "Brethren and sisters may not go to each other's shops to learn songs," points to music repertoire as ever expanding.[12] Although Shakers were discouraged from owning personal possessions and from decorating their rooms with paintings and colorful textiles, they were "allowed to make plain bound books for writing hymns, anthems, etc. or for Journals."[13] This suggests that writing and copying songs were among the few creative outlets available to Believers and positively reinforced by the Ministry.

An intriguing aspect of democratized music production is the habitual use of individual names and initials to mark the specific composers of songs. This would seem to contradict the Millennial Laws, which stated that "No one should write or print his name on any article of manufacture, that others may hereafter know the work of his hands."[14] The apparent discrepancy is explained when one ceases to think of Shaker songs as products of personal skill and talents. Instead, Shakers regarded songs as spiritual "gifts" given to the entire community, often through a specific individual who simply acted as the "instrument" of that gift. Marking the source or instrument of a song, then, did not elevate a particular person's musical skill or talent. Rather, it amounted to yet another musical innovation, namely, to permit the entire community to "unite with the gift—in other words, to allow the instrument's identity to remind the community of the potential for any Believer to act as instrument of a spiritual gift, thus instilling confidence and reassurance, especially in those who had not ever acted as instruments. Identifying instruments by name, then, allowed others to share vicariously in their gifts, and it permitted the effects of the gifts to be multiplied.

It has been observed that as Shaker worship entered the highly charged visionary phase known as the "Era of Manifestations" or "Mother Ann's Work" after 1837, new songs poured from Believers in all villages at an incredible rate.[15] Not only did an even wider array of Shakers create songs, but songs poured forth spontaneously during worship meetings, from young and old, male and female, in the course of spiritual labors. Many display a sense of immediacy because they articulate Believers' experiences in a given moment (Figure 5). Songs began to display different characteristics, reflecting the further democratization of music production—fewer stanzas, simpler messages, and more repetition of words or phrases. They named an amazing array of "heavenly" objects that were being brought into the worship meetings and distributed among Believers: animals, golden chains, fruits, baskets, cups, even guns and swords. Another innovation was the tendency to record songs in other languages and dialects in an effort to reproduce the languages of angels, Native Americans, or other "foreign" spirits who visited meetings and commonly circulated among Believers.[16]

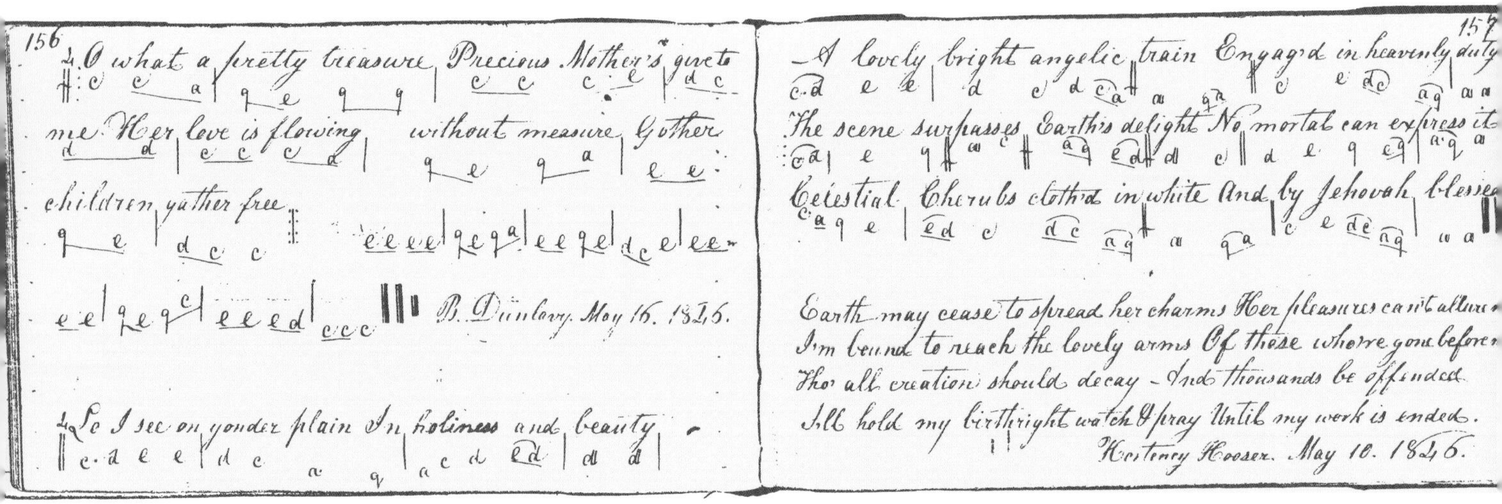

The number of hymnals representing the Era of Manifestations alone easily runs into the hundreds, as the outpouring of songs was overwhelming and often spontaneous. At the same time, documentation of this music by the Shakers was painstakingly thorough. For the rank and file of such a small religious sect to have recorded prodigious quantities of original music in minute detail is itself a noteworthy innovation, standing as it does in stark contrast to the dominant practice in America, where composing church music was the province of a select few, accomplished only through a distant and formalized process.

Figure 5. This page from a manuscript hymnal compiled by Benjamin Dunlavy of Pleasant Hill contains many apparently spontaneous "gift songs" from the Era of Manifestations, including this one attributed to Hortency Hooser, whose opening words, "Lo, I see on yonder plain," appear to describe what she was experiencing as she received the song. (Courtesy of Warren County Historical Society Library, Shaker Manuscripts Collection.)

Technical Innovation

The elaborate system of musical notation developed after 1825 served several purposes. It permitted a wider range of Shakers to participate in the production of music by re-organizing notation around the alphabet, something that most Shakers knew anyway. Although what the Shakers called "letteral notation" took various forms,[17] some incorporating the five-line staff and some not, a basic form could convey a tune in a mere string of lower-case letters accompanied by the simplest of diacritical markings (Figure 6). This sidestepping of the complexities of standard notation, it serviced the Shakers' desire for democratization and unity. During the more fertile phases of musical output, the ease of executing songs in letteral notation ensured that Believers could uphold Mother Ann's spiritual injunction that no "gifts" be lost. To be sure, the system also allowed the Shakers to reinforce their desire for separation from the world's practices. Indeed, because the system appeared indecipherable to the uninitiated, it was an innovation that shielded Shaker music against the world's gaze. Eventually, this led Shaker musicians

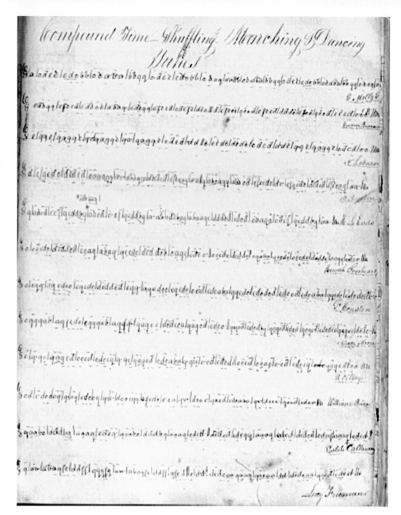

Figure 6. This page from a hymnal compiled by Betsy Smith of South Union, Kentucky, opens a section of wordless dance tunes of several genres, most of which are attributed to individuals. Begun in 1835, the hymnal contains some of the earliest letteral notation recorded in the west. (Courtesy of Kentucky Museum and Library Manuscripts Collection.)

to develop instructional materials in hopes of improving the musical skills present within the various communities (Figure 7).

Shaker historian and musician Isaac Newton Youngs devised a five-line staff pen, and many Shaker music manuscripts place letteral notation on a staff (Figure 4). But just as often, tunes simply appear as strings of lower-case letters interlined with words. The problem of how to convey the movement of the melody stimulated another innovative feature of Shaker notation, namely, the graphic meandering of the letters. In an overwhelming number of music manuscripts, songs appear as strings of individual letters, and the movement of the melody is signaled by the meandering of the string of letters uphill or downhill relative to the horizontal plane of each written line.

As letteral notation was being developed, Shaker musicians were already using the conventional round-note and shape-note systems that dominated the churches and singing schools of early America. Several early Shaker songwriters had prior experience as church choirmasters or singing school leaders, and they brought these skills into the Shaker community. Because so many different Shakers were actively involved in creating music simultaneously, and because these practitioners held varying levels of skill in both the worldly and Shaker-invented music notation, the contemporary student of Shaker music is confronted with an overlapping array of notation systems, often in the same manuscript or even on the same page, reflecting the Shakers' adaptive approach to notation.

Figure 7. "Musical Key" by D. A. Buckingham of Watervliet, New York, 1848. (Courtesy of Western Reserve Historical Society.)

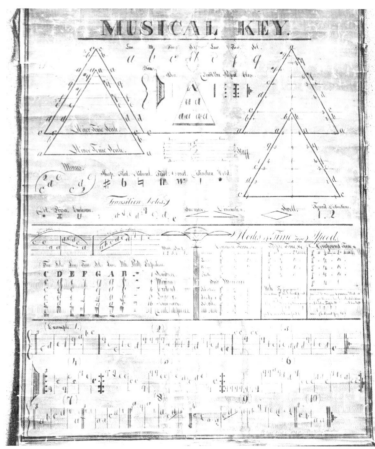

The most profound aspects of musical innovation among the Shakers are reflected in how music serves the sect's core values. Shakers' emphasis on the spiritual equality of members led to a degree of democratization in music production that has no known analogue in other religious sects. A small and far-flung sect that was paradoxically defined by "union," they successfully applied music to the problem of geographic separation. Manuscripts suggest that music was used innovatively to bring Shakers across the widely spaced communities into uniform action or practice on specific days. In one example, Believers across both East and West were directed in 1835 to pause on March 1 at six o'clock in the evening and sing two specific hymns from *Millennial Praises* to mark Mother Ann's birthday, because, "the consideration that all the faithful in every Society throughout the land are, at the same time, ingaged cannot fail to . . . animate the zeal and cheer the spirits of all her faithful children."[18] One hymnal records that an 1850 New Hampshire song called "All Glean With Care," was "appointed to be universally sung among Believers, Sept. 1, 1850."[19] Also, many mid-century hymnals, Eastern and Western, record a song entitled "Saturday Evening," which promoted a period of collective spiritual reflection across the entire Shaker world as the Sabbath neared:

Behold we now come to the close of the week,
And have we been faithful & humble & meek,
Have we in our calling been faithful & good,
Been kind to each other & done as we should,
If all have been faithful & done what is right,
We surely may worship with freedom tonight.[20]

Today, Shaker music innovations are invisible to most people. The complex letteral notation that structured most of their music is a quaint and illegible relic to most who view it. Alone among the Shakers' vast musical output, "Simple Gifts" is likely to be recognized by the average American. Some may even realize its Shaker origin, but without an appreciation of the complex and revolutionary musical tradition that contributed to its production. For anyone who seeks to better understand them, the many innovations in Shaker music still have the power to awe, impress, astonish, and inspire, as they reach across the years to touch our contemporary lives. ❧

Brother Isaac Newton Youngs (1793-1865) of New Lebanon created his own style of pen for drawing 5-line musical staffs some time before 1840. (Pen: brass and unknown hardwood with paint, 1 -4⅛". Courtesy of Hancock Shaker Village.)

This pen may be used either side up: -- but if it will not make good lines without bearing on too hard, it needs some repair. I.N.Y.

NOTES

Introduction

1. Mount Lebanon, New York was called New Lebanon until late 1861 when it was granted its own post office. The latter name will be used here. Watervliet, New York, should not be confused with an entirely different community of the same name in Ohio.

2. This attribution is based on an editorial published in the *Hartford Courant*, August 27, 1897, in which publisher Charles D. Warner wrote: "A well-known U.S. writer once said that while everyone talks about the weather, nobody seemed to do anything about it."

3. Throughout this introduction I will observe the occasional Shaker practice of using an uppercase W for the non-Shaker world. This emphasizes their "apartness."

4. Stephen J. Stein, *The Shaker Experience in America* (New Haven: Yale University Press, 1992). This is the most complete general history of the Shaker movement to date. An exceptional history of the movement in condensed form, written by Shaker historian Stephen J. Paterwic, may be found in M. Stephen Miller, *From Shaker Lands and Shaker Hands* (Hanover, N.H.: University Press of New England, 2007). The latter publication is also a survey of many of the Shaker communal industries.

5. Stephen J. Paterwic, *Historical Dictionary of the Shakers* (Lanham, Md.: Scarecrow Press, 2008), pp. 223–24. It is argued here that the name often applied to them as their "official" name—The United Society of Believers in Christ's First and Second Appearing—is of unknown origin and was not used by them.

Although called a "dictionary," this reference work is really more an encyclopedia.

6. George Bishop, *New England Judged by the Spirit of the Lord*, 1703, cited in Steven Waldman, *Founding Faith* (New York: Random House, 2008), p. 221, n40.

7. Brother Theodore Johnson, *Life in the Christ Spirit: Observations on Shaker Theology* (Sabbathday Lake, Me.: United Society, 1969).

8. Sister Marguerite Frost, *The Shaker Story* (Penacook, N.H.: Hazen Printing Co., 1963), n.p.

9. The Sabbathday Lake Shakers, "Who Are the Shakers," in Miller, *From Shaker Lands and Shaker Hands*, p. 21.

10. Personal communication from Magda Gabor-Hotchkiss. I thank her for her lucid expression of this philosophical point.

11. Stephen J. Paterwic, "Who Were the Shakers?" in Miller, *From Shaker Lands and Shaker Hands*, p. 7.

12. See in particular Elizabeth A. De Wolfe, *Shaking the Faith* (New York: Palgrave, 2002). This is a fascinating study of apostate Mary Marshall Dyer (1780–1867), who made a career of challenging the Enfield, New Hampshire, Shakers in writings, lectures, and in court.

13. Personal communication from Magda Gabor-Hotchkiss.

14. Paterwic, *Historical Dictionary of the Shakers*, pp. 152–55.

15. Ibid., pp. 36–37.

16. Lauren Stiles, "'Rather Than Ever Milk Again': Shaker Sisters Refusal to Milk at Mount Lebanon and Watervliet, 1873–1877," *American Communal Societies Quarterly* 3 (2009): 13–25. Stiles documents the important role that sisters played in milking their community's dairy herds in the nineteenth century. They were often responsible for feeding the calves as well.

17. Paterwic, "Who Were the Shakers?" in Miller, *From Shaker Lands and Shaker Hands*, pp. 12–16.

18. Patents were issued, for example, to Luther Copley, New Lebanon, N.Y. for a "Water Mill, or Machine, and Applying Water, Wind or Steam thereto," Patent granted May 15, 1834 (Patent No. Lacking); Amos Stewart, New Lebanon, N.Y., "Water Wheel," Patent granted November 22, 1864, No. 45191; Harvey K. Annis, Enfield, N.H., "Improvement in Water-Wheel (With Controlling Gate)," Patent granted November 15, 1864, No. 45,114.

19. *The American Heritage Dictionary of the English Language* (Boston: Houghton Mifflin Company, 1992). This question will arise again with the discussion of "patent medicines"—an often-confused concept.

20. This has had some unfortunate consequences. At Hancock, Massachusetts, the Shakers decided to raze their historic Meeting House in 1938 in order to save on taxes. After the Shakers left there in 1960, the non-profit Hancock Shaker Village, Inc., moved a nearly identical Meeting House from the former Shirley, Massachusetts, community. It fit Hancock's foundation almost exactly!

21. New Lebanon Brother George O. Donnell patented a metal "tilting" device on March 2, 1852, Patent No. 8771, "a new and improved mode of preventing wear and tear of carpets and the marring of floors caused by the corners of the back posts of chairs as they take their natural motion of rocking backward and forward."

22. United States Department of Commerce, Patent and Trademark Office. Patent No. 90,380, May 25, 1869.

23. This structure was initially built in 1826 with a main and an upper level. After fire destroyed most of it in 1864, the barn was rebuilt in the same form but with a lower level—the manure pit—added. The final modification came in about 1875 with the addition of a fourteen-sided superstructure that allowed for additional light and air circulation. It is internationally recognized today as a supreme example of functional architecture.

24. *Testimonies of the Life, Church, Revelations and Doctrines of our Ever Blessed Mother Ann Lee . . .* (Hancock: J. Tallcott and J. Deming, Junrs. 1816), p. 309. This saying of Mother Ann and reported by Mother Lucy Wright reads: "A certain young man came to Mother, with some peach and plum stones in his hand, and asked her if he might plant them. 'Yes; (answered Mother;) do all your work . . .'"

25. Glendyne R. Wergland, ed., *Visiting the Shakers* (Hamilton, N.Y.: Richard W. Couper Press, Hamilton College, 2007), p. 179.

26. A number of men actually joined after that date, but only Brother Ted Johnson died in the faith, in 1986. As of this writing, Brother Arnold Hadd, who entered the Sabbathday Lake community in 1978, is the only brother there.

27. Priscilla J. Brewer, *Shaker Communities, Shaker Lives* (Hanover, N.H.: University Press of New England, 1986), p. 219. It should be noted here that this book concentrates on the eleven eastern communities with little attention given to those in the West. Western Shakerism was a very significant force in its own right and deserves more consideration than is possible here. I thank Stephen Paterwic for providing the statistical data for the Shaker West.

28. The present day Shakers at Sabbathday Lake, Maine, use "Father/Mother God" when referring to the Deity.

Innovations in Shaker Architecture and Planning

1. Scott T. Swank, *Shaker Life, Art, and Architecture* (New York, London, Paris: Abbeville Press Publishers, 1999). This is a general overview of Canterbury, its patterns of growth and development as well as its achievements over a period of two-hundred years.

2. Joseph S. Wood, *The New England Village* (Baltimore and London: The Johns Hopkins University Press, 1997).

3. Robert P. Emlen, *Shaker Village Views* (Hanover and London: University Press of New England, 1987).

Equality of the Sexes as Shakers' Inspired Innovation

1. Lee Virginia Chambers-Schiller, *Liberty, a Better Husband: Single Women in America . . . 1780–1840* (New Haven: Yale University Press, 1984), chapter 1.

2. Rick Geddes and Dean Lueck, "The Gains from Self-Ownership and the Expansion of Women's Rights," *American Economic Review* 92 (2002): 1079–80. JSTOR, accessed April 22, 2009.

3. Catherine A. Brekus, *Strangers and Pilgrims: Female Preaching in America, 1740–1845* (Chapel Hill: University of North Carolina Press, 1998), pp. 343–46.

4. Anonymous, "A Short Account of the People known by the Name of Shakers, or Shaking Quakers," *Theological Magazine* 1 (September–October 1795): 81–87, in Wergland, *Visiting the Shakers*, pp. 21–22.

5. Jean Humez, "Weary of Petticoat Government": The Specter of Female Rule in Early Nineteenth-Century Shaker Politics," *Communal Societies* 11 (1991): 1–17.

6. Wergland, *Visiting the Shakers*, pp. 174, 237, 317.

7. Hester A. Pool, "Among the Shakers," *The Manifesto* 18 (1888): 252.

8. Lawrence Pitkethly, 1842, in Wergland, *Visiting the Shakers*, p. 301. A Shaker wash mill is at Hancock Shaker Village. See also Edward D. Andrews, *Community Industries of the Shakers*, New York State Museum handbook 15 (1933; repr.; Charlestown, Mass.: Emporium Publications, 1971), pp. 43–44, 270. Enfield, New Hampshire, Shakers had a "centrifugal dryer." Charles Nordhoff, *Communistic Societies of the United States* (1875; repr., New York: Dover Publications, 1966), p. 188.

9. Worn-out farm wives: Sally McMurray, *Families and Farmhouses in Nineteenth-Century America* (New York: Oxford University Press, 1988), chapter 4.

10. Betsy Bates, Journal of Events (1833–35), March 22, 1835, microfilm reel 35, V:B-128, Western Reserve Historical Society Shaker Collection (hereinafter WRHS); Giles Avery, Historical Sketches (1834–43), 41, microfilm reel 4:53, Library of Congress Shaker Collection, (hereinafter LC).

11. Isaac N. Youngs, Family and Meeting Journal, August 17, 1816 (frame 350), LC 3:42.

12. "Writer," Lower Canaan Journal, [13, 23, 25, 30–31, 33], WRHS 33, V:B-84.

13. Glendyne R. Wergland, *Sisters in the Faith: Shaker Women, 1780–1890*, forthcoming.

14. Dianne Avery and Alfred S. Konefsky, "The Daughters of Job: Property Rights and Women's Lives in Mid-Nineteenth-Century Massachusetts," *Law and History Review* 10 (1992): 323–56. JSTOR, accessed April 22, 2009.

15. *New York Tribune* quoted in J. M. Brown, Domestic Journal (1856–77), June 11, 1869, WRHS 32, V:B-71.

16. Nordhoff, *Communistic Societies*, 165–66. Google Books, accessed April 22, 2009.

17. Elie Reclus, "A Visit to Mount Lebanon in 1878," translated and edited by Marius B. Péladeau, *Shaker Quarterly* 11 (Spring 1971): 26.

18. "Among the Shakers," *Boston Daily Globe*, August 7, 1881, 6, reprinted from the *New York Tribune*. Proquest, accessed January 18, 2009.

19. "In the East," *Deseret News*, March 7, 1888, Utah Digital Newspapers, http://digitalnewspapers.org/, accessed February 24, 2009.

20. Stephen J. Paterwic, *Historical Dictionary of the Shakers*, pp. 35–36, explains this term.

21. Lida A. Kimball, "A Visit to the Shakers," *North Adams Transcript*, June 4, 1897. NewsArchive.com, National Archives, accessed January 16, 2009.

1. Garden Seeds

1. Wergland, ed., *Visiting the Shakers*, p. 176. This volume of visitors' accounts to the Watervliet and New Lebanon, New York, and Tyringham and Hancock, Massachusetts communities offers valuable insights into, and presents contemporary biases for and against, the Shakers that are not otherwise readily available.

2. Medicinal Herbs and Preparations

1. Henry Clay Blinn, "Historical Record of the Society of Believers, 1792–1842, Canterbury, N.H.," Canterbury, N.H. (hereafter SVI #763).

2. Henry Clay Blinn, "Church Record, 1784–1879," SVI #764, Canterbury, N.H., pp. 142–43.

3. Isaac Hill, "The Shakers," *The Farmer's Monthly Visitor*, No. 2 (1840), Concord Public Library, Concord, N.H.

4. "Shakers' Sarsaparilla: The oldest and best of all medicines called Sarsaparilla," *The Shakers' Manual* [Canterbury, N.II.], January 1, 1880, New Hampshire Historical Society, Concord, N.H.

5. Galen Beale and Mary Rose Boswell, *The Earth Shall Blossom: Shaker Herbs and Gardening* (Woodstock, Vt.: Countryman Press, 1991); "Catalogue of Medicinal Plants and Vegetable Medicine prepared by the United Society, Canterbury, N.H., printed at Shaker Village 1835," Microfiche Collection #230, Western Reserve Historical Society, Cleveland, Ohio (hereafter WRHS).

6. "Facts Concerning Brown's Shaker Pure Fluid Extract of English Valerian (*Valerianan officinalis*) made at Enfield, N.H.," n.d., Enfield, N.H., Microfiche Collection, #235, WRHS.

7. "Jerub Dyer, Obituary Notice," *Free Press*, December 8, 1886, Enfield Shaker Museum Collection, Enfield, N.H.

8. John N. McClintock, "The Shakers," *The Granite Monthly*, January 1880, New Hampshire State Library, Concord, N.H.

3. Planting Perfection

1. U. P. Hedrick, assisted by N. O. Booth, O. M. Taylor, R. Wellington, and M. J. Dorsey, *The Grapes of New York*, State of New York Department of Agriculture Fifteenth Annual Report, Vol. 3, Part II (Albany: J. B. Lyon Company, State Printers, 1908), p. 415. An examination of this book fails to turn up any mention of the Union Village.

2. U.S. Commissioner of Patents, *Report of the Commissioner of Patents for the Year 1856: Agriculture* (Washington, D.C., 1857), p. 433. [This also printed also as U.S. 34th Congress, 3d Session, Senate Document No. 53, Pt. 4].

3. Andrew Jackson Downing, *The Fruit and Fruit Trees of America*, revised and corrected by Charles Downing. (New York: John Wiley, 1860), p. 346.

4. Brian Cole, horticulturist from West Hartland, Conn., in conversation to Darryl Thompson, April 10, 1994; Hedrick, et al., *Grapes of New York*, p. 415; U.S. Commissioner of Patents, *Report . . . for the Year 1856*, 433; Downing, *Fruit and Fruit Trees*, p. 346; Andrew S. Fuller, *The Grape Culturist: A Treatise on the Cultivation of the Native Grape* (New York City: "Printed for the Author by Davies & Kent, N.Y.", 1864), p. 231; Peter B. Mead, *An Elementary Treatise on American Grape Culture and Wine Making* (New York: [Peter Mead?], 1867), pp. 198–99.

5. Hedrick, et al., *Grapes of New York*, p. 416.

6. Hedrick et al., *Grapes of New York*, pp. 3–4; Michael Goc, "Searching for the Ideal Northern Grape," *The Old Farmer's Almanac* (1989), p. 177; Charles "Bud" Thompson, Shaker historian, letter to Darryl Thompson, March 3, 1996.

7. Fuller, p. 231.

8. C. M. Hovey, "Grapes," *The Magazine of Horticulture, Botany, and All Useful Discoveries and Improvements in Rural Affairs*, 25 (January 1859). [This volume is also listed as Vol. V, Third Series, (Boston: Hovey and Co., 1859), p. 35.]

9. Hedrick, et al., *Grapes of New York*, pp. 415–16.

10. T. V. Munson, *Foundations of American Grape Culture* (New York: Orange Judd Company, 1909), p. 166.

11. *Facts for Farmers*, p. 659.

12. Hedrick, et al., *Grapes of New York*, p. 416.

13. Antoinette Doolittle, "God's Love Universal," *The Shaker Manifesto*, 8 (October 1878): 238–39.

14. These additional resources are available to those who wish to pursue this subject further. S. A. Beach, *Gooseberries* [Bulletin No. 114, New Series, January 1897, New York Agricultural Experiment Station, Geneva, N.Y.], p. 13; U. P. Hedrick, assisted by G. H. Howe, O. M. Taylor, Alwin Berger, G. L. Slate, and Olav Einset, *The Small Fruits of New York*, Department of Farms and Markets, State of New York, Thirty-third Annual Report, Part II (Albany, N.Y.: J. B. Lyon Company, Printers, 1925), p. 274; Daniel J. Hawkins and Philemon Stewart, "Statement of Daniel J. Hawkins and Philemon Stewart, of the United Society of Shakers, at New Lebanon, Columbia county, New York," *Report of the Commissioner of Patents for the Year 1854, Agricultural Volume*, printed also

as U.S. 33d Congress, 2d Session, Senate Ex. Doc. No. 42, Series No. 155 and H. of R. Ex. Doc. No. 59, Series No. 787 (Washington, D.C.: Government Printing Office, 1855), p. 315; U. P. Hedrick, assisted by N. O. Booth, O. M. Taylor, R. Wellington, and M. J. Dorsey, *The Grapes of New York* (Albany, N.Y.: J. B. Lyon Company, State Printers, 1908), pp. 365–66.

15. Edward D. Andrews, *The Community Industries of the Shakers* (Albany: University of the State of New York, 1933), p. 82.

16. Isaac Newton Youngs, "A Concise View of the Church of God," MS. no. SA 760, Winterthur, Delaware.

17. This is especially remarkable because it was they who developed a huge industry selling garden seeds in individual packages. The only remnants of their packaging dried sweet corn are a large wooden crate with paper label (located at Hancock Shaker Village) and a colorful, round label made to be affixed to a barrel-head (located at the Berkshire Athenaeum, Pittsfield, Massachusetts).

18. Cheryl Bauer, *The Shakers of Union Village* (Charleston, S.C.: Arcadia Publishing, 2007), pp. 36–37 and Katherine Lollar Rowland, "Union Village's Vineyards and Winery at Wickliffe, Ohio," HYPERLINK "http://www.rootsweb.ancestry.com/~ohwarren/shaker/vineyard.htm" www.rootsweb.ancestry.com/~ohwarren/shaker/vineyard.htm.

19. Charles Nordhoff, *The Communistic Societies of the United States* (1875; repr. New York: Dover Printing, Inc., 1966), pp. 193–94.

4. Woodenwares

1. Youngs' notes on trades were incorporated into his "A Concise View of the Church of God . . . New Lebanon," 1856, 1860, the Edward Deming Andrews Memorial Shaker Collection, McKinstry #861, Henry Francis du Pont Winterthur Museum. This history was edited and published as "History of the Church of Mt. Lebanon, N.Y. No. 15," *The Manifesto* 20 (September 1890): 193.

2. For example Elder Daniel Crosman commented in a journal that he was planing cedar heading for boxes around 1860, and fortunately several boxes survive with cedar tops and bottoms. Distinctive marks left by Smith's Revolving Timber Plane can occasionally be found on Mount Lebanon boxes.

3. Mary Earle Gould, *Early American Wooden Ware* (Springfield, Mass.: The Pond-Ekberg Company, 1948).

4. Box-making at Alfred, Maine, is better documented by extant boxes than through written records. Reference to the production of boxes is noted in Sister R. Mildred Barker, *Holy Land: A History of the Alfred Shakers* (Sabbathday Lake, Me.: The Shaker Press, 1983). The box-making career of Elder Delmer C. Wilson at Sabbathday Lake is nicely told by John Wilson in, "Brother Delmer and the 1083 Carriers," *The Shaker Quarterly* 15 (Winter, 1987): 115–119, and 16 (Spring, 1988): 18–23.

5. In 1841 the Ministry at Union Village requested the assistance of the Mount Lebanon Shakers in helping them set up an oval box and half-bushel measure business. To support the request the Ministry sent Brother Micajah Burnett from Pleasant Hill to build box-making equipment following plans developed by Brother Isaac Newton Youngs at Mount Lebanon. By 1842 the machinery was made and put in motion, but by February 1846 the oval box part of the business was found to be unprofitable and discontinued. This seems to be the entire history of oval box–making in the western Shaker communities. Western Reserve Historical Society, V:B-230, 1841–1846.

6. Jethro Turner, "Memoranda," July 13, 1801, Mss. No. V:B-76, Western Reserve Historical Society.

7. "Domestic Journal of Daily Occurrences, [Mount Lebanon, N.Y.], 1834–1846," Mss. No. 13500, New York State Library; "Domestic Journal of Daily Occurrences, [Mount Lebanon, NY], 1847–1877," Mss. No. V:B-70-71, Western Reserve Historical Society.

8. *An Illustrated Catalogue and Price-list of the Shakers' Chairs. Manufactured by the Society of Shakers.* Mount Lebanon, N.Y. (R. M. Wagon & Co., [n. d.]).

9. Jerry V. Grant, "The Last of the Old Shaker Cabinetmakers," *Report* 2 (August 1991): [1–2].

10. Sister Sadie Neale, Mount Lebanon, N.Y., to Mrs. L. J. Petersen, Cincinnati, Ohio, 1945. Private collection.

11. This is one of the clearest distinctions between Shaker-made and reproduction boxes. An intimate knowledge of the characteristics of wood and the steam bending process, as well as unhurried time, give the advantage to Shaker-made boxes.

12. It is usual practice for the Shakers to number wood-enwares in this manner—the largest having the lowest number. This will be seen again with the nest of oval carriers, illustration p. 89.

13. Edward D. Andrews, *The Community Industries of the Shakers* (Albany: University of the State of New York, 1933), 145-146.

14. Glendyne Wergland, *Visiting the Shakers: 1778-1849* (Hamilton, N.Y.: Richard W. Couper Press, Hamilton College, 2007), 29.

15. Both are illustrated in *Shaker: Furniture and Objects from the Faith and Edward Deming Andrews Collections commemorating the Bicentenary of the American Shakers* (Washington, D.C.: Smithsonian Institution Press, 1973), 85.

16. *The Shaker Quarterly* 15, no. 4, 1987 and 16, no. 1, 1988. This is the definitive source for information about the beginnings of this major industry, one that helped both Maine communities survive into the twentieth century.

5. Shaker Basket Making

1. Martha Wetherbee and Nathan Taylor, *Shaker Baskets* (Sanbornton, N.H.: Martha Wetherbee Basket Shop, 1988), p. 111.

2. M. Stephen Miller, "The Copley-Lyman Shaker Family of Enfield, Connecticut: An Annotated Genealogy," *American Communal Studies Quarterly* 1 (April 2007): 51–68.

3. Wetherbee and Taylor, *Shaker Baskets*, p. 210.

6. Cooperage

1. Robert P. Emlen, "The Story of the Enfield, New Hampshire Shaker Sap Buckets," *Maine Antiques Digest*, vol. 7, no. 4 (May 1979) first explored this subject, and I am deeply indebted to him for reading and making important suggestions about improving this essay. I am also grateful to scholar Galen Beale for much of the material used here. It can be found in "The New Hampshire Shakers' Wooden Tub and Pail Industry," *The Chronicle of Early American Industries*, 47 (September 1994): 69–78.

2. I am again grateful to Robert P. Emlen for this insight. (Personal communication.)

3. Some confusion results from the inconsistent spelling of the last name of Brother Henry. In articles he wrote for the *Enfield Advocate* newspaper in 1905, he spelled it Cumings, and it appears that way on a billhead (1879) in the author's collection. However, in an advertisement published in *The Shaker Manifesto* in July 1878 and on four other billheads in the author's collection (1875–1879) it is spelled Cummings. One also finds the spelling of his natural brother John's and natural sister Rosetta's last names spelled both ways.

7. Shaker Textiles

1. Cloaks shipped on October 20, 1888, to Miss H. Brandegee, New London, Conn., and on October 25, 1888, to Mrs. M. E. Brandegee, New London, Conn., in "Cloaks Shipped, [Church Family, Mount Lebanon, NY, 1888–1928]," Mss. No. 10415, Shaker Museum and Library, Old Chatham, New York.

2. "Trademark Certificate. 'Long Cloaks,' Emma J. Neale & Co., Church Family, Mount Lebanon, NY, 1901," Mss. No. 11555, Shaker Museum and Library.

3. [Dyers' Journal, Church Family, Mount Lebanon, NY, 1849–1866]. Shaker Museum and Library, Mss. 8515

4. "Records Kept by Order of the Church, [Church Family, Mount Lebanon, NY, 1871–1905, 1916]," Mss. No. 10343, Shaker Museum and Library.

5. "A Domestic Journal Kept by Order of the Deaconesses, [Church Family, Mount Lebanon, NY]," Mss. No. 8856, Shaker Museum and Library.

6. "Account of Cloaks Made by the North Family for Emma J. Neale & Co., Church Family, Mount Lebanon, NY, 1890–1904." Mss. No. 8906, Shaker Museum and Library.

7. "Cloaks Shipped, [Church Family, Mount Lebanon, NY, 1888–1928]," Mss. No. 10415, Shaker Museum and Library.

8. ". . . to NYC to consult with authorities there relative to Woman's Industrial Exposition to be held in Madison Square from Oct 6th to 18th. An urgent invitation to our Sisterhood has been extended, to be there in person and represent their industries. . . ," in "Records Kept by Order of the Church, [Church Family, Mount Lebanon, N.Y., 1871–1905, 1916]," Mss. No. 10343, Shaker Museum and Library.

9. "Account of Cloaks Made by the North Family for Emma J. Neale & Co., Church Family, Mount Lebanon, N.Y., 1890–1904."

10. "Order. Emma J. Neale & Co., Dealers in Genuine Shaker Cloaks, Mount Lebanon, Columbia County, N.Y., 191?," Acc. No. 10567a, Shaker Museum and Library.

11. Mrs. Grover Cleveland wore her Shaker cloak to her husband's second inauguration in 1893.

12. "A Domestic Journal Kept by Order of the Deaconesses, [Church Family, Mount Lebanon, N.Y.]."

13. Elmer R. Pearson and Julia Neal, *The Shaker Image: Second and Annotated Edition*, by Magda Gabor-Hotchkiss (Pittsfield, Mass.: Hancock Shaker Village, 1994), p. 202.

14. Beverly Gordon, *Shaker Textile Arts* (Hanover, N.H.: University Press of New England, 1980), p. 27.

15. Charles R. Muller and Timothy D. Rieman, *The Shaker Chair* (Winchester, Ohio: The Canal Press, 1984), pp. 152–55.

8. Shaker Chairs

1. Nancy Goyne Evans, *American Windsor Chairs* (New York: Hudson Hills Press in association with the Henry Francis du Pont Winterthur Museum, 1996), pp. 65, 67.

2. Freegift Wells, "Memorandum of Events," 1812–1965; "No. 1 Ledger Book, 1804, Alfred," United Society of Shakers, Sabbathday Lake, Maine; "Financial Accounts of the Shaker Community in the Miami Valley, Ohio," 1807–1815, Library of Congress; Andrews, *Community Industries of the Shakers*.

3. Andrews, *Community Industries of the Shakers*, p. 233; "A domestic journal of domestic occurrences at Mount Lebanon, New York," 1814–1833, Western Reserve Historical Society.

4. "Number of Chairs left at the Second Family," The Henry Francis DuPont Museum, Wintherthur, Delaware.

5. "Diary of Henry Blinn," 1872, Shaker Village, Canterbury, New Hampshire.

6. Account Book, "Order book – Chair Room, New Lebanon, N.Y.," 1884–1885, Henry Francis DuPont Winterthur Museum.

7. Muller and Rieman, *The Shaker Chair*, p. 213.

8. "Checks written on the Agricultural National Bank of Pittsfield by The R. M. Wagan & Co.," 1884–1921, Pearson Collection, Chicago.

9. *Berkshire Evening Eagle*, December 9, 1923.

10. Edward Deming and Faith Andrews, *Religion in Wood* (Bloomington: Indiana University Press, 1966), p. xiii.

11. "A Crowd of Female Strikers," *New York Times*, August 23, 1879. The article describes a strike at the Arnold & Co. chair factory in Poughkeepsie, New York, when management informed the 300–400 women who were taking chairs home and adding seats that the price for seating was going to be cut by a half-cent because of competition.

12. Muller and Rieman, *The Shaker Chair*, p. 90.

13. Account Book, "Order book – chair Room, New Lebanon, N.Y.," 1884–1885, Henry Francis DuPont Winterthur Museum, Winterthur, Delaware.

14. This earliest known broadside relating to the Shaker chair manufactory is located at the Western Reserve Historical Society, Cleveland, Ohio (R-249).

15. "A domestic journal of domestic occurrences at Mount Lebanon, New York," 1814–1833.

16. Freegift Wells.

17. Benjamin Lyons, "A Journal of Work," 1834–1838, Library of Congress.

18. Jefferson White, "Letter from City of Union," August 31, 1853.

19. George O. Donnell, "Specification of Letters Patent No. 8,771, dated March 2, 1852," New Lebanon, N.Y.

9. Fancy Goods

1. *Community Industries of the Shakers*, pp. 202–5, 285.

2. Anna White and Leila S. Taylor, *Shakerism. Its Meaning and Message, Embracing an Historical Account, Statement of Belief and Spiritual Experience of the Church from Its Rise to the Present Day* (Columbus, Ohio: Fred J. Heer, 1904), p. 313.

3. Elsie A. McCool, "Shaker Woven Poplar Work," *The Shaker Quarterly* 2 (Summer 1961): 55–59.

4. James Elliot, "Shaker Collecting," *Maine Antiques Digest*, February 1974, pp. 24–25. James Elliot was a pseudonym used by Brother Theodore E. Johnson of the Sabbathday Lake, Maine, Shaker community.

5. Philemon Stewart and Daniel Crosman, "A Confidential Journal Kept in the Elders' Lot," Lebanon, N.Y., 1842–81, microfilm V: B-136, December 1862, Western Reserve Historical Society.

6. Beverly Gordon, *Shaker Textile Arts* (Hanover, N.H.: University Press of New England, 1980), p. 216.

7. Wetherbee and Taylor, *Shaker Baskets*, pp. 78, 130.

10. Health and Sanitation

1. *The Boston Medical and Science Journal*, Vol. XLVIII, No. 23, July 6, 1853.

2. Nordhoff, *Communistic Societies of the United States*, p. 181 and passim.

3. Edward Deming Andrews, *The People Called Shakers* (1953; repr., New York: Dover Publications, 1963), p. 198.

4. "Designed for Sale: Shaker Commerce with the World," M. Stephen Miller in *Shaker Design: Out of this World* (New Haven: Yale University Press, 2008), p. 73.

5. Sally M. Promey, *Spiritual Spectacles: Vision and Image in Mid-Nineteenth-Century Shakerism* (Bloomington and Indianapolis: Indiana University Press, 1993). This thoughtful study gives many examples of the uses of Order. See pp. 44, 55–56, 66, 68–70, 71–75, 238, and 240. Also, Paterwic, *Historical Dictionary of the Shakers*, pp. 165–66.

6. For an expansive treatment of the importance of order in furniture design, see especially John Kirk, *The Shaker World: Art, Life, Belief* (New York: Harry N. Abrams, Inc., 1997).

7. An anonymous visitor designated only as "S" and recorded in Wergland, *Visiting the Shakers*, p. 186.

8. Ibid. p. 28.

9. Ibid. p. 77–78

10. Ibid. p. 228

11. "The Millennial Laws or Gospel Statutes and Ordinances . . . ," 1821, revised in 1845. This manuscript appeared edited with an introduction by Theodore E.

Johnson in *Shaker Quarterly* 7 (Summer 1967): 35–58. See Edward Deming Andrews, *The People Called Shakers*, p. 260.

12. Edward Deming Andrews and Faith Andrews, *Work and Worship Among the Shakers* (Greenwich, Conn.: New York Graphic Society, 1974), p. 73.

13. Ibid., quote on p. 73.

14. *The Shaker Manifesto*, 19 (May 1889). This is a reprint of a report by Charles Frederick Wingate, "Shaker Sanitation," *The Plumber & Sanitary Engineer* 3, September 1880, p. 397.

11. Retiring Rooms

1. See, for example, Edward Deming and Faith Andrews, *Shaker Furniture* (New Haven: Yale University Press, 1937) or more recently, a portfolio of photographs produced by David Schorsch, *The Photographs of William F. Winter, Jr.: 1899–1939* (New York: Published by the author, 1989). All of these images are in black and white, which unfortunately distorts the historical record, for the woodwork in retiring rooms—furniture, floors, baseboards, and peg rails—were often painted in vibrant colors.

2. Edward Deming Andrews, *The People Called Shakers*, p. 181.

3. Ibid., pp. 271–72.

4. Ibid., p. 272.

5. Julie Nicoletta, *The Architecture of the Shakers* (Woodstock, Vt.: The Countryman Press, 1995), pp. 49–75.

12. Shaker Inventions

1. Norman Ball, "Circular Saws and the History of Technology," *Bulletin of the Association of Preservation Technology* 7, no. 3 (1975): 87.

2. Anonymous, "An Oration, [Illegible] Citizen of the United States, on [Illegible] 11th of July, 1800," *American Citizen and General Advertiser*, [New York], July 16, 1800, http://www.newsbank.com/readex/?content=96.

3. Henry Disston and Sons, Inc., *The Saw in History* (Philadelphia: n.p., 1916), p. 13.

4. Shakers, "Advertisement of the Shakers," *The United States' Gazette for the Country* [Philadelphia], December 8, 1813. I thank Jerry Grant for sharing this article with me. The rest of the Shakers' advertisement refers to a planing machine, and an augur machine.

5. See for example: Samuel Paxton & Co., "By Samuel Paxton & Co." [Advertisement], *Mercantile Advertiser* [New York], April 5, 1814.

6. Isaac Newton Youngs, *A Concise View of the Church of God*, 1856, p. 236, Andrews Collection SA 760, Winterthur, Del.

7. Henry Disston and Sons, Inc., *The Saw in History*, p. 13.

8. Orville W. Carroll, "Mr. Smart's Circular Saw Mill c. 1815," *Bulletin of the Association of Preservation Technology* 5, no. 1 (1973): 58–64.

9. Anon., "Valuable Improvement," *Daily National Intelligencer* [Washington, D.C.], July 21, 1817, http://www.newsbank.com/readex/?content=96.

10. Anon., [Advertisement], *Dedham [Mass.] Gazette*, October 10, 1817, http://www.newsbank.com/readex/?content=96.

11. Henry Disston and Sons, Inc., *The Saw in History*, p. 13.

12. John O. Curtis, "The Introduction of the Circular Saw in the Early 19th Century," *Bulletin of the Association of Preservation Technology* 5 (1973): 162–89.

13. Anon., "Mechanics," *The Times, and Weekly Adviser* [Hartford, Conn.], July 24, 1821. http://www.newsbank.com/readex/?content=96.

14. "A Historical Narrative of the Rise and Progress of the United Society of Shakers. Enfield N.H. 1858," p. 99. New Hampshire Historical Society ms. 9765. I thank Rob Emlen for sharing this reference with me.

15. New York State Agricultural Society, *Transactions of the New York State Agricultural Society* (New York: The Society, T. Weed, 1870), p. 595. I thank Jerry Grant for this reference.

16. Anon., "The Philosopher's Corner," *The Shaker*, 6, no. 1 (1876): 7.

17. David Austin Buckingham, "Epitomic History of the Watervliet Shakers, No. 1," *The Shaker* 7, no. 8 (1877): 59.

18. Franklin Ellis, *History of Columbia County, New York* (Philadelphia: Press of J. B. Lippincott & Co., 1878), p. 308. I am very grateful to Jerry Grant for bringing this reference to my attention.

19. Anon., "Eldress of the Harvard Shakers," *The Manifesto*, 29, no. 2 (1899): 23.

20. White and Taylor, *Shakerism: Its Meaning and Message*, p. 312.

13. Music and Song

1. Russel Haskell, "A Record of Spiritual Songs . . . in Twelve Parts, Compiled by Leading Singers and Lovers of Heavenly Devotion in the Church, Enfield, Conn. 1845," M2131.S4E5 Music 3139 Item 5, Music Manuscripts, Library of Congress.

2. Daniel W. Patterson, *The Shaker Spiritual*, Second, Corrected edition (Mineola, N.Y.: Dover Edition, 2000), p. 56.

3. A music manuscript owned by White Water, Ohio, Shaker descendants contains wordless dance tunes dating from the 1870s. Local newspaper accounts reflect that the Shakers of White Water continued to dance enthusiastically into the late 1870s. See Marjorie Burress, *Whitewater, Ohio Village of Shakers, 1824–1916* (North Bend, Ohio: Friends of White Water Shaker Village, 2003). But Daniel Patterson reports that in nearby Union Village, Ohio, dancing was executed with relatively less success in 1874 (*The Shaker Spiritual*, p. 388).

4. Harold E. Cook, *Shaker Music: A Manifestation of American Folk Culture* (Lewisburg, Pa.: Bucknell University Press, 1973), pp. 34–35.

5. Haskell, "A Record of Spiritual Songs," p. 11.

6. Patterson, *The Shaker Spiritual*, pp. 240–41.

7. "A Collection of Hymns, Anthems, and Tunes, Adapted to Worship, by Betsy Smith, Born 28th August 1813, South Union, Kentucky," Item 143 B1F3, Manuscripts, Kentucky Library and Museum, Western Kentucky University.

8. D. A. Buckingham's innovative "Harmony of Angels," Western Reserve Historical Society Shaker Collection Catalog (hereinafter WRHS) Section IX, Subsection B, Item Shaker Music (OM) 9, is discussed in Cook, *Shaker Music*, pp. 95–97. Subsequent references to

music manuscripts from WRHS will reflect the catalog format of WRHS IX B SM #. For clarification of the cataloging of WRHS Shaker manuscripts, see Kermit J. Pike, *A Guide to Shaker Manuscripts in the Library of The Western Reserve Historical Society* (Cleveland: The Western Reserve Historical Society, 1974).

9. White and Taylor, *Shakerism: Its Meaning and Message*, pp. 338–40.

10. *Millennial Praises* (Hancock: Josiah Tallcott, 1813 edition), from "Preface," iv. Preface is reprinted in *Millennial Praises: A Shaker Hymnal*, edited by Christian Goodwillie and Jane F. Crosthwaite (Amherst: University of Massachusetts Press, 2009), pp. 45–46.

11. I am drawing from the *Millennial Laws of 1845*, included as an Appendix in Andrews, *The People Called Shakers*, pp. 251–89. Although Steve Paterwic correctly reminds us that the *Millennial Laws of 1845* "were the ones least adhered to and the ones in effect for the shortest period of time," (*Historical Dictionary of the Shakers*, p. 278) and should therefore be utilized cautiously, they nonetheless offer a sense of aspired norms and values, if not an accurate representation of actual practice at all times and places.

12. In Part II, Section II, "Orders concerning the Spiritual Worship of God, Attending to Meetings, &c."

13. In Part II, Section XI, "Orders Concerning Books, Pamphlets, and Writings in General."

14. In Part II, Section XII, "Concerning Marking Tools and Conveniences."

15. For analysis of how "Mother's Work" shaped Shaker music, see Mary Ann Haagen, "On Gift Songs," in *Heavenly Visions: Shaker Gift Drawings and Gift Songs*, Frances Morin, Curator (New York: The Drawing Center, 2001), pp. 135–51. See also Daniel W. Patterson, *Gift Drawing and Gift Song: A Study of Two Forms of Shaker Inspiration* (Sabbathday Lake, Me.: The United Society of Shakers, 1983), and Patterson's discussion in *The Shaker Spiritual*, 316–23. I wish to acknowledge Mary Ann Haagen for her exceptional help in reading my initial approach to this subject and offering insightful suggestions for its presentation here.

16. See the examples illustrated and discussed in Haagen, "On Gift Songs," pp. 136, 144.

17. Full discussions of the Shaker notation system can be found in Cook, *Shaker Music*, pp. 75–107; and Patterson *The Shaker Spiritual*, 41–56.

18. Letter from New Lebanon, January 11, 1835, WRHS IV A 37.

19. WRHS IX B SM 376, np.

20. WRHS IX B SM 76, 35–37.

ABOUT THE AUTHORS

Galen Beale

Galen Beale's introduction to the Shakers came about quite by accident while driving her children to school through Canterbury Shaker Village in the late 1970s. She soon took over their herb gardens there and as a result of walks and talks with the sisters, especially Sister Mildred Wells, became conversant with the 150-year tradition of herbal culture at the village. Intensive research in primary sources led to her publication with Mary Rose Boswell of *The Earth Shall Blossom* in 1991.

The last eldresses at Canterbury also taught Galen how they made poplarware, even though the practice had been discontinued many years earlier. This allowed that unique craft tradition to continue in her hands when it was on the verge of being lost. Galen continues to demonstrate poplarware making at many Shaker museums to this day. Her commitment to the craft also led to the publication of *Shaker Baskets & Poplarware*, which she co-authored in 1992. She is currently researching Shaker apostasy in the mid-nineteenth century for a book in progress.

Richard Dabrowski

Richard is president of Shaker Workshops, located in Ashburnham, Massachusetts, with showrooms in nearby Arlington. Founded in 1970 with the goal of offering the public accurate and affordable reproductions of some of the most treasured Shaker crafts, the company has also sold their furniture as do-it-your-self kits since 1972. A portion of their mission statement reads: "Shaker furniture is a major creative force in our decorative arts heritage, because it is the one truly original American style of furniture. Its clear crisp lines and singular lightness (with no sacrifice in strength) fit equally well into a modern interior or more traditional setting. Shaker Workshops was founded [with] the purpose of reproducing original Shaker furniture and oval boxes as faithfully and as economically as possible."

Dabrowski has a long-time interest in the unique Shaker-originated and perfected craft of poplarware making and has assembled a remarkable collection of examples from the villages where it was produced. He has lectured on the subject at various gatherings of Shaker enthusiasts and contributed to several texts.

Christian Goodwillie

A self-described "fateful" visit to the former Shaker village of Pleasant Hill, Kentucky in 1998 was "an epiphany . . . shifting the course of my life and studies completely." His majors at Indiana University were history and music; he subsequently completed a master's degree program in historic preservation at the School of the Art Institute of Chicago in 2001. The focus of his thesis was the 1846 Ministry Shop at the former Shaker village of South Union, Kentucky. Two summers of interning at Hancock Shaker Village led to his appointment as curator of collections there in 2002.

While at Hancock he was responsible for five major exhibitions, the last of which, "Gather Up the Fragments: The Andrews Shaker Collection," will be touring four museums, from Maine to California in the years ahead.

Goodwillie has published many magazine articles and the following books: *Shaker Songs* (2002), *Handled With Care: The Function of Form in Shaker Craft* (with M. Stephen Miller, 2006), *Gather Up the Fragments: The Andrews Shaker Collection* (with Mario DePillis, 2008), and *Millennial Praises: A Shaker Hymnal* (with Jane Crosthwaithe, 2009). He is currently working with Carol Medlicott on *As Branches of One Living Tree: Richard McNemar and the Music of the Shaker West.* He, wife Erika, and their son Douglas live in Clinton, New York, where he is curator of special collections and archives at Hamilton College.

Jerry V. Grant

Jerry is presently Director of Research and Library Services at the Shaker Museum and Library, Old Chatham, New York, a position he has held since 1987. His interest in Shakers began in the mid-1970s with the study of oval boxes and their written documentation in order to learn about their history and construction. He subsequently made reproduction boxes at Hancock Shaker Village, where he also worked as an interpreter, librarian, and administrator. Jerry is a graduate of Michigan State University and earned a master's degree in library and information science from the State University of New York at Albany.

Jerry has been an invaluable resource over the years to myriad scholars who have researched Shaker-related topics of all kinds. He has also written a number of articles and monographs on Shaker subjects including "Noble but Plain: The Shaker Meetinghouse at Mount Lebanon" (1994) and, with his wife Sharon Duane Koomler, "An Eye Toward Perfection" (2008) for the Shaker Museum and Library. He was the co-author (with Douglas R. Allen) of *Shaker Furniture Makers* (1989). Grant and wife Sharon Koomler live in East Chatham, New York—an area rich in Shaker history.

Sharon Duane Koomler

Sharon is an independent Shaker scholar, author, and curator. She holds a bachelor of arts degree in Folklore from Indiana University, a master's degree in historic preservation from Western Kentucky University, and is a Fellow in Shaker Life and Material Culture at Winterthur Museum and Gardens. She has worked with Shaker materials at the Shaker Museum at South Union, Kentucky; Hancock Shaker Village, Pittsfield, Massachusetts; Shaker Museum and Library, Old Chatham, New York; and with numerous private collections. Among the exhibitions she has curated are "Seen & Received: The Shakers' Private Art" (Hancock Shaker Village, 2000), "Coming Full Circle: Shaker Faith, Community, Industry, and Design" (Shaker Museum and Library 2003), "Crafting Utopia: The Art of Shaker Women" (International Arts & Artists, (2000–2003), and "An Eye Toward Perfection: The Shaker Museum and Library" (Winter Antiques Show, 2008).

Sharon has spoken to groups on a variety of Shaker subjects throughout the eastern United States. Publications include *Seen & Received: The Shakers' Private Art* (2000), *Shaker Style: Form, Function, Furniture* (2000), and *In the Shaker Tradition* (2002), as well as numerous articles in periodicals. She lives on a small farm in East Chatham, New York, with her husband, Jerry Grant, and "too many chickens."

Carol Medlicott

Dr. Medlicott is an assistant professor of geography at Northern Kentucky University. She received her PhD in geography from the University of California at Los Angeles in 2003. Her research considers a range of topics in historical and cultural geography. A post-doctoral fellowship at Dartmouth College in 2004–2005 brought her into contact with the former Shaker community at nearby Enfield, New Hampshire. This sparked an interest in Shaker culture, particularly their music (which she performs frequently). A subsequent move to Cincinnati opened up a "second front" of interest in the western Shakers. She presently serves on the Board of Directors of Friends of White Water Shaker Village, near Cincinnati.

Medlicott's work in cultural geography has been published in a number of scholarly journals, including *Historical Geography* and *National Identities*. Recently, her Shaker research led to a major article in *Timeline: A Publication of the Ohio Historical Society*. Entitled "Issachar Bates: Shaker Missionary," it is part of a book-length treatment of this important Shaker elder now in progress. She is also collaborating on a critical edition of an 1833 Ohio Shaker hymnal compiled by Richard McNemar—another towering figure in the early history of the Shaker West.

M. Stephen Miller

When Steve and wife Miriam happened upon Hancock Shaker Village in the summer of 1977, a whole new world opened up. The following summer they made their first purchases of Shaker materials, a worktable and paper can label. Since that time, hundreds more hand-crafted items entered their home, along with approximately sixteen thousand pieces of paper—printed by or for the Shakers to serve their many industries—called "ephemera." Theirs is now regarded as one of the most comprehensive collections of these materials. At the same time that he conducted a busy dental specialty practice, with offices in New Britain and Southington, Connecticut, Miller managed to fit in many hours of research and to publish a number of articles on Shaker subjects.

In 1988 he served as co-curator for an exhibit, "Marketing Community Industries 1830–1930: A Century of Shaker Ephemera," at Hancock Shaker Village. He also wrote, photographed, and self-published an annotated catalog for it. Since that time he has been actively involved in the Shaker world as contributor to dozens of books and articles and a number of exhibitions. Miller also served on the boards of Hancock Shaker Village and Canterbury Shaker Village, and chaired the board of the Ephemera Society of America, from 1995 to 1997.

In 2006 he co-curated the exhibition "Handled With Care," shown at Hancock Shaker Village

and the National Heritage Museum, Lexington, Massachusetts, and photographed and co-wrote its catalog. His 2007 publication, *From Shaker Lands and Shaker Hands*, was the first comprehensive study of the Shaker industries in seventy-five years, and the Communal Studies Society named it "Book of the Year." In 2008 he was the major contributor to "Shaker Design: Out of this World" at the Shelburne Museum in Vermont and the Bard Center in New York City. He continues to collect, research, publish, and—most importantly—share his ideas and materials with the World.

Charles R. Muller

For twenty-five years Chuck was the editor and co-owner of the *Ohio Antiques Review*, produced in Worthington, Ohio. In 1979 he gathered forty articles from the *OAR* and published them as *The Shaker Way*, and followed that with *The Shaker Chair*, co-authored with Timothy D. Rieman, in 1984. This is still considered the definitive study of this subject. Chuck's most recent book is *Soap Hollow: The Furniture and Its Makers*, about a small group of Amish/Mennonite craftsmen in Western Pennsylvania. It was published in 2004.

Muller was guest curator for "Ohio Furniture: 1788–1888" at the Columbus (Ohio) Museum of Art in 1984 and "The Shakers: Abiding Inspiration in Faith and Design" at the Ohio Decorative Arts Center in Lancaster, Ohio, in 2009. Now retired, Chuck served for forty years—first full time and later part time—as pastor in the United Methodist Church. One of that denomination's predecessors acquired the large Union Village, Ohio, property from the Shakers in 1912. Muller's first church was on Shaker Road, leading to the village.

Stephen J. Paterwic

A native of Springfield, Massachusetts, Steve has taught mathematics in high schools and middle schools in and around that city since 1983. He presently teaches at West Springfield Middle School and also reviews mathematics for the Great Source division of the Houghton-Mifflin Company. Blessed with a near-photographic memory, and having read deeply in Shaker manuscripts, as well as primary and secondary texts, he is a frequent presenter at meetings, seminars, and forums. He was the keynote speaker at both the Annual Communal Studies Association Conference in 2004 and the Centennial Celebration of the 1905 Mount Lebanon Peace Conference.

Paterwic's numerous articles have appeared in the *Shaker Quarterly, American Communal Studies Quarterly,* the *Historical Journal of Massachusetts,* and *New England Ancestors.* He has contributed to many books with Shaker subjects including, *The Shaker Image: Second and Annotated Edition* (1994), *Shaker Medicinal Herbs* (1998), and *From Shaker Lands and Shaker Hands* (2007). His *Historical Dictionary of the Shakers* was published in 2008. He has had a life-long friendship with the Shakers at Sabbathday Lake, whom he credits with providing inspiration for his own spiritual life.

Scott T. Swank

Dr. Swank was born and raised in Amish farm country in Lancaster County, Pennsylvania. He received a bachelor's degree in history from Elizabethtown College (where he later taught for eight years) and a master's and doctoral degrees from the University of Pennsylvania. He served as Director of Education and Deputy Director of Interpretation at Winterthur Museum and Gardens in Delaware. Fifteen years later he assumed the position of director, and later president, of Canterbury Shaker Village in New Hampshire, from 1990 to 2005. Here he directed the restoration of twenty-five original historic buildings and the reproduction of four former Shaker buildings. He is currently Executive Director of Heritage Museums and Gardens in Sandwich, Massachusetts. With one hundred acres and three distinct museums, it is the largest cultural institution on Cape Cod.

Dr. Swank has published extensively on the arts and architecture of the Pennsylvania Germans and Shakers. His books include *Perspectives on American Folk Art* (1979), *Arts of the Pennsylvania Germans* (1983), *Shaker Art, Life, and Architecture* (1997)—an extensive study of the historic Canterbury Shaker community—and, *Shaker Family Album* (1999). He is active professionally in the American Association of Museums and the New England Museum Association and now lives in Sandwich, the oldest town on Cape Cod.

Darryl Thompson

Darryl grew up with the Shakers at Canterbury, New Hampshire, arriving there with his parents at the age of one year. Altogether, he lived at the community for thirty-one years and was a favorite of the last sisters residing there. He earned bachelor's and master's degrees in American history from the University of New Hampshire; his master's thesis focused on historic plant varieties developed by Shakers in the nineteenth and early twentieth centuries. He and his father Bud, the former curator at Canterbury Shaker Village, were consultants for the Ken Burns documentary film, "The Shakers: Hands to Work and Hearts to God" (1984).

Thompson has lectured widely, written many articles, and led elderhostel programs about the Shakers at Canterbury. He has also led tours of that village for many years. Darryl wrote the preface to Jeffrey S. Paige's *The Shaker Kitchen* (1994) and the liner notes for several collections of Shaker music on compact discs. He was also featured in articles about Canterbury Shaker Village that have appeared in the *New York Times, London Times,* and *Yankee* magazine. Darryl teaches American history at the New Hampshire Institute of Art in Manchester.

Glendyne R. Wergland

Born in Okmulgee, Oklahoma, Dr. Wergland pursued her education around the United States. At the age of forty, after raising children and settling in the Berkshire hills of western Massachusetts, where she worked as an executive with the Girl Scouts for nine years, Glendyne returned to school and earned a bachelor's degree at Mount Holyoke College in 1992—with honors,

Phi Beta Kappa. She attended graduate school and received her doctorate in United States history at the University of Massachusetts, Amherst, in 2001.

Now an independent scholar with occasional teaching and speaking engagements, she is making up for "lost" time by writing about the Shakers. Dr. Wergland has two books in print: *One Shaker Life: Isaac Newton Youngs, 1793–1865* (2005) and *Visiting the Shakers, 1778–1849* (2007). A companion volume, *Visiting the Shakers, 1850–1899,* from the Couper Press, Hamilton College, and *Sisters in the Faith: Shaker Women, 1780–1890* are forthcoming.

Martha Wetherbee

Martha has devoted the past thirty-one years to the preservation of the art of Shaker basket making through a careful examination of manuscript records—shop journals and ledgers—and ultimately, a meticulous study of surviving examples. The latter led her into the storage rooms of museums and former Shaker villages throughout the Northeast. Her studies sometimes meant deconstructing badly damaged examples to learn the unseen details of their fabrication. Her quest began in the 1970s when she learned that even the surviving sisters at Canterbury Shaker Village had long since lost knowledge of basket construction, which had once been an important endeavor there. Her tenacity, discoveries, and great love for the subject resulted in the publication (with Nathan Taylor) of the definitive *Shaker Baskets* (1988).

As an author, lecturer, teacher, and recognized authority on Shaker baskets, Wetherbee has appeared on NBC, PBS, HG TV, and the Martha Stewart Show. She has also been featured in many national magazines such as *Country Living, Country Home, The Magazine Antiques*, and *Fine Woodworking*. When not on "the road" teaching throughout the country, she can be found either pounding brown ash logs at her camp in New Hampshire to make basket material, or in Florida. Most of the "Shaker style" baskets seen today, as well as their names, are the result of her research discoveries.

INDEX